Intermarket Analysis

Founded in 1807, John Wiley & Sons is the oldest independent publishing company in the United States. With offices in North America, Europe, Australia, and Asia, Wiley is globally committed to developing and marketing print and electronic products and services for our customers' professional and personal knowledge and understanding.

The Wiley Trading series features books by traders who have survived the market's ever changing temperament and have prospered—some by reinventing systems, others by getting back to basics. Whether a novice trader, professional or somewhere in-between, these books will provide the advice and strategies needed to prosper today and well into the future.

For a list of available titles, please visit our Web site at www.WileyFinance.com.

Intermarket Analysis

Profiting from
Global Market Relationships

JOHN MURPHY

WILEY

John Wiley & Sons, Inc.

For general information on our other products and services, or technical support, please contact our Customer Care Department within the United States at 800-762-2974, outside the United States at 317-572-3993 or fax 317-572-4002.

Wiley also publishes its books in a variety of electronic formats. Some content that appears in print may not be available in electronic books.

For more information about Wiley products, visit our web site at www.wiley.com.

ISBN: 0-471-02329-9

Printed in the United States of America.

10 9 8 7 6 5

To Anne, a great poet
and
to Tim, a great brother

Contents

Acknowledgments

I owe thanks to a lot of people who helped put this book together: Pamela van Giessen, Executive Editor at Wiley, for talking me into doing it in the first place; Jennifer MacDonald and Joanna Pomeranz for making sure that everything wound up in the right place; Heidi Shelton and Pete Behmer at Stockcharts.com for producing great looking charts; John Carder at Topline Investment Graphics for his innovative historical charts; Tim Murphy for his help with the cover design and computer graphics; those market analysts who generously allowed me to draw from their work including Ned Davis, Ken Fisher, Ian Gordon, Martin Pring, and Sam Stovall. And, finally, the McTooles family who kept my spirits up while I was writing this book.

Introduction
to Intermarket
Analysis

In 1990, I completed a book entitled *Intermarket Technical Analysis: Trading Strategies for the Global Stock, Bond, Commodity, and Currency Markets.* My point in writing it was to show how closely related all the financial markets really are, both domestically and internationally. The book's main thesis was that technical analysts need to broaden their chart focus to take these *intermarket* correlations into consideration. Analysis of the stock market, for example, without consideration of existing trends in the dollar, bond, and commodity markets was simply incomplete. The book suggested that financial markets can be used as leading indicators of other markets and, at times, confirming indicators of related markets. Because the message of my earlier text challenged the *single market* focus of the technical community, some questioned whether this newer approach had any place in the technical field. Many questioned whether intermarket relationships existed at all—and whether they could be used in the forecasting process. The idea that global markets are linked to each other was also viewed with some skepticism. How things have changed in just one decade.

Intermarket analysis is now considered a branch of technical analysis and is becoming increasingly popular. The *Journal of Technical Analysis* (Summer–Autumn 2002) asked the membership of the Market Technicians Association to rate the relative importance of technical disciplines for an academic course on technical analysis. Of the fourteen disciplines included in the poll, intermarket analysis ranked fifth. Intermarket work has come a long way in ten years.

EARLIER BOOK COVERED THE 1980s

My earlier text focused on events in the 1980s starting with the end of the *commodity bubble* at the start of that decade. This ended the hyperinflation of the 1970s when hard assets like commodities soared and paper assets (like bonds and stocks) soured. The 1980 peak in commodities ushered in a two-decade disinflationary trend that coincided with major bull markets in bonds and stocks. The biggest financial event of the 1980s—the 1987 stock market crash—provided a textbook example of how markets are related to each other and the necessity for paying attention to those related markets. A surge in commodity prices—and a collapse in bond prices—during the first half of 1987 gave ample warning of an impending stock market decline during that year's second half. Three years later during 1990, as the previous book was going to press, global financial markets were just starting to react to Iraq's invasion of Kuwait in August of that year. Gold and oil prices surged—while stock markets around the world fell. Interestingly, thirteen years later (at the start of 2003), market observers were facing the prospect of another Iraq war and were studying anew the 1990–1991 market reactions to look for parallels. History has a way of repeating itself, even in intermarket work.

JAPANESE BUBBLE BURSTS IN 1990

Another important event which happened at the start of 1990 is still having global repercussions more than a decade later. The bubble in the Japanese stock market burst. This started a thirteen-year descent in that market (which represented the world's second largest economy) that turned into a *deflation* (a decline in the prices of goods and services). Over a decade later, western central bankers were studying the Japanese deflation model to find ways to combat increasing signs of deflation in western economies. Some of the charts presented in this book also bolster the view that Japanese deflation was one of the major contributing factors to the *decoupling* of bonds and stocks in the United States years later when rising bond prices starting in 2000 coincided with falling stock prices.

THIRD ANNIVERSARY OF 2000 MARKET TOP

March 10, 2003 marked the third anniversary of the ending of the Nasdaq bubble that signaled the start of the worst bear market in decades. A 50 percent decline in the S&P 500 was the worst since 1974. The Nasdaq's loss of 78 percent was the worst since the stock market crash from 1929–1932 in the midst of the Great Depression. Market historians had to go back to study these two periods to gain some insight into market behavior. What made comparisons between these two earlier periods complicated was that each of them was caused by a different economic event. The bear market in stocks during the 1970s was associated with a period of rising commodity prices—and hyperinflation. The bear market of the 1930s, however, was associated with a period of economic deflation. While both situations are bad for stocks, deflation is the more difficult to counter.

Starting in 1998, the word *deflation* was being heard for the first time since the 1930s. This happened as a result of the Asian currency crisis that gripped the world during 1997 and 1998. Within five years, global deflation had spread from Asia and was starting to infect global bond and stock markets everywhere—including the United States. More than any other factor, the reappearance of deflation changed intermarket relationships that had existed over the prior forty years. These changes are why I am writing this book—to show what has worked according to the older intermarket model and, more importantly, what has changed. Intermarket analysis is based on relationships (or correlations) between markets. It is not, however, a static model. Correlations between financial markets can change over time. They do not change randomly, however; there is usually a good reason. The main reason for some of the changes that started in the late 1990s was the growing threat of deflation.

THE DEFLATION SCENARIO

In the 1999 revision of my book *Technical Analysis of the Financial Markets*, I included a chapter on intermarket analysis which reviewed the historic relationships that had been working for several decades. I also added a new section which was entitled "Deflation Scenario." This section described the collapse in Asian currency and stock markets starting in the middle of 1997; the severe decline had an especially depressing effect on global commodity markets like copper, gold, and oil. For the first time in generations, analysts starting expressing concern that a beneficial era of *disinflation* (when prices are rising at a slower rate) might turn into a harmful *deflation* (when prices of goods actually fall). How the markets reacted to that initial threat of deflation defined the intermarket model for the next five years. Commodity prices fell while bond prices rose. This was nothing new—falling commodity prices usually produce higher bond prices. What changed, though, was the relationship between bonds and stocks. During 1998, stocks were sold all over the world while money poured into U.S. Treasury bonds in a global search for safety. In other words, stocks fell while bonds rose. This was unusual and represented the biggest change in the intermarket model. Disinflation (which lasted from 1981 through 1997) is bad for commodities but is good for bonds and stocks. Deflation (which started in 1998) is good for bonds and bad for commodities—but is also bad for stocks. In a deflationary climate, bond prices rise while interest rates fall. Falling interest rates, however, do not help stocks. This explains why a dozen easings by the Federal Reserve in the eighteen months after January 2001 were unable to stop a falling stock market that had peaked at the start of 2000.

INTERMARKET MODEL FROM 1980 TO 1997

This book begins with a quick review of the 1980s, starting with the big intermarket changes that helped launch the greatest stock bull market in history. We will also revisit the 1987 stock market crash—because of its importance in the development of intermarket theory and its role in changing this theory into reality. The 1990 bear market was just starting as I was completing my earlier book. We will study this year in more depth, especially given its relevance to global events thirteen years later. Traditional intermarket relationships held up quite well during the 1994 bear market and continued to do so until 1998.

THEN CAME 1998 AND THINGS CHANGED

The rest of this book deals with market events from 1998 onwards. That year represented a sea change in the intermarket model. We will study market forces leading up to the bursting of the stock market bubble in the spring of 2000—and the ensuing three years of stock market decline. Deflation plays a key role from 1998 on. Global markets became very closely correlated during the late 1990s and the first three years of the new millennium. This was mainly due to global overinvestment in technology stocks during the latter stages of the Nasdaq bubble—and the ensuing global collapse after the bubble burst. Deflationary trends were also global in scope. The fact that virtually all world markets collapsed together after 2000 called into question the wisdom of *global diversification* (when stock investments are made in foreign markets to reduce overall risk). During global bear markets in stocks, all world markets become closely correlated to the downside. This happened during the crash of 1987—and again after 2000. It was also another manifestation of the intermarket reality that financial trends are usually global in nature. This includes the direction of stock markets, interest rates, currency markets, and trends in inflation and deflation.

THE ROLE OF OIL

In 1999, rising oil prices set in motion a series of events that led to the start of a bear market in stocks in the spring of 2000 and the onset of a recession a year later in the spring of 2001. Rising oil prices have contributed to virtually every U.S. recession in the last forty years. 1999 was no exception. The surge in oil prices led the Federal Reserve to tighten interest rates, which helped end the longest economic expansion since the 1960s. This action by the Fed led to an *inverted yield curve* as 2000 started; this is a classic warning sign of stock market weakness and impending recession. All of these trends were clearly visible on the price charts at the time, a fact which is demonstrated in the book. Unfortunately, the economic community—together with most Wall Street analysts—either did not see the classic warning signs of trouble or simply chose to ignore them.

Another change from my previous book is the increasingly important role that *sector rotation* plays in intermarket work. Different stock market sectors take over market leadership at different points in the economic cycle. In 1999, oil stocks were the market's strongest sector. This is usually a bad sign for the economy and the stock market. You will see how valuable sector "signals" were during the crucial years of 1999 and 2000—and how some defensive market sectors started new uptrends just as the Nasdaq peaked.

THE RESURGENCE OF GOLD

During the twenty years from 1980 to 2000, gold was in a major downtrend. This was due to the disinflationary trend of that two-decade period and to the fact that gold generally does poorly during bull markets in stocks. Because gold is bought mainly during times of crisis, there is not much need for it during a super bull market in stocks. A strong dollar during most of those years also kept gold out of favor. This started to change in 2000, however. During that watershed year, the twenty-year bull market in stocks came to an end. At the same time, a seven-year bull market in the U.S. dollar was ending. These two factors combined to light a fire under a moribund gold market. Over the next three years, gold stocks were the top-performing stock market sector. Interestingly, the gold rally started in 2000—right around the time that deflationary talk started to get louder. This puzzled investors, who believed that gold could only be used as an inflation hedge. History shows that gold stocks did very well in the deflationary climate of the 1930s. Gold's historic role has been as a store of value during times of economic upheaval. Another reason for gold's popularity in deflationary times is the Federal Reserve's attempt to *reflate* the economy. It does this by weakening the dollar in an attempt to create a little inflation, which in turn boosts the price of gold. The Fed tried this in the 1930s and in its more recent battle against deflation in the early 2000s. The strategy worked during the 1930s and appears to be working again seventy years later.

ASSET ALLOCATION AND ECONOMIC FORECASTING

Intermarket work has important applications in the areas of *asset allocation* and economic forecasting. It has long been accepted that the stock market is a leading indicator of the economy. A classic example of this occurred when the U.S. market peaked in March of 2000. It took the economic world twelve months—until March of 2001—to officially declare that a U.S. recession had started. Markets have a way of looking into the future to "discount" economic trends as far away as six months. This is true for all, including the dollar, bonds, and commodities markets. Commodities give us an early warning of deflationary or inflationary trends. The dollar does the same. The direction of bonds tells us whether interest rates are rising or falling—which tells us a lot about the strength or weakness of the economy. And all of these trends subsequently affect the direction of the economy and the stock market.

More importantly, intermarket work helps us to determine which part of the financial spectrum offers the best hope for potential profits. From 2000 through 2002, for example, deflationary tendencies made bonds a much stronger asset class than stocks. At the same time, a falling dollar made gold an attractive alternative to stocks. By charting these intermarket trends, investors have a better of chance of being in the right asset class at the right time—and out of the wrong ones.

By the end of 2002, longer-term intermarket charts were hinting that *hard assets* (like gold and other commodities) were starting to take precedence over *paper assets* (like bonds and stocks) for the first time in twenty years. Charts also showed that the housing sector was one of the few bright spots in an otherwise disappointing stock market and a sluggish economy. Intermarket analysis showed that the resiliency in REITs and homebuilding stocks was closely linked to the historic drop in interest rates to their lowest level in forty-five years. Charts also showed that 2003 started to see some rotation out of bonds and back into stocks for the first time in three years. This was good for the stock market and the economy, but hinted that the boom in Treasury bonds was nearing completion. Weakness in the dollar and firmer commodity prices also threatened to boost long-term interest rates. This could be bad for the housing sector which had been thriving on falling long-term rates. Although there are no guarantees that those trends will continue, they are examples of how some knowledge of intermarket charting can play an important role in economic analysis and the asset allocation process.

IMPORTANCE OF CHARTS

All of this may start sounding like a lot of economic theory. This is partially the case, for intermarket analysis is based on economic principles. However, it is not theory. Intermarket work is market-driven. There is nothing theoretical about a profit and loss statement. Economists look at statistics to determine the direction of the economy and, by inference, the direction of financial markets. Chartists look at the markets themselves. This is a big difference. While economic statistics are usually *backward-looking*, the markets are *forward-looking*. It is much like comparing the relative merits of using a lagging or a leading indicator. Given the choice, most people would choose the leading indicator. This goes to the heart of technical analysis. One of the basic premises of the technical approach is that the price action in each market (and each stock) is also a leading indicator of its own fundamentals. In that sense, chart analysis is just a shortcut form of economic and fundamental analysis. This is also why the intermarket analyst uses charts.

Another reason that chartists have such a big advantage in intermarket work is that they look at so many different markets. Charts make a daunting task much simpler. In addition, it is not necessary to be an expert in any of the markets. All one needs to do is determine if the line on the chart is going up or down. Intermarket work goes a step further by determining if two related markets are moving in the same direction or in the opposite direction. It does not matter if the charts being compared are those of gold, bond yields, the dollar, the Dow, or the Japanese stock market. You do not have to be a charting expert to do intermarket work, either. The ability to tell up from down is all that is needed. And an open mind.

CHAPTER 1

A Review
of the 1980s

To fully understand the dramatic turns in the financial markets that started in 1980, it's necessary to know something about the 1970s. That decade witnessed a virtual explosion in commodity markets, which led to spiraling inflation and rising interest rates. From 1971 to 1980, the Commodity Research Bureau (CRB) Index—which is a basket of commodity prices—appreciated in value by 250 percent. Bond yields rose by 150 percent during the same period and, as a result, bond prices declined. Figure 1.1 shows the close correlation between the CRB Index and the yield on 10-year Treasuries between 1973 and 1987. Long-term rates rose with commodities during the inflationary 1970s and fell with them during the disinflationary 1980s.

The 1970s were not good for stocks, either. The Dow Jones Industrial Average started the decade near 1,000 and ended the decade at about the same level. In the middle of that 10-year period of stock market stagnation, the Dow lost almost half its value. The 1970s were a decade for tangible assets; paper assets were out of favor. By the end of the decade, gold prices had soared to over $700 per ounce. A weak dollar during that period also contributed to the upward spiral in gold and other commodity prices—as well as the relative weakness in bonds and stocks. All this started to change in 1980, when the bubble burst in the commodity markets. Figure 1.2 is a ratio of the Dow Industrials divided by the gold market. The plunge in this ratio during the 1970s reflected the superior performance by gold and other hard assets in that inflationary decade. The ratio bottomed in 1980 after gold peaked. The Dow then bottomed in 1982.

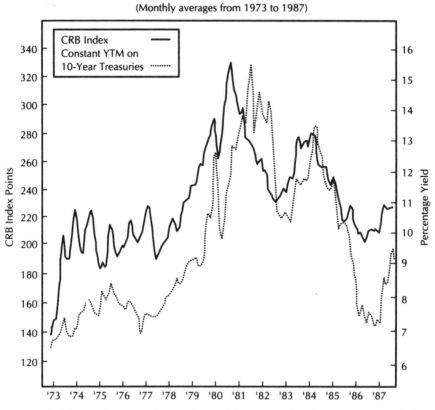

FIGURE 1.1   A demonstration of the positive correlation between the CRB index and 10-year Treasury yields from 1973 to 1987.

COMMODITIES PEAK IN 1980

In late 1980, the bubble in commodity prices suddenly burst. The CRB Index started to fall from a record level of 330 points—and began a 20-year decline during which it lost half of its value. During these same 20 years, gold prices fell from $700 to $250, losing over 60 percent of their value. (It was not until after the stock market peak in 2000 that gold prices started to show signs that their twenty-year bear hibernation had ended.) The 1980 peak in commodity markets ended the inflationary spiral of the 1970s and ushered in an era of falling inflation (or disinflation) that lasted until the end of the twentieth century. Figure 1.3 shows the dramatic rally in a number of commodity indexes during the 1970s and the major peak that occurred in 1980. Commodity prices declined for the next 20 years. Another financial market

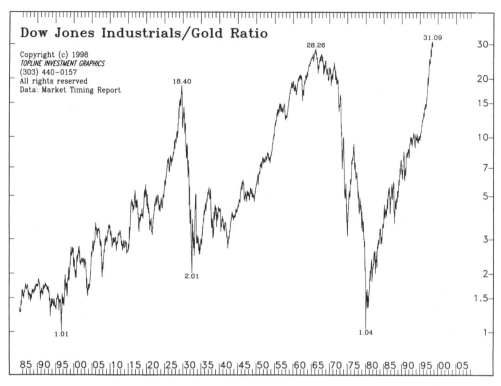

FIGURE 1.2 The plunge in the ratio during the 1970s reflected the superior performance of gold during that inflationary decade.

made a big turn in 1980 that had a lot to do with the big peak in commodities: the U.S. dollar.

DOLLAR BOTTOMS IN 1980

The U.S. dollar hit a major bottom in 1980 and doubled in price over the next five years. One of the key intermarket relationships involved is the *inverse* relationship between commodity prices and the U.S. dollar. A falling dollar is inflationary in nature, and usually coincides with rising commodity prices (especially gold). A rising dollar has the opposite effect and is bearish for commodities and gold. This is why the significant upturn in the U.S. currency in 1980 was such an important ingredient in the historic turn from hyperinflation to disinflation that characterized the next 20 years. (Starting in year 2002, a major decline in the U.S. dollar contributed to a major upturn in gold and other commodities.)

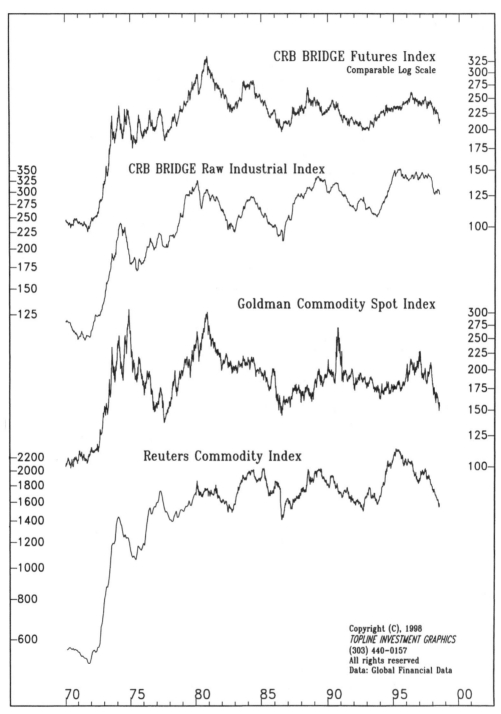

FIGURE 1.3   A number of commodities indexes show the dramatic rally during the 1970s and the major commodity peak during 1980.

BONDS BOTTOM IN 1981

Another key intermarket relationship has to do with bond and commodity prices. They trend in opposite directions. Rising commodity prices (like those seen in the 1970s) signal rising inflation pressure, which puts upward pressure on interest rates and downward pressure on bond prices. (Bond prices and bond yields trend in opposite directions.) Commodity prices often change direction ahead of bonds, which also makes them leading indicators of bonds at important turning points. At the start of the 1980s, it took a year for the drop in commodities to push the bond market higher.

During the second half of 1981, bond yields peaked near 15 percent. They fell to half that level (7 percent) within five years, which caused a major upturn in bond prices. The tide had turned. The stock market, which had been held back for a decade by rising interest rates, soon got an enormous boost from falling bond yields (and rising bond prices).

STOCKS BOTTOM IN 1982

During the summer of 1982, within a year of the bond market bottom, the biggest bull run in stock market history started—and lasted for almost two decades. The fact that the bond market bottomed ahead of stocks is also part of the normal pattern. The bond market has a history of turning ahead of stocks and is therefore viewed as a leading indicator of the stock market. The intermarket scenario had completely reversed itself at the start of the 1980s. Hard assets (like commodities) were in decline, while paper assets (bonds and stocks) were back in favor.

This turning point was one of the clearest examples of how intermarket relationships play out. Notice that four different market groups were involved: currencies, commodities, bonds, and stocks. All four played a major role as the inflationary 1970s ended and the disinflationary 1980s began. Let's review the groundrules for how the financial markets normally interact with each other, which form the basis for our intermarket work.

HOW THE FOUR MARKET GROUPS INTERRELATE

Intermarket analysis involves the simultaneous analysis of the four financial markets—currencies, commodities, bonds, and stocks. It is how these four markets interact with each other that gives them their predictive value. Here is how they interrelate:

- The U.S. dollar trends in the opposite direction of commodities
- A falling dollar is bullish for commodities; a rising dollar is bearish
- Commodities trend in the opposite direction of bond prices
- Therefore, commodities trend in the same direction as interest rates
- Rising commodities coincide with rising interest rates and falling bond prices
- Falling commodities coincide with falling interest rates and rising bond prices
- Bond prices normally trend in the same direction as stock prices
- Rising bond prices are normally good for stocks; falling bond prices are bad
- Therefore, falling interest rates are normally good for stocks; rising rates are bad
- The bond market, however, normally changes direction ahead of stocks
- A rising dollar is good for U.S. stocks and bonds; a falling dollar can be bad
- A falling dollar is bad for bonds and stocks when commodities are rising
- During a deflation (which is relatively rare), bond prices rise while stocks fall

The list sums up the key intermarket relationships between the four market groups—at least as they are in a normal inflationary or disinflationary environment, the likes of which existed during the second half of the last century. This held up especially well during the 1970s, the 1980s, and most of the 1990s. (The last item in the preceding list which refers to deflation was not normal in the postwar era. Later in the book I explain how deflationary pressures starting in 1997 and 1998 changed the normal relationship that had existed between bonds and stocks.) With a basic understanding of intermarket relationships, it is easier to see how well the markets followed that script at the start of the 1980s. A rising dollar led to falling commodities, which led to rising bond prices, which led to rising stock prices. Things stayed pretty much this way until 1987.

1987 STOCK MARKET CRASH REVISITED

The stock market crash during the second half of 1987 was an even more dramatic example of the necessity for intermarket awareness. It happened swiftly and the results were dramatic and painful. Those who ignored the action in related markets during the first half of that year were blindsided by the market collapse during the second half. As a result, they sought out scapegoats like *program trading* and *portfolio insurance* (futures-related strategies that can exaggerate stock market declines) to explain the carnage. While these two factors no doubt added to the steepness of the stock market decline, they did not cause it. The real explanation for the stock market crash that year is much easier to explain, but only if viewed from an intermarket perspective. It started in the bond and commodity pits in the spring of that year.

COMMODITIES RISE, BONDS FALL DURING SPRING OF 1987

During the four years after 1982, two of the main supporting factors behind the stock market advance were falling commodity prices (low inflation) and rising bond prices (falling interest rates). In 1986, both of those markets started to level off; commodities stopped going down and bond prices stopped going up. The intermarket picture did not really turn dangerous, however, until the spring of 1987. In April of that year, the CRB Index of commodity prices turned sharply higher and "broke out" to the highest level in a year. At the same time, bond prices went into a virtual freefall. (Rising commodity prices usually produce lower bond prices.) These intermarket trend changes removed two of the bullish props under the stock market advance and gave an early warning that the market rally was on weak footing. Figure 1.4 shows the inverse relationship between bond and commodity prices from 1985 to 1987. It shows the CRB Index rising above a *neckline* (a trendline drawn over previous peaks) in the spring of 1987 (which completed a bullish *head and shoulders* bottom) just as bond prices were falling under the lower trendline in a yearlong triangular pattern—a bad combination for stocks since it suggested that rising inflation was pushing interest rates higher.

STOCK MARKET PEAKS IN AUGUST

The stock market rally continued for another four months into August 1987 before finally peaking. The fact that bond prices peaked four months ahead of stocks demonstrates the tendency for bonds to turn ahead of stocks. Again,

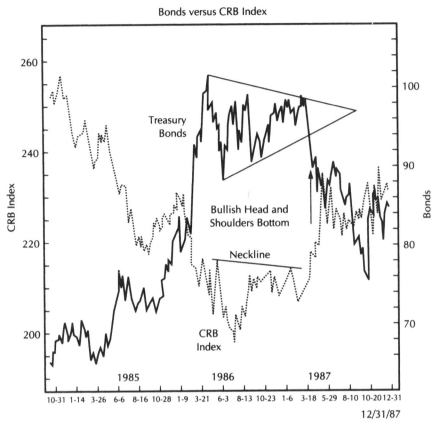

Bonds versus CRB Index

FIGURE 1.4   The inverse relationship between bond prices and commodities can be seen from 1985 through 1987. The bond market collapse in the spring of 1987 coincided with a bullish breakout in commodities.

bonds are considered to be leading indicators of stocks. Figure 1.5 shows the divergence between bond and stock prices from the spring of 1987 (when bonds peaked) until August (when stocks peaked). Bonds fulfilled their role as a leading indicator of stocks. By October, bond yields had climbed above 10 percent. Probably more than any other factor, this jump in interest rates to double-digit levels caused the October stock market crash. Figure 1.6 shows that the October 1987 plunge in stocks followed closely after bond yields climbed over 10 percent. In addition, the U.S. dollar played a role.

DOLLAR FALLS WITH STOCKS

The dollar, which had been declining earlier in the year, started a rebound in May that lasted into the summer. This rebound ended in August as the stock

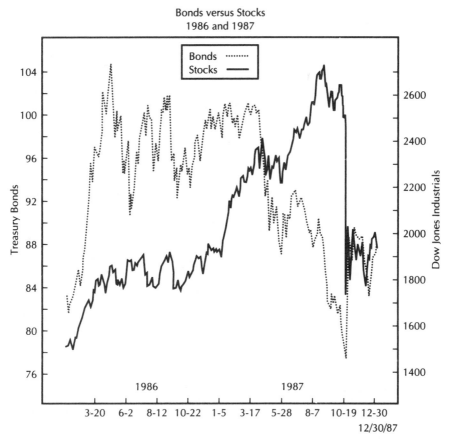

FIGURE 1.5 Bonds versus stocks during 1986 and 1987. Bonds collapsed in April of 1987 and preceded the August peak in stocks by four months.

market peaked. Both markets then fell together. A second rally attempt by the dollar during October also failed, and its subsequent plunge coincided almost exactly with the stock market crash. Figure 1.7 shows the close correlation between the peaks in the dollar and stocks during August and October 1987. Consider the sequence of events going into the fall of 1987. Commodity prices had turned sharply higher, fueling fears of renewed inflation. At the same time, interest rates soared to double digits. The U.S. dollar suddenly went into freefall (fueling even more inflation fears). Is it any wonder that the stock market finally ran into trouble? Given all of the bearish activity in the surrounding markets, it is surprising that the stock market held up as well as it did for as long as it did. There were plenty of reasons why the stock market should have sold off in late 1987. Most of those reasons were visible in the action of surrounding financial markets—like commodi-

FIGURE 1.6 The surge in bond yields in the summer and fall of 1987 had a bearish influence on stocks. From July to October of that year, Treasury bond yields surged from 8.50 percent to over 10.00 percent. The surge in bond yields was tied to the collapsing bond market and rising commodities.

ties and bonds—but not necessarily in the stock market itself. The events of 1987 provide a textbook example of how intermarket linkages work. That traumatic market year also makes a compelling argument as to why stock market participants need to monitor the other three financial markets.

THE 1987 MARKET CRASH WAS GLOBAL

Another important lesson of 1987 is the fact that the market crash was global in scope—world markets fell together. This is important for two reasons. First, it is a dramatic demonstration of how global stock markets are linked.

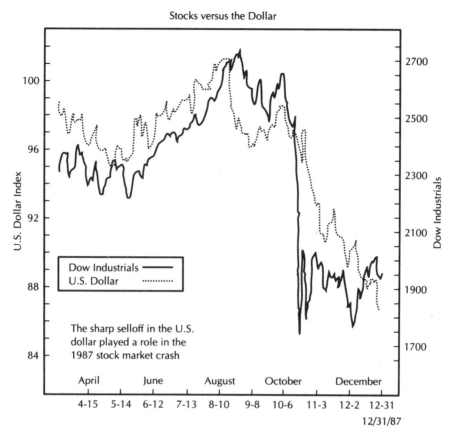

Stocks versus the Dollar

FIGURE 1.7   The falling U.S. dollar during the second half of 1987 also weighed
on stock prices. The twin peaks in the U.S. currency in August and
October of that year coincided with similar peaks in the stock
market. The collapse in the U.S. dollar in October also paralleled
the drop in equities.

Second, it shows that world stock markets become even more closely linked
during serious downturns than they are normally. At such times, global diversification becomes a myth. (The same phenomenon of a global bear market in
stocks is apparent starting in 2000.) Global linkages are not limited to stock
markets, either. Foreign currencies are linked to the U.S. dollar. Trends in
inflation and deflation (which are reflected in commodity prices) are global.

There is another lesson having to do with the global nature of the 1987
stock market crash. Many market observers at the time took the narrow
view that various futures-related strategies—like program trading and portfolio insurance—actually caused the selling panic. They reasoned that there
did not seem to be any economic or technical justification for the stock

market collapse. The fact that the equity crash was global in nature, and not limited to the U.S. market, argued against such a narrow view, especially since most foreign markets at the time were not affected by program trading or portfolio insurance.

LATER EXAMPLES OF GLOBAL LINKAGES

During the Iraq crisis of 1990 and again in 2003, rising energy prices slowed global economic growth and contributed to weakness in all of the world's major stock markets. The rise in oil prices during 1990 also pushed interest rates higher all over the world and once again showed how global interest rates rise and fall together. After 1998, a close correlation developed between falling global interest rates—including those in the United States—and a falling Japanese stock market, which was caught in the grip of deflation. Figure 1.8 shows interest rates moving higher around the globe during the inflationary 1970s and then falling together during the disinflationary 1980s and the deflationary 1990s.

THE DOLLAR'S IMPACT CAN BE DELAYED

Of the four financial markets used in intermarket work, the dollar is probably the most difficult to fit into a consistent intermarket model. Long delays between trend changes in the dollar and other markets are part of the reason for that. The events leading up to 1987 provide a good example of why this is so. After rallying for five years, the dollar started to drop in 1985, largely due to the Plaza Accord, a five-nation agreement designed to drive down the price of the dollar. Normally, a falling dollar would give a boost to commodity prices. But this boost did not come—at least not right away. It was not until a year later—in 1986—that the commodity decline that started in 1980 started to level off and bond prices stopped going up. When commodities started to rally during the spring of 1987, the real problems started. It took almost two years for the falling dollar to stimulate a serious rally in commodities—and cause problems for bonds and stocks. Figure 1.9 shows the lag time between two events (the 1985 dollar peak and the 1986 bottom in commodity prices) and the upturn that took place during the spring of 1987. The falling dollar eventually had an impact, but it took a year or two for it to take effect.

Intermarket trends during the 1980s also show why the impact of the dollar's direction on bonds and stocks needs to be filtered through the com-

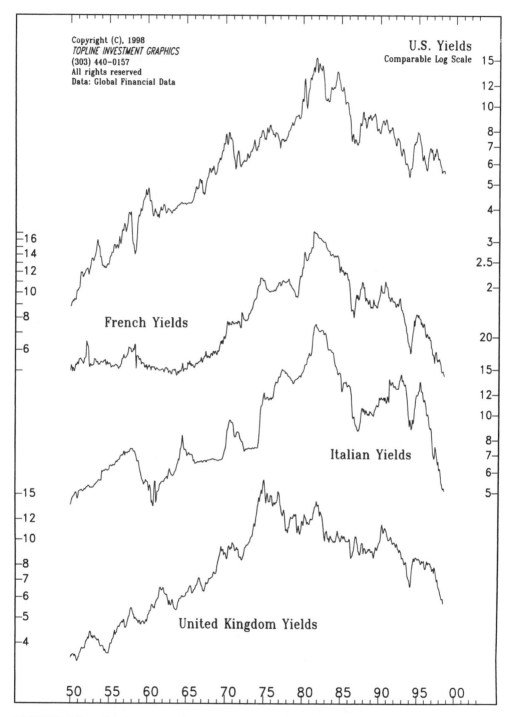

FIGURE 1.8   Global bond yields rose during the inflationary 1970s and fell during the disinflationary 1980s and 90s. Global rates usually rise and fall together.

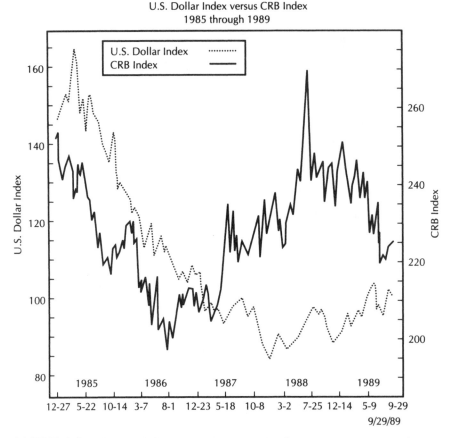

FIGURE 1.9   The U.S. dollar versus the CRB index from 1985 through the fourth quarter of 1989. A falling dollar will eventually push the CRB index higher. The 1986 bottom in the CRB index occurred a year after the 1985 peak in the dollar.

modity markets. A falling dollar can be bearish for bonds and stocks, but only if it coincides with rising commodity prices. (It can also be said that a falling dollar is not a serious problem until it starts to push interest rates higher, which is usually the result of rising commodity prices.) A falling dollar can coexist with rising bond and stock prices, as long as commodity prices do not rise. The decline of the dollar that started in 1985 did not have much of an impact on either bonds or stocks—until commodity prices (and interest rates) turned up during April 1987. Figure 1.10 shows the delayed effect of a falling dollar on interest rates. The dollar peaked in 1985. Bonds peaked one year later, but did not really start tumbling until the spring of 1987. A falling

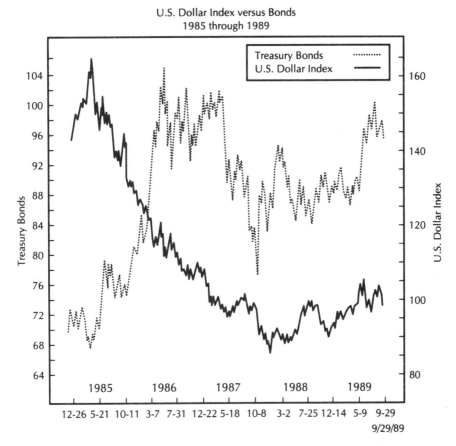

U.S. Dollar Index versus Bonds
1985 through 1989

FIGURE 1.10   The U.S. dollar versus Treasury bond prices from 1985 through 1989. A falling dollar is eventually bearish for bonds. During all of 1985 and most of 1986, bonds were strong while the dollar was weak.

dollar became a problem for stocks when its inflationary impact pushed bond prices lower and interest rates higher.

Some have argued that the generally weak dollar in the years between 1985 and 1995 did not have much of a negative impact on bonds and stocks. There is some validity to this argument, since bonds and stocks continued to enjoy major advances during those 10 years. However, it is also true that dollar peaks in 1985 and 1989 preceded the 1987 and 1990 bear markets (in bonds and stocks) by two years and one year, respectively. In addition, commodities rallied during both bear markets as a result of that dollar weakness. It is also true that the 1994 bear trend in bonds and stocks followed another peak in the dollar and an upturn in commodity prices.

ONWARD AND UPWARD TO 1990

Bond and stock prices stabilized during the fourth quarter of 1987 and began a two-year advance that lasted from the start of 1988 to the end of 1989. The intermarket picture during those two years had reverted to a more benign alignment: a strong dollar, weak commodities, and rising bond and stock prices. At the start of 1990, however, things took a turn for the worse. It started with a drop in bond prices, a selloff in the dollar, and a rally in commodities, all of which are negative signs for the stock market. Then came the Iraqi invasion of Kuwait in early August of that year. Oil prices spiked to $40 per barrel. The result was a bear market in stocks and a recession. Because of the lessons that can be learned from studying the intermarket relationships of 1990 and their relevance to geopolitical events 13 years later, we will examine that landmark year in more depth in the next chapter.

CHAPTER 2

1990 and the First Persian Gulf War

I n the fall of 1990, my earlier book on intermarket analysis was just going to press.[1] In the Appendix, I included charts of the most important intermarket relationships through the third quarter of that year. It was gratifying to see how well the markets followed their intermarket script despite the Mideast crisis that gripped the global financial markets during the summer of 1990. But that was only part of the story. Iraq invaded Kuwait in August of that year, which made a bad situation even worse. However, intermarket relationships had started to deteriorate at least six months earlier. As was the case during 1987, the deterioration started in the bond and commodity pits during the first half of the year. Bonds started to fall at the start of the year, while commodity prices rose. The dollar was weak. Then things went from bad to worse.

After the Kuwait invasion, crude oil soared to $40 a barrel which pushed stock markets lower all over the world. Gold prices also jumped as the dollar and stocks weakened. These are both classic intermarket relationships. Interest rates jumped all over the world in reaction to higher energy prices. The result was the start of a recession in the United States a month after the invasion. (This was not the only time that rising oil prices had contributed to a U.S. recession. The U.S. economy had suffered four recessions since 1970. Three of the four—those that took place in 1974, 1980, and 1990—were accompanied by surging oil prices. Nine years later, surging oil prices in 1999 contributed to the onset of another recession and, in the process, helped burst the bubble in the Nasdaq market.) Interestingly, the stock market suffered its biggest losses during the five months following the 1990 Iraq invasion.

---

[1]*Intermarket Technical Analysis: Trading Strategies for the Global Stock, Bond, Commodity, and Currency Markets*, John Wiley & Sons, 1990.

Once the war actually started (on January 16, 1991), all of the preexisting intermarket relationships reversed. Gold and oil tumbled while stocks soared. Both at the start and at the end of this earlier Mideast crisis, the traditional intermarket relationships held. Some intermarket trends had already started to change, however, at the start of 1990 in the futures pits. Let's start there.

BONDS TURN DOWN IN EARLY 1990

At the beginning of 1990, treasury bond prices had been rising for almost two years. Starting in January, however, bond prices started to drop sharply and continued to do so until October of that year (more on that later). To use intermarket parlance, a *negative divergence* was created between bonds and stocks. As was the case in 1987, it was an early warning of stock market problems to come. Part of the reason that bond prices were falling was a rise in commodity prices—also just like the situation in 1987. Figure 2.1 is a snap-

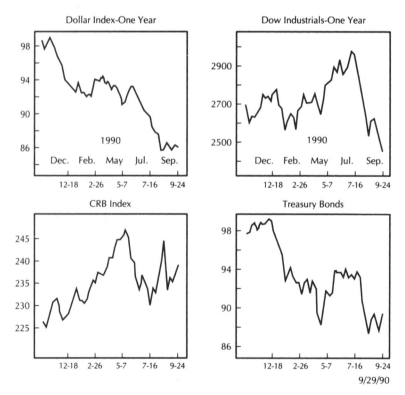

FIGURE 2.1   Charts of the four sectors—the dollar, CRB Index, stocks, and bonds—through the third quarter of 1990. A weak dollar during most of 1990 helped support commodity prices and put downward pressure on bonds and stocks.

shot of the four markets—the dollar, the CRB Index, stocks, and bonds— through the first three quarters of 1990. A falling dollar boosted commodities and hurt bonds during the first half of the year, which hurt stocks during the second half of the year.

CRB TURNS UP IN EARLY 1990

The CRB Index of commodity markets was rising at the start of 1990. That was partly due to a drop in the dollar during the second half of 1989, which coincided with a rebound in commodity markets. As 1990 wore on, the dollar dropped even more sharply. During most of 1990, a weak dollar helped support commodity prices and put downward pressure on bonds and stocks. Figure 2.2 shows how the falling dollar from the fourth quarter of 1989 to the fourth quarter of 1990 gave a big boost to commodity prices. The CRB rally

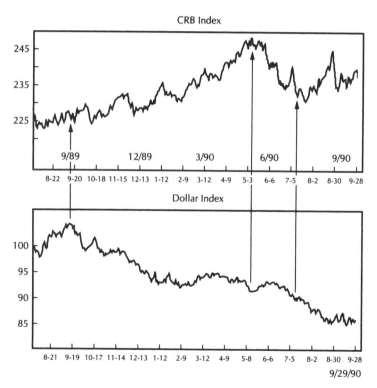

FIGURE 2.2   A comparison of the CRB Index to the U.S. dollar from late 1989 to September 1990. The falling dollar, which is inflationary, helped commodity prices advance during 1990. A bounce in the dollar during May contributed to the CRB peak that month. Commodities firmed again during the summer as the dollar dropped to new lows.

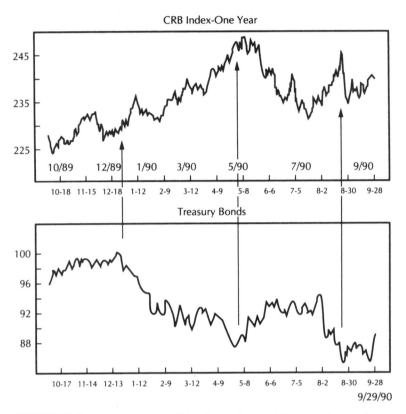

FIGURE 2.3   A comparison of the CRB Index and Treasury bonds from
late 1989 through the third quarter of 1990. During the
first half of 1990, commodities rallied while bonds
weakened. The bond bottoms in early May and late
August (see arrows) were accompanied by peaks in
commodity prices.

from late 1989 through the first half of 1990 was caused by rising agricultural
markets, many of which peaked by that summer. This explains the top in the
CRB Index during May of that year. Gold and oil both turned up that summer
and carried the CRB rally into October when it peaked for good. Those CRB
peaks during May and October coincided with bond bottoms. Figure 2.3
shows that commodity prices rose during the first half of 1990, coinciding
with a downturn in the bond market. It also shows two peaks in the CRB
Index producing bond rallies.

BONDS AND STOCKS DIVERGE

By May of 1990, bond prices had fallen more than 10 percent, while stock
prices remained relatively flat. From May to August, bonds and stocks re-

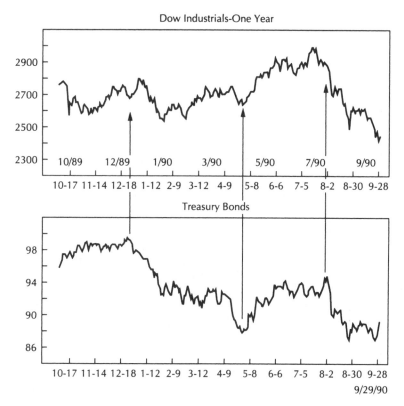

FIGURE 2.4 Stocks versus bonds from late 1989 through September 1990. After falling through the early portion of 1990, the bond trough in early May helped support the stock rally. Bonds failed to confirm the Dow's move to new highs during the summer. Both markets then tumbled together.

bounded together. During these three months, the Dow Industrials gained 300 points (10 percent) and reached a record high. Bonds regained only 50 percent of their first half's losses, and never came close to reaching their earlier highs. This set up a *bearish divergence* between bonds and stocks. By August, both tumbled together. Figure 2.4 shows the negative divergence that existed between bonds and stocks heading into the summer of 1990, months before the dramatic geopolitical events that started during August.

GLOBAL MARKETS DON'T CONFIRM U.S. RALLY

Major world markets like Britain, Japan, and the United States weakened at the beginning of 1990 and then rallied in the spring. Only the U.S. market, however, rallied to a new high. Neither of the other foreign markets confirmed the U.S. move into record territory during the summer of 1990. When any one

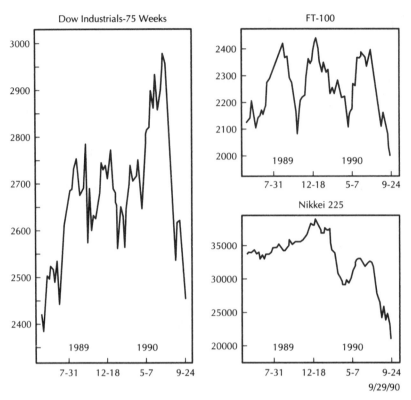

FIGURE 2.5 A comparison of American, British, and Japanese stock markets in the 18-month period ending in the third quarter of 1990. All three markets dropped sharply at the beginning of 1990 and then rallied in the spring. Neither of the foreign markets confirmed the American rally to new highs during the summer of 1990. The "triple top" in Britain and the collapse in Japan held bearish implications for American equities. Global markets then collapsed together.

global market (even one as big as the United States) is the only one to reach a new high, it qualifies as a *global divergence*. Figure 2.5 shows that the U.S. stock market was the only one to hit a new high during the summer of 1990. A bearish *triple top* pattern was forming in Britain. The Japanese market, which had peaked at the end of 1989, never recovered. It fell for another 13 years. The triple top in Britain and the collapse in Japan held bearish implications for U.S. equities.

IRAQ INVADES KUWAIT IN AUGUST

On August 2, 1990, Iraq invaded Kuwait, which set events in motion that led up to the 1991 Persian Gulf War. As it turns out, it was not much of a war.

But it threw a scare into the financial markets for the six months leading up to the actual outbreak of hostilities. How the markets reacted to the geopolitical situation was in itself another lesson in intermarket linkages. Each and every market did pretty much what was expected of it during the period leading up to the war. Bonds and stocks fell, as did the dollar. Gold and oil prices rose sharply. This was also a global phenomenon that affected bond and stock prices all over the world. From August to October, major declines were seen in the bond markets of Britain, Germany, Japan, and the United States—while oil prices soared. With oil rising all over the world, and global bonds falling, major stock markets everywhere tumbled as well. Figure 2.6 shows how rising crude oil prices in 1990 pushed bond prices downward in the United States, Britain, Germany, and Japan. It was truly a global event.

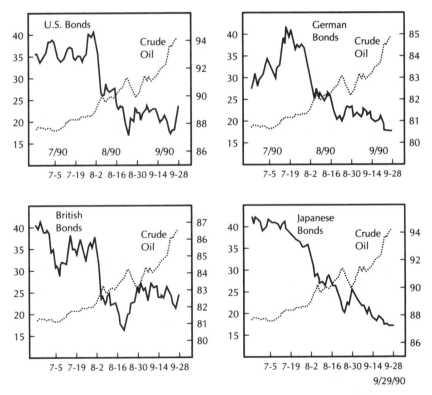

FIGURE 2.6 A comparison of the American, British, German, and Japanese bond markets during the summer of 1990. Global bond markets tumbled as oil prices surged following Iraq's invasion of Kuwait on August 2, 1990. Japanese bonds turned in the worst performance (owing to Japan's greater dependence on oil), not only leading global bond prices lower but also accounting for the collapse of Japanese equities.

OIL AND GOLD SOAR

The inflationary impact of rising oil prices during the summer of 1990 took a bearish toll on equity prices around the globe. Oil became the dominant commodity during that year and demonstrated in dramatic fashion how sensitive bond and stock markets are to action in the commodity sector. Gold prices also jumped, although not as dramatically as oil. Starting in August, gold prices rose over $60 (almost 20 percent) before finally peaking. (Like oil, gold has a history of trending in the opposite direction of the stock market.) Any comparison of gold or oil during the second half of 1990 (and early 1991) will show the two key commodities moving in the opposite direction of the stock market, which is their normal pattern. Figures 2.7 and 2.8 show the

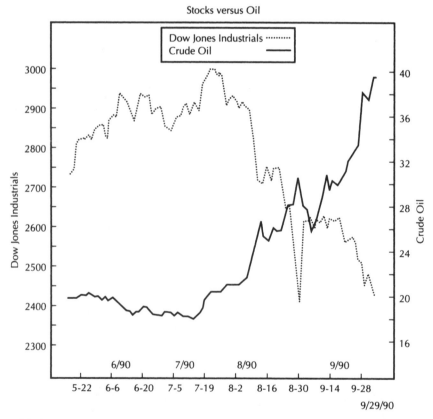

FIGURE 2.7   Dow Industrials versus crude oil during the summer of 1990. The inflationary impact of surging oil prices during the summer of 1990 took a bearish toll on equity prices everywhere on the globe. Oil became the dominant commodity during 1990 and demonstrated how sensitive bond and stock markets are to action in the commodity sector.

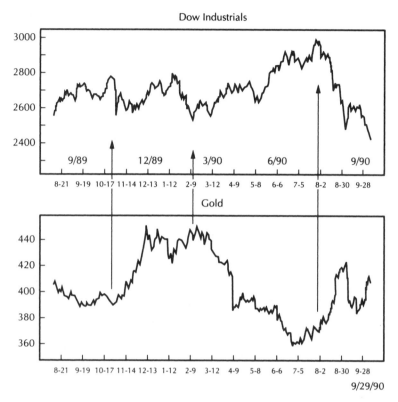

FIGURE 2.8   Gold versus the Dow Industrials from the summer of 1989 to the autumn of 1990. The gold rally in the fall of 1989 coincided with stock market weakness. The February 1990 peak in gold coincided with a rally in stocks. Gold rose during the summer of 1990 as stocks weakened. Throughout the period shown, gold did best when the stock market faltered.

inverse correlation between the two key commodities—gold and oil—and the stock market in 1990. The weak dollar fell even harder after the invasion, which added more strength to the rallies in oil and gold. Gold and oil stocks continued to rally while the rest of the market tumbled. Figure 2.9 shows how the falling dollar in 1990 gave a boost to gold prices, especially at the start of the year and at mid-year.

EVERYTHING REVERSES AT THE START OF WAR

As so often happens in the financial markets, the anticipation of an event is usually worse than the event itself. The markets discount expected events well before they happen. The event can be anything from a bad earnings report to a war. And, as so often happens, the markets reverse on the actual

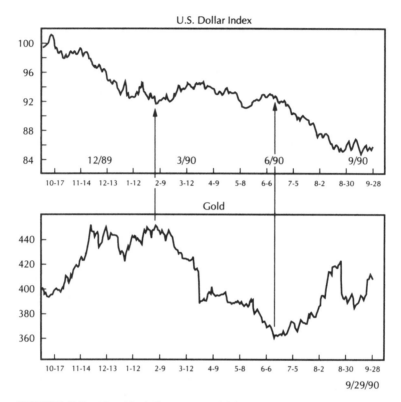

FIGURE 2.9   The U.S. dollar versus gold from late 1989 through
September 1990. The declining dollar during most of 1990
wasn't enough to turn the gold trend higher. However, the
inverse relationship can still be seen, especially during
the dollar selloffs in late 1989 and June 1990, when gold
rallied. The interim bottom in the dollar in February 1990
was enough to push gold prices lower.

event when it does occur. At least this is what happened in mid-January 1991
when the Persian Gulf War started. The bombing of Iraq started on the
evening of January 16, 1991. The following trading day, gold and oil prices
tumbled while stocks soared. Within a month, the dollar had put in a bottom
and turned higher.

Figure 2.10 shows gold and oil prices tumbling at the outbreak of war in
mid-January 1991. Both commodities had turned up that August just after the
Iraq invasion of Kuwait. Oil had actually peaked at $40 during October but
was attempting another rebound during January 1991. The outbreak of war
caused oil to lose almost half of its value within a month. Gold declined from
$400 to $350 in the three months after the war started. A big bounce in the
dollar contributed to the commodity selloff. At the same time, a major rotation took place after the war started. Only this time it was out of commodities and back into the dollar, bonds, and stocks.

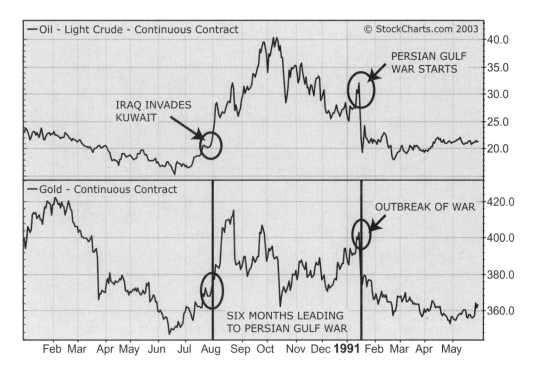

FIGURE 2.10   Gold and oil tumbled at the outbreak of war in mid-January 1991.

Bonds rallied at the start of the war, but not as dramatically as stocks. Part of the reason for the more muted reaction in bonds was that U.S Treasuries had already risen 15 percent since October in an apparent "flight to safety." When the war started, stocks did better than bonds for the first month thereafter as traders moved money from the safety of bonds back into the stock market. Figure 2.11 shows the dollar bottoming within a month after the outbreak of war. This contributed to the tumble in commodity prices but was good for bonds and stocks. Figure 2.11 also shows that bond prices had bottomed during October (as oil peaked) and had acted as a safe haven for the next three months leading up to the war. Bonds hit a temporary peak after the war when they lost some of their safe haven status and money rotated back into stocks.

The Dow also hit its lowpoint in October, but had shown only modest gains until the following January. From mid-January to mid-February (the month following the start of the war), the Dow had risen nearly 500 points (a 20 percent gain) while Treasury bonds gained a much smaller 5 percent. It is interesting to once again see bond prices acting as a leading indicator for stocks. Bonds peaked before stocks during the first half of 1990, and rallied more than stocks during the second half. (One of our intermarket principles

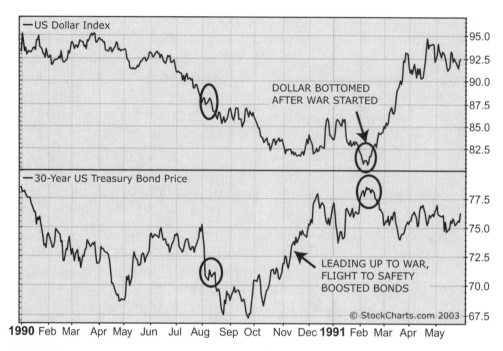

FIGURE 2.11 The dollar bottomed a month after the outbreak of the Persian Gulf War. Bonds bottomed the prior October.

FIGURE 2.12 The Dow soared in the months after the Persian Gulf War started.

is that bonds usually lead stocks.) Figure 2.12 shows the Dow Industrials soaring in the months after the war started. The Dow had fallen from 3,000 to 2,400 in the three months after the Iraq invasion before bottoming in October along with bonds (as oil peaked). The January pullback retraced about half of the rally from October to December and has been described by chartists as a *right shoulder* in a bullish head and shoulders bottom (the right shoulder is the third and final trough in a head and shoulders bottom).

1990 DIVERGENCE BETWEEN OIL AND OIL SHARES

The action of oil stocks throughout 1990 provides us with another intermarket lesson. During that year, oil stocks acted as a leading indicator for crude oil, both on the way up and on the way down. Although oil stocks soared with oil prices over the summer, they had actually turned up two months earlier. More importantly, oil stocks peaked a couple of months before the commodity did that October. As the price of crude was nearing $40 that autumn, oil shares had already started dropping. This gave an early warning of an oil top.

While putting the finishing touches on my earlier manuscript in the autumn of 1990, I included the following words: "As the third quarter of 1990 ended . . . falling oil shares have set up a negative divergence with the price of oil, which is testing its all-time high at $40." Figure 2.13 is the same chart that I included in the earlier book. You can see the obvious negative divergence to which I referred. I wrote these words because one of the intermarket relationships has to do with how a commodity relates to its shares. They should move in the same direction. For example, rising oil shares should accompany rising oil prices. When they start to diverge, it is usually an early warning of an impending trend change. In addition, stocks usually change direction ahead of their related commodity. This makes energy shares a leading indicator for oil. Anyone who was aware of this relationship in 1990 got an early warning that the oil rally was nearly done, which also meant that the bear markets in bonds and stocks were nearing completion as well. Both markets hit their lows in October, just as oil was peaking near $40.

THE IMPORTANCE OF $40 OIL

The $40 price level plays an important role in the history of crude oil. This resistance level has stopped every major advance in the price of crude in

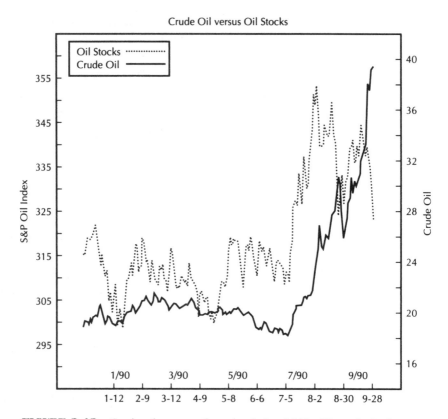

FIGURE 2.13   Crude oil versus oil stocks during 1990. Oil stocks had spent
the first half of 1990 in a holding pattern while oil prices
weakened. Oil stocks exploded to new highs in early July
when oil bottomed. As the third quarter of 1990 ended,
however, falling oil shares have set up a "negative divergence"
with the price of oil, which is testing its all-time high at $40.

over 30 years. Oil peaked at $40 in 1980 just as the commodity bubble was
bursting. It reached that level again during Desert Storm in 1991, then turned
back down again. Twelve years later, during the second Iraq crisis (in the
early part of 2003), oil prices reached that key level once again before falling
sharply at the start of that war.

INTERMARKET LESSONS LEARNED DURING 1990

Some of the intermarket relationships that manifested themselves during
1990 were:

- Bond prices and commodity prices moved in opposite directions
- A falling dollar boosted commodities and hurt both bonds and stocks

- Bonds peaked ahead of stocks and then led them higher after October
- Gold and oil prices moved in the opposite direction of stocks all year
- All major global markets trended together, including bonds and stocks
- Oil shares provided an early warning of the October top in crude oil prices
- Rising oil prices contributed to another recession

COMPARISONS BETWEEN 2003 AND 1991

Intermarket trends witnessed during the Desert Storm era were remarkably similar to those witnessed during the second Iraq crisis over a decade later in 2002–2003. In the later conflict, gold and oil prices soared (while the dollar and stocks fell) in the months leading up to the second Iraq invasion just as they had in 1990. In 2003, traders were expecting a replay of the events of 1990–1991 at the outbreak of war—and they were not disappointed. The week that hostilities started (March 20, 2003) the U.S. stock market recorded a gain of 8 percent—the biggest in 20 years. Oil prices (which had peaked at $39.99 on February 28) fell $13 for a loss of 33 percent. Gold prices (which peaked at $390 on February 5) had fallen $60, or 15 percent. The U.S. dollar jumped 4 percent as gold fell and stocks rose. Bond prices, which had been rising as stocks fell, had their biggest drop in two years; there was a massive switch from the relative safety of bonds back into stocks.

International reactions were equally dramatic. Global bond yields jumped as geopolitical tensions eased. In currency markets the Euro, the Japanese yen, and the Swiss franc (which had previously acted as a safe haven) fell sharply. Stock markets all over the world jumped markedly. The German DAX (which had been the weakest market in Europe) gained 10 percent, Korea's index rose 7 percent, and Brazil's 3 percent, to name just a few examples. Within a week of the start of the 2003 Iraq war, all the preexisting intermarket trends had been reversed—just as had happened in 1991. In addition, each market did exactly what it was expected to do. The two situations were not completely the same, however.

While the intermarket reactions during the two wars in the Mideast were remarkably similar, long-term trends were not. In 1990, the stock market was in the midst of a major bull market that had another eight years to run. Commodity markets were in the middle of a major bear market that lasted another decade. The rise in commodities—and the decline in stocks—in 1990 were short-term corrections to long-term trends. After January 1991, stocks resumed their bull market while commodities resumed their downtrend. At the start of 2003, however, the situations were reversed. The 20-year secular bull market in stocks had ended, and commodities had entered a new bull market. This situation was very different from 1990. The intermarket reactions were similar in both Iraq wars; what differed, though, were the major trends of the key markets.

JAPAN NEVER RECOVERS

All the major global stock markets resumed their long-term bull trends at the start of 1991—with one notable exception. The Japanese stock market, which had peaked near the end of 1989, kept dropping even after resolution of the first Persian Gulf War. By the start of the second Iraq war in 2003, the Nikkei 225 (the main index of Japanese stocks) had just fallen to the lowest level in 20 years. During this 13-year decline, the Nikkei dropped from 39,000 to 8,000, losing close to a staggering 80 percent of its value. This was the biggest crash in a major stock market since 1929. Although the Japanese collapse did not have an immediate influence on other global markets, its bearish influence was felt a decade later when Japanese deflation was exported to other parts of the world. The 78 percent decline in the Nasdaq market after 2000 also provoked comparisons to the deflationary years in the United States from 1929–1932. As is described later in the book, deflation became a big issue at the start of the new millennium and changed some important intermarket relationships. Although nobody knew it at the time, the deflationary problems of the early 2000s actually started with the bursting of the Japanese bubble just as the 1980s were ending and the 1990s were starting.

CHAPTER 3

The Stealth Bear Market of 1994

THINGS LOOK GOOD FROM 1990 THROUGH 1993

Immediately after the Persian Gulf War, intermarket trends turned favorable again for the next three years. From early 1991 to the end of 1993, bond and stock prices rose together. Commodities were generally weak. The U.S. dollar, which bottomed early in 1991, was firm. A dip in the dollar from mid-1991 to mid-1992 did not cause much damage to bonds and stocks, mainly because commodities remained weak. (Recall that a falling dollar only hurts bonds and stocks when commodities are rising.) Things started going badly for stocks, however, during the first quarter of 1994, then got steadily worse as the year progressed. Bond prices fell along with stocks as commodity prices rose. The rise in commodities was aided by a falling U.S. dollar, which peaked at the start of 1994 and fell during the rest of the year. Rising commodity prices and a falling dollar proved to be a bad intermarket recipe for bonds and stocks. As is usually the case, however, early warning signs showed up in the bond and commodity markets the previous year. Let's take a look.

A DESCRIPTION OF THE CRB INDEX

The CRB Index is the most widely followed measure of commodity price direction. During 1993 and 1994, it was made up of 21 commodity markets. Changes to the index in late 1995 reduced the number from 21 to 17. However, it still includes all of the major commodity groups: industrial metals, precious metals, energy, grain, livestock, and tropical commodities. Any long-range chart that compares the CRB Index to Treasury bond prices will show that they generally trend in opposite directions. However, the CRB Index is not the only commodity index. (It should be noted that the CRB Index has recently been renamed the CRB/Reuters Futures Price Index.)

THE CRB INDEX TURNS UP IN EARLY 1993

Heading into 1993, commodity prices were falling as bond prices were rising. During the first quarter of 1993, however, the CRB Index turned higher and rose through the balance of that year. Commodity and bond prices rose together until the fourth quarter of 1993, when bond prices suffered their worst collapse in half a century. Since these two markets generally trend in opposite directions, the rise in the CRB Index provided an early warning that the uptrend in bonds was unsustainable. The interplay between bonds and commodities during 1993 showed how activity in one asset class can affect another—and how one market can act as a leading indicator for another. (Commodity prices usually turn up before bond prices turn down.) It is also an excellent demonstration of how intermarket relationships can sometimes seem "out of line" for a period of time but still carry a warning.

In this case, the amount of time from the CRB bottom (in February) to the bond peak (in September) was a relatively lengthy seven months, but the end result was a virtual collapse in the bond market. Figure 3.1 shows the CRB Index and Treasury Bond prices rising together from February 1993 until that autumn. The rise in commodity prices eventually contributed to the collapse in bond prices during the fourth quarter of that year. Although the CRB Index did a good job at warning investors of a serious downturn in bond prices, it gets bad marks in 1993 for precision timing because it turned up half a year ahead of the peak in bonds. This brings us to the need to watch other commodity indexes and key individual commodities in order to get a more accurate read on the direction of commodity prices. And also to improve the timeliness of their signals. This is done by a closer monitoring of commodity prices more directly tied to the economy.

WATCH INDUSTRIAL PRICES

The CRB Index is often influenced by agricultural markets. This was true in early 1993; these markets accounted for most of the Index's upturn. (Gold also rose during that spring and summer.) Agricultural markets, however, are

FIGURE 3.1 Commodity Research Bureau Index of 17 commodity markets. The rise in commodity prices that started in early 1993 (point A) eventually caused the bond market peak at point B. Bond and commodity prices usually trend in opposite directions. *(MetaStock, Equis International, Inc.)*

more often affected by weather than economic trends. For this reason, it is a good idea to consult other measures of general commodity price trends and certain commodity sectors like industrial metals. Industrial metals like aluminum and copper are especially sensitive to economic trends because they are used in the building of autos and homes and have other industrial applications. For this reason, industrial commodities usually have a much closer correlation to bond prices than other commodities that are more weather-related, like grain and produce markets.

Copper prices actually fell during most of 1993 and only turned up that October, just when bond prices were peaking. Figure 3.2 shows that the

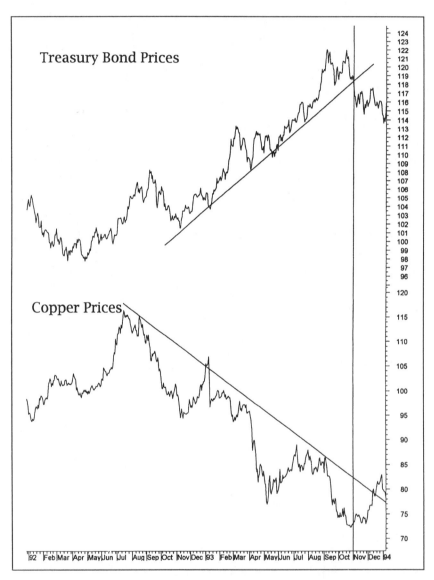

FIGURE 3.2   The bond price peak in late 1993 coincided with a major bottom in copper. Falling copper prices imply economic weakness which is bullish for bond prices. The dramatic rally in copper that began in late 1993 helped push bond prices lower. *(MetaStock, Equis International, Inc.)*

upturn in copper during the fourth quarter of 1993 coincided almost exactly with the bond market peak. The chart also shows a strong inverse correlation between copper and bond prices. Copper fell throughout most of 1993 as bond prices rose. Copper turned up during the fourth quarter just as bond prices were peaking. Figure 3.2 shows that bond prices fell below a rising support line just as copper rose above a falling resistance line. (A support line is drawn under price lows in an uptrend. A resistance line is drawn over price peaks in a downtrend. The breaking of those lines usually means that existing trends are reversing.) Not only did the copper bottom coincide with the bond top in late 1993, but the bulk of 1994 saw falling bond prices accompanied by surging copper prices.

Figure 3.3 is an overlay comparison of the copper and bond markets during 1993 and 1994. The chart shows them turning together during the fourth quarter of 1993. It also shows that copper prices rose through most of 1994 while bond prices fell. During both years, bonds and copper maintained a close inverse relationship. The rotation from a weak bond market to a strong copper market accounted for an important sector rotation within the stock market. While *interest rate sensitive* stocks like utilities followed bonds lower, industrial metal shares followed copper higher during 1994. Given their strong influence over interest rates and the fact that they are more closely tied to economic trends, industrial prices are preferred by most economists. It was only a matter of time until economists created a commodity index of industrial prices.

THE JOURNAL OF COMMERCE (JOC–ECRI) INDEX

The most widely followed index of industrial commodity prices is the Journal of Commerce (JOC)–Economic Cycle Research Institute (ECRI) Industrial Price Index. The original JOC index was created in 1986 by Geoffrey H. Moore[1] and his research staff located in New York. The latest JOC-ECRI Index was revised at the start of 2000 by the same team of researchers. What distinguishes this index from the others is the careful selection of commodities that have been shown to have the best cyclical relationship to inflation. What also distinguishes the JOC-ECRI Index from the others is the fact that it includes only industrial prices—it excludes food, grains, and precious metals. The JOC-ECRI Index includes 18 industrial prices grouped into textiles, metals, petroleum products (including crude oil), and miscellaneous prod-

---

[1]Dr. Moore, now deceased, was one of this country's leading experts on the business cycle.

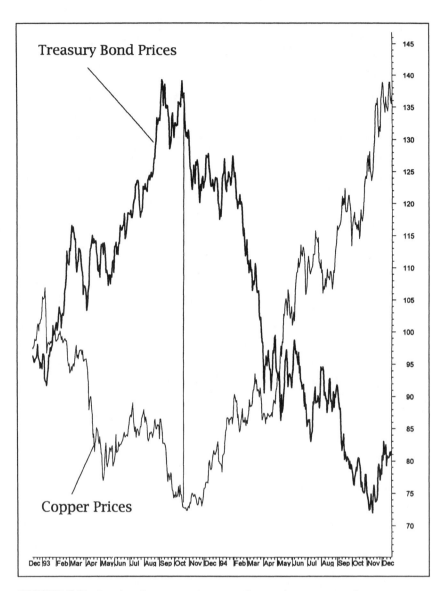

FIGURE 3.3   Bond and copper prices usually trend in opposite directions.
The 1993 bond peak coincided with a major bottom in copper.
(MetaStock, Equis International, Inc.)

ucts (including plywood). The metals markets include aluminum, copper,
lead, tin, zinc, and nickel.

In 1993, the JOC Index tracked bond yields very closely. (Industrial commodities trend in the opposite direction of bond prices. Since bond prices
and yields trend in opposite directions, that means that industrial prices trend

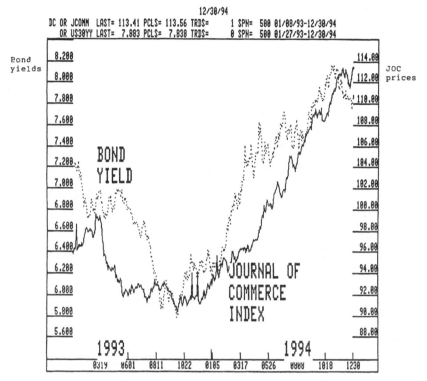

FIGURE 3.4   The upturn in the JOC Index of Industrial Material Prices coincided exactly with the major bottom in bond yields in late 1993.

in the same direction as bond yields.) Figure 3.4 shows both markets falling together throughout most of the 1993 and turning up together during the fourth quarter. They rose together for most of the following year. The JOC Index gave traders a much more precise read on when interest rates were more likely to trough—and when bond prices were about to begin their major decline. (More information on the JOC-ECRI index can be found on the website of the Economic Cycle Research Institute *(www.businesscycle.com)*. We will refer to the pioneering work of Geoffrey Moore in Chapter 12 when we discuss the rotation of bonds, stocks, and commodities at different stages in the business cycle.)

GOLD AND OIL ARE ALSO IMPORTANT

In addition to industrial metals, two other commodities that should be watched closely are gold and oil. Gold is viewed as a traditional leading indicator of inflation and carries important psychological weight. Investors may not be very concerned about rising soybean prices, but a jump in the price of gold makes headlines. The Federal Reserve Board also watches gold prices to determine if monetary policy is on course. Gold price direction also has a major influence on the trend of gold mining shares.

The price of energy has more than a psychological effect on the inflation picture. It also has an important impact on the economy. The previous chapter discusses the fact that rising oil prices have been a contributing factor in most recent recessions. Oil-related stocks are also largely dependent on the trend of oil.

A sharp rise in either of these two key commodities sends an *immediate* warning to bond traders and an *early* warning to stock traders. A rise in both commodities is especially dangerous for bonds and stocks. During the summer of 1993, gold prices rose but oil prices continued to drop. As a result, the bond and stock markets were not impacted by the rise in gold. Oil prices started jumping early in 1994. Rising gold and oil prices together added to the bearish sentiment in bonds and stocks that year.

GOLDMAN SACHS COMMODITY INDEX

The Goldman Sachs Commodity Index (GSCI) is the newest of the three indexes. It includes most of the same commodity markets as the CRB Index, but is a trade-weighted index. In other words, it weights the various commodities according to their importance in world trade. As a result, energy prices comprise over half of its weighting. It is thus not as useful in measuring overall commodity price trends, but is helpful in monitoring the impact of energy prices on the overall commodity price trend. The GSCI was the last of the commodity indexes to turn up during the 1993–1994 time period. It bottomed just as 1994 was starting and oil prices were starting to firm. This meant that all three commodity indexes—the CRB, the JOC, and the GSCI—were rising at the start of 1994. Figure 3.5 shows the GSCI turning up sharply at the start of 1994. This was a sign that energy prices (which dominate the GSCI) were rising. An upside breakout in late 1995 also signaled higher energy inflation.

Since none of these commodity indexes is perfect, it is a good idea to keep an eye on all of them. The most convincing evidence of commodity price trends occurs when all of the commodity indexes are trending in the same direction, as they were at the start of 1994. The GSCI and the CRB Indexes are both traded as futures contracts and their prices are readily available and easily charted.

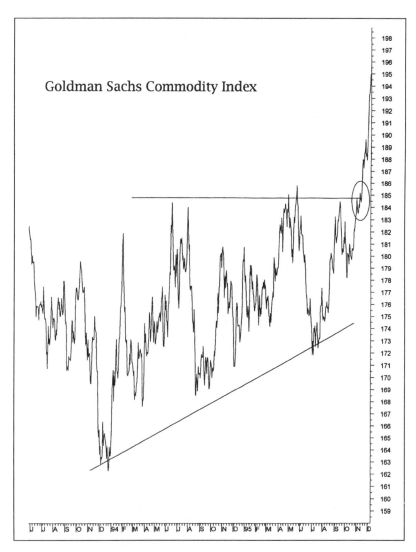

FIGURE 3.5 A bullish breakout in late 1995 by this energy-dominated index signaled higher energy inflation. *(MetaStock, Equis International, Inc.)*

BONDS PEAK AHEAD OF STOCKS

Commodity prices affect the direction of bond prices. Bond prices, in turn, affect the direction of stock prices. Rising bond prices (falling bond yields) are positive for equity prices. Falling bond prices (rising bond yields) are negative for equities. Turns in the bond market, however, usually precede similar turns in the stock market by several months. As such, important turns in the direction of bond prices can provide an early warning of an impending turn in stocks. This was certainly the case in the months leading up to the 1994 bear market in stocks. The bond market peaked during September 1993. The stock market peaked during February 1994, five months after the bond peak. Figure 3.6 overlays the Dow Industrials and Treasury Bond prices

FIGURE 3.6 Bond prices usually lead stock prices. The bond market top in late 1993 (point A) warned of a stock market top within six months (point B). *(MetaStock, Equis International, Inc.)*

during 1993 and 1994. The chart shows the stock market peaking within six months of the bond market peak. It also shows the bond bottom during the fourth quarter of 1994 coinciding with a bottom in the Dow.

THE STEALTH BEAR MARKET

Bonds suffered their worst fall in decades. The major stock averages lost little more than 10 percent from peak to trough. The relatively small declines in the major averages that year masked more serious damage in some sectors of the market, which is why it is often called a "stealth" bear market. Smaller stocks, as represented in the Russell 2000 and the Nasdaq market, lost 15 percent. Figure 3.7 compares the Dow Industrials with the New York Stock Exchange (NYSE) Advance–Decline line during 1994. The contrast between the two lines is striking; it shows that the broader market suffered much bigger losses than the major stock averages.

The stocks that bore the brunt of that bear year were in the transportation and interest rate groups. The Dow Transports lost 26 percent, probably owing to rising oil prices. The Dow Utilities were the hardest hit of all. Although they lost 26 percent from the start of 1994, they had actually started falling along with bonds the previous September. The utilities' total loss was closer to 34 percent from peak to trough.

A LOSS FOR UTILITIES IS A GAIN FOR METALS IN 1994

In addition to the negative macro effect that rising commodity and falling bond prices have on the stock market, it is important to consider the dynamic rotation that is caused within certain stock sectors. This consideration leads to an extremely important element in intermarket analysis: the interplay between the three asset classes (bonds, stocks, and commodities) which helps to explain the rotation within the stock market from sector to sector. This insight helps determine which sectors of the stock market to invest in at certain times to ensure that an investor is always in the sector that is outperforming the general market—and out of the ones that are doing the worst. The events of 1993 and 1994 had dramatically different effects on two stock market sectors.

Utility stocks are considered to be driven by interest rates and, as a result, track bond prices very closely. Figure 3.8 shows the remarkably close correlation between Treasury Bond prices and the Dow Utilities in 1993 and

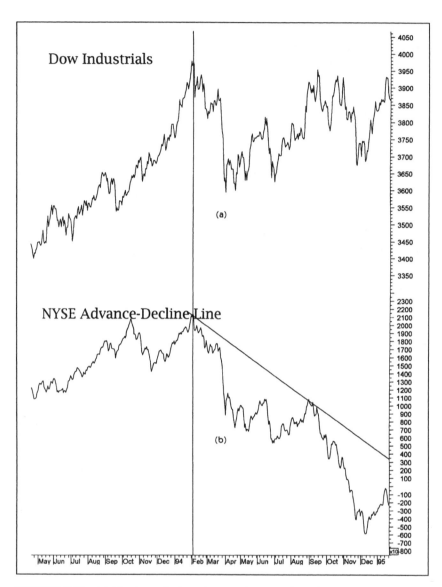

FIGURE 3.7 (*a*) The Dow decline during 1994 was less than 10 percent. (*b*) The NYSE AD Line failed to support the Dow rally to new highs in early 1994, creating a negative divergence. The broader market suffered much greater losses during 1994 in a "stealth" bear market. (*MetaStock, Equis International, Inc.*)

1994. Utilities peaked right along with bonds in September 1993 and continued to fall with bonds for the following year. During this time span, utilities lost 34 percent of their value. In a climate of falling bond prices, utilities are often among the stocks that suffer the greatest damage. (Financial stocks also often suffer more when bonds are falling.)

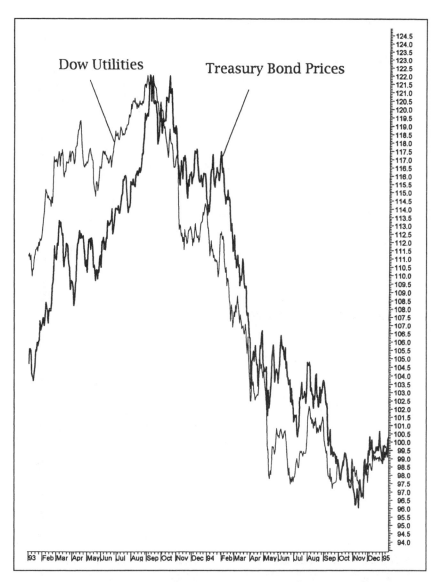

FIGURE 3.8   Bond prices and utility stocks usually trend in the same direction. They peaked together in late 1993 and bottomed together in late 1994. *(MetaStock, Equis International, Inc.)*

With industrial metals rising throughout the year, copper and aluminum stocks (and basic material stocks in general) did well in 1994 despite the fact that it was an otherwise dismal year. Figure 3.9 shows nonferrous metal stocks rising along with copper during 1994 and profiting accordingly. In the stock market as in real estate, the name of the game is *location*. In 1994, aluminum and copper stocks were a good place to be while utilities were not. (We will cover sector rotation more thoroughly in Chapter 13.)

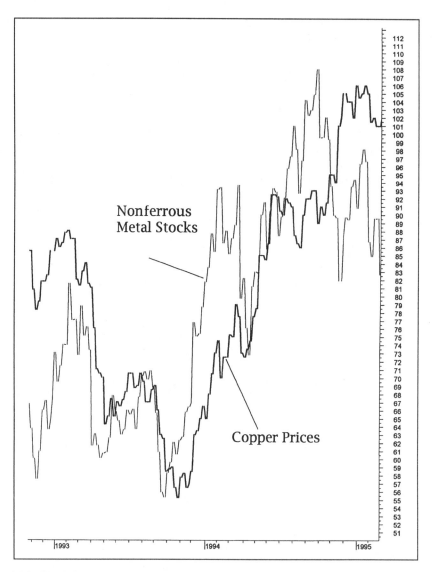

FIGURE 3.9   The bottom in copper prices may have been bearish for bonds
and utilities, but was bullish for related metal stocks.
(MetaStock, Equis International, Inc.)

INTERMARKET PICTURE REVERSES IN 1995

The normal rotation among the three assets classes is this: commodities turn
first, bonds turn second, and stocks turn last. A *bottom* in commodity prices
in 1993 preceded a *top* in bond prices, which was followed by a *top* in stock
prices. This is the normal rotation. The intermarket rotation that unfolded
in late 1994 and early 1995 followed this same order, but in the opposite

direction. The CRB Index peaked in the middle of 1994 (and traded sideways for the next year). Bond prices bottomed during November. Stocks bottomed within a month of bonds. Once again, the normal intermarket rotation occurred. Commodities peaked first, followed by a bottom in bonds, followed by a bottom in stocks. Once again, copper proved to be a *coincident* as opposed to a *leading* indicator for bond prices and utilities.

Figure 3.10 shows copper peaking near the end of 1994 just as the bond market was bottoming. Utilities bottomed along with bonds just as the price

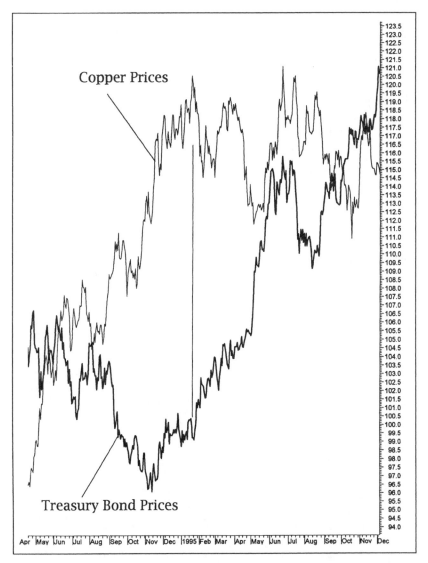

FIGURE 3.10   At the start of 1995, the peak in copper prices coincided with an important bottom in bond prices. *(MetaStock, Equis International, Inc.)*

of copper was peaking. Figure 3.11 shows the bond bottom in late 1994 occurring just ahead of a major bottom in the stock market. The U.S. dollar, which had been falling throughout 1994, turned up in the spring of 1995 and began a seven-year bull market. The stronger dollar had a dampening effect on commodities, but helped bonds and stocks.

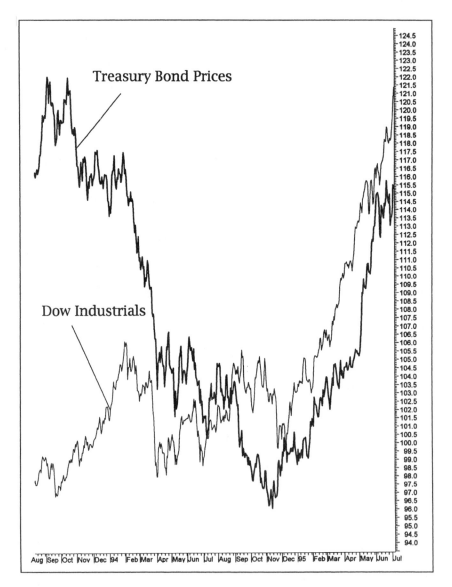

FIGURE 3.11 Weakness in bond prices during 1994 caused a 10 percent correction in stock prices and a year of consolidation. The late 1994 bottom in bonds helped launch another bull leg in stocks. *(MetaStock, Equis International, Inc.)*

THE CRB/BOND RATIO

Another simple indicator which is especially helpful in determining whether one's portfolio should be emphasizing *inflation-* or *rate-sensitive* stocks is the CRB/bond ratio. This simple ratio divides the price of the CRB Index (or any commodity index) by the price of Treasury Bonds (or T-Notes). The ratio is a measure of *relative strength*, a concept that is explored more fully later in the book. When the CRB/bond ratio is rising, commodity prices are outperforming bond prices. In such a climate, commodity markets (or commodity-related stocks) should be emphasized. Commodity-related stocks include basic materials and natural resources, such as aluminum, copper, gold mining, and energy. These are stocks that tend to outperform the general market during periods of rising inflation. Figure 3.12 shows the CRB/bond ratio advancing during most of 1994 and then peaking during the fourth quarter.

The CRB/bond ratio turned up in late 1993 and continued to rise for almost a year. This was during a period of time when copper stocks rose and utilities tumbled. A rising CRB/bond ratio is generally negative for the stock market, since it signals rising inflation and higher interest rates. (The negative influence of rising commodities on stocks holds true during inflationary and disinflationary periods—but not necessarily during a deflation. In a deflation, rising commodity prices are generally positive for stocks.) This also helps explain why 1994 was a difficult year for stocks and rate-sensitive stocks in particular. The peak in the ratio in November 1994 signaled a shift in the asset allocation mix away from commodity-type stocks and back to rate-sensitive stocks (and stocks in general). The peak in the CRB/bond ratio near the end of 1994 helped set the stage for a strong stock market advance that lasted until 2000.

BONDS AND STOCKS RISE TOGETHER UNTIL 1998

From their bottom during the fourth quarter of 1994, stocks began a phenomenal bull run that lasted until the end of the decade. During those five years, the Dow went from under 4,000 to nearly 12,000—more than a tripling in price. This gain was dwarfed by the technology-dominated Nasdaq market—it rose from 700 to 5,000 in those same five years, increasing its 1994 value by seven times. The stock market got a lot of help from the U.S. dollar during the five-year bull run. The U.S. Dollar Index rose from a value of 85 near the start of 1995 to 120 by 2000 for a gain of 40 percent. Commodity prices fell

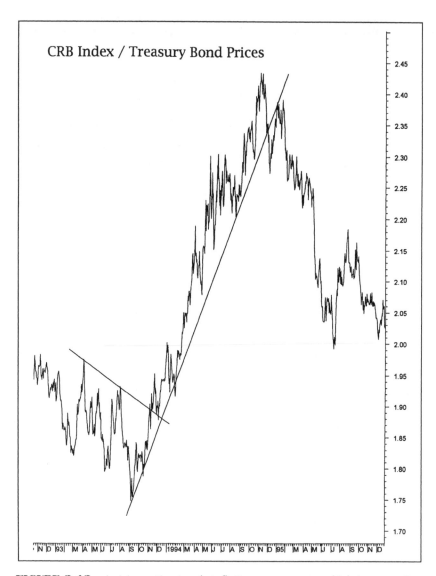

FIGURE 3.12 A rising ratio signals inflationary pressure, which is generally
negative for stocks (1994). The peak in the ratio in early
1995 was negative for commodities, but bullish for both
bonds and stocks. *(MetaStock, Equis International, Inc.)*

throughout most of that period and did not hit bottom until 1999. Treasury
bond prices, which had bottomed during November 1994, rose for the next
four years into the autumn of 1998. Until 1998, the intermarket relationships
that had held throughout most of the postwar era remained intact. A rising
dollar and falling commodities supported bull markets in bonds and stocks.
In 1998, however, some key intermarket relationships started to change.

CHAPTER 4

The 1997 Asian Currency Crisis and Deflation

ASIAN CURRENCY CRISIS STARTS IN 1997

The intermarket principles that I have described are based on market trends since 1970. The 1970s saw runaway inflation, which favored commodity assets. The 1980s and 1990s were characterized by falling commodities (disinflation) and strong bull markets in bonds and stocks. Starting in 1997, however, some changes started showing up in the traditional intermarket model. The problems started with a currency crisis in Thailand during 1997 and climaxed with another one in Russia during 1998. The events of 1997 and 1998 provided a dramatic example of how closely linked global markets really are, and how a crisis in one part of the world can quickly spread to other parts.

During the summer of 1997, the currency of Thailand started to tumble. It was a trend that soon spread to other currencies in that region. The collapse in Asian currency markets caused a corresponding collapse in Asian stock prices, which had a ripple effect around the globe. Fears of global deflation pushed commodity prices into a free fall and contributed to a worldwide rotation out of stocks into bonds. Over the following year and a half, the CRB fell to the lowest level in 20 years. The reaction of Asian central bankers to the crisis provided a lesson in intermarket relationships. In an attempt to stabilize their falling currencies, they raised interest rates. This jump in interest rates pushed Asian stocks into a sharp decline that lasted for at least a year and had a pronounced effect on all global financial markets. Throughout these hectic two years, all traditional intermarket relationships held up quite well—except for one.

BONDS AND STOCKS START TO DECOUPLE

The most important result of the events of 1997 and 1998 was the *decoupling* of bonds and stocks. *Decoupling* means that bond and stock prices trend in opposite directions, rather than adhere to their traditional tendency to trend in the same direction. During the second half of 1997, stock prices in the United States declined while Treasury bond prices rose. During the first half of the following year, stocks rose while bonds declined. During the third quarter of 1998, stocks fell even more sharply as Treasury bond prices soared. From July to October of 1998, the Dow Industrials fell 20 percent. Stock markets sold off all over the world. While stocks were falling, U.S. Treasury bond prices surged to record highs. During these three months of panic stock selling, U.S. Treasuries became the strongest market in the world.

By the end of the fourth quarter of 1998, perceptions that the crisis had passed caused bonds to tumble and stocks to soar in a complete role reversal of the prior three months. Bonds continued to fall throughout the entire year of 1999 while stocks soared to new highs. The events of 1997 and 1998 contributed to a major decoupling of bonds and stocks, which was to last for several years. The changing relationship between bonds and stocks started in the midst of the Asian currency crisis when a new word started circulating in financial circles—deflation.

THE DEFLATION SCENARIO

In 1998, I was in the process of revising my first book *Technical Analysis of the Futures Markets*, which included a new chapter on intermarket analysis. After explaining the normal intermarket relationships that had prevailed up to that point, I inserted a section entitled "The Deflation Scenario." In it I noted that for the first time since the 1930s, market analysts were worried that a beneficial period of disinflation (when prices of goods rise at a slower rate) might turn into a harmful deflation (when prices of goods actually fall) as a direct result of the Asian meltdown. *Asian contagion* became a familiar phrase in the financial world. (The Japanese stock market decline that started during 1989 had pushed the world's second largest economy into a deflationary spiral.) To add to these worries, producer prices in the United States fell on an annual basis for the first time in more than a decade.

During the Asian currency crisis that started in the middle of 1997, investors started selling stocks and buying bonds. The reason for this switch in trading patterns is that deflation changes some of the normal intermarket relationships, but not all. In a deflationary climate, bond prices rise while commodity prices fall. This is what happened from the middle of 1997 through the fourth quarter of 1998. However, the stock market can react negatively in such an environment. To quote what I wrote back in 1998: "If and when deflation does occur, intermarket relationships will still be present but in a different way. Disinflation is bad for commodities, but good for bonds and stocks. Deflation is good for bonds and bad for commodities, but may also be bad for stocks." The section ended with the following paragraph:

> *The deflationary trend that started in Asia in mid-1997 spread to Russia and Latin America by mid-1998 and began to hurt all global equity markets. A plunge in commodity prices had an especially damaging impact on commodity exporters like Australia, Canada, Mexico, and Russia. The deflationary impact of falling commodity and stock prices had a positive impact on Treasury bond prices, which hit record highs. Market events of 1998 were a dramatic example of the existence of global intermarket linkages and demonstrated how bonds and stocks can decouple in a deflationary world.*

1997 AND 1998 WERE ONLY A DRESS REHEARSAL

The way the financial markets reacted to the initial deflationary threat during 1997 and 1998 was only a "dress rehearsal" for the devastating bear market in stocks that started in the spring of 2000. During the worst three stock market years since the Great Depression, bond prices rose continuously while stock prices fell. The Fed lowered interest rates 12 times over an 18-month period with no apparent effect on stocks. Stocks kept falling along with rates, which fell to the lowest level in over 40 years. Those who heeded the warnings of 1997 and 1998 were on alert that rising bond prices (and falling rates) do not help stocks in a deflationary climate. Those traders and investors who scoffed at the deflationary threat and kept playing by the old rules paid a heavy price in stock market losses and missed big profit opportunities in bonds.

INTERMARKET PICTURE DURING 1997 AND 1998

In this chapter, we discuss the intermarket relationships surrounding the Asian currency crisis that started during the summer of 1997 and climaxed in the fall of 1998. The main focus is how the markets reacted to each other from the middle of 1997 to the end of 1998. We discuss which relationships changed and which ones did not. In the next chapter, the analysis is extended into 1999 to show how intermarket trends led to the bursting of the stock market bubble the following year.

THE DOLLAR VERSUS COMMODITIES

From the start of 1994 through the end of 1998, the Dollar Index and commodity prices maintained their normal inverse pattern, as shown in Figure 4.1. The U.S. dollar bottomed out during the first part of 1995 and began a bull market climb that lasted until the end of that decade. Normally, a rising dollar has a bearish impact on commodity prices. And this is exactly what happened, but with a time lag. After trading sideways from the middle of 1994 through the middle of 1995, the CRB Index rose into the early part of 1996. 1995 thus saw an unusual pattern of rising commodity prices coinciding with

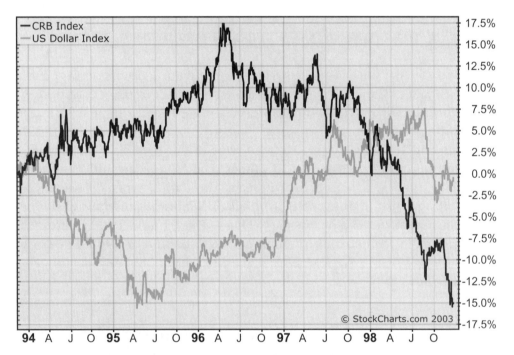

FIGURE 4.1 Commodities and the dollar moved inversely from the start of 1994 to the end of 1998.

a rising dollar. By the start of 1996, however, the CRB Index hit a major peak and fell for the following three years. For these three years, commodity prices fell while the dollar rose. The normal inverse relationship between these two markets was particularly evident during 1997 and 1998.

Immediately after the Asian crisis started in the summer of 1997, the dollar sold off from August through October after which it turned higher again (see Figure 4.2). The CRB Index did just the opposite. It bounced first (as the dollar dipped). By November of 1997 the dollar was rallying again; the CRB Index, however, had started a serious decline. The dollar stayed firm from November 1997 to August 1998. During these 10 months of dollar strength, the CRB tumbled to the lowest level in twenty years as fears of commodity price deflation intensified. During 1997 and 1998, the gold market mirrored dollar moves almost perfectly. Gold hit an interim low during August 1997 just as the dollar started another downside correction that lasted into October. When the dollar rebounded during the fourth quarter, gold resumed its downtrend. Nothing had changed in the intermarket relationship between the dollar and commodities. During 1997 and 1998, the dollar rose while commodities fell.

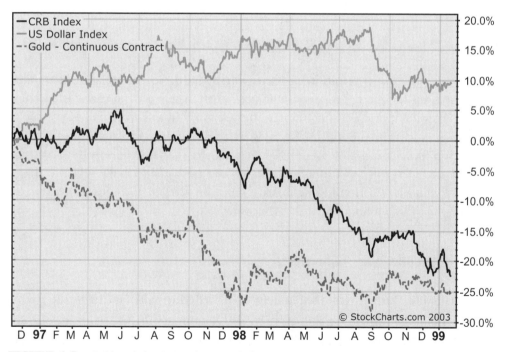

FIGURE 4.2 Gold and the CRB Index trended inversely to the dollar during 1997 and 1998.

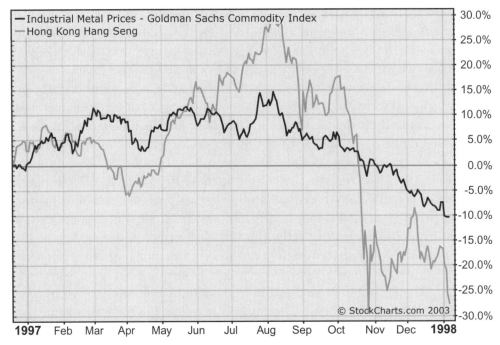

FIGURE 4.3   Industrial metals and the Hang Seng Index peaked together during the summer of 1997.

HONG KONG AND INDUSTRIAL METALS PEAK TOGETHER

Industrial metal prices were hit especially hard. The collapse in Asian markets raised fears of an economic downturn in that part of the world, which put a damper on all global economies. A comparison of industrial metal prices and Hong Kong's Hang Seng Index shows a remarkably close correlation (see Figure 4.3). Both indexes peaked at the end of July 1997 and fell together for at least another year. In the next chapter, we will see that a rebound in the Hong Kong market near the start of 1999 contributed to an upturn in commodity markets that year.

COMMODITIES VERSUS BONDS

This intermarket relationship held up also during 1997 and 1998. After commodities peaked at the start of 1996, they maintained an almost perfect inverse correlation with Treasury bond prices until the end of 1998, as shown in Figure 4.4. The CRB peak in the spring of 1996 coincided with a bottom in bond prices. The early months of 1997 saw a downside correction in bond prices,

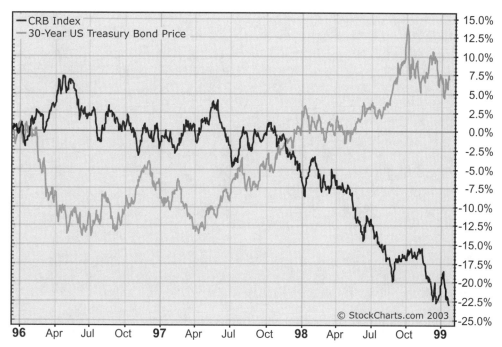

FIGURE 4.4 The CRB Index and Treasury bond prices traded inversely from 1996 through 1998.

which coincided with a rebound in the CRB Index. During the spring of that year, however, bonds began a major advance that lasted until the end of 1998. Commodities peaked within a month of the bond market bottom and fell through the remainder of the year. In October 1997 (three months after the Asian currency crisis started), bond prices soared to a new high for the year while commodities tumbled. By the end of 1997, bond prices had touched a record high, whereas the CRB Index had fallen to the lowest level in three years. These inverse trends continued through the balance of 1998. (We will see in the next chapter that both of those trends reversed in 1999.) Both markets did exactly what they would normally be expected to do in the midst of a deflationary threat. Bond prices rose drastically while commodities fell drastically. Here again, nothing had changed in this key intermarket link. What did change, though, was the relationship between bonds and stocks.

BONDS VERSUS STOCKS

After 1994, bonds and stocks resumed their long-term bull markets. During the first quarter of 1997, both markets experienced relatively modest down-

FIGURE 4.5   Stocks and bonds started diverging after the Asian currency crisis in July 1997.

side corrections that lasted into April (see Figure 4.5). Both markets bottomed together that month and rose together through the end of July 1997—when the Asian currency crisis hit. Initially, bonds and stocks dipped together for a month or so before rebounding in September. In October, their relationship changed. Stocks fell sharply during that month. The Dow Industrials dropped over a thousand points, losing about 12 percent. At the same time, however, bond prices rose; they continued to rise until January. The bond rally ended at the start of 1998 just as stocks started to rally again. In the past, bonds and stocks had decoupled for short periods of time, especially in market crises like that of 1987. What few people could have suspected during the fourth quarter of 1997 was that this decoupling of bonds and stocks would last for at least another five years and would change one of the most important intermarket relationships. Things got even worse in 1998.

BONDS AND STOCKS DIVERGE IN 1998

A comparison of bond and stock prices in 1998 shows dramatically divergent trends (see Figure 4.6). Stocks rose from January through April, while bonds

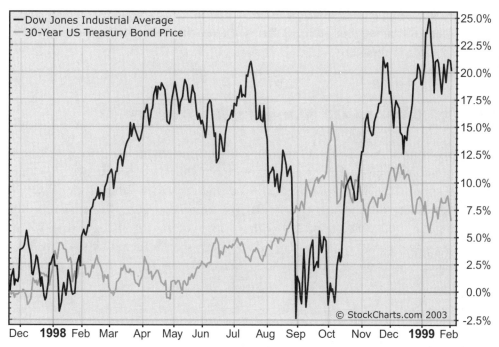

FIGURE 4.6   The decoupling of bonds and stocks became more obvious during 1998.

sold off. The stock market corrected that spring, but bond prices started to rise. During June and early July, stocks made one more run to the upside; bonds pulled back. In the middle of July, stocks started to tumble. From its July peak to its October bottom, the Dow dropped almost 2,000 points (about 20 percent). During these three months, bond prices soared to a new record high. Panic selling in global stock markets caused a massive asset allocation move out of stocks into U.S. Treasury bonds. (Matters were made worse when a financial crisis in Russia during August 1998 crushed the ruble and raised fears of Russian debt defaults. The failure of a major hedge firm, Long-Term Capital Management, did not help either.) With some help from the Fed, however, the stock market stabilized to form an October 1998 bottom.

From the October bottom, the stock market turned higher and by the start of 1999 was trading at a new record high. Just as stocks were bottoming throughout October, bond prices peaked and began a major decline that lasted almost a year. For all of 1999, bond prices fell while stocks rose. The bond-stock decoupling had now lasted for more than a year. This decoupling would last for several more years and would confound those who failed to recognize that a major change had taken place in this key intermarket relationship. This change was being driven by fears of deflation emanating from

Asia. The Japanese market was already in the grip of deflation. The Asian currency crisis that started in 1997 raised fears that Asian deflation was starting to spread elsewhere.

THE CRB/BOND RATIO AND SECTOR ROTATION

We studied the CRB/bond ratio in the previous chapter and showed how its direction could influence sector rotation within the stock market. We know that a rising CRB/bond ratio favors inflation stocks; a falling ratio, however, favors interest rate-sensitive stocks. We are going to study the same ratio during the 1997–1998 period but with a couple of new wrinkles added. We are going to expand the notion of which sectors are affected by the CRB/bond ratio. In addition, we are going to expand on the use of *relative strength analysis*, which is so crucial in sector work.

CONSUMER VERSUS CYCLICAL STOCKS

Two major sectors of the stock market that are always competing for investor funds are consumer and cyclical stocks. As their name implies, cyclicals are *economically sensitive* stocks that rise and fall with the business cycle. They tend to do especially well when the economy is strong and badly when the economy is weak. Many of the stocks in this group are tied to commodities like aluminum, copper, and paper & forest products. As a result, this group is closely tied to the fortunes of commodity prices. Consumer stocks, by contrast, include consumer staples like beverage, food, drug, tobacco, and personal products. These stocks hold relatively steady in good and bad economic times. When the economy is strong, cyclicals usually do better than consumer staples. When the economy is weak, consumer staples usually do better than cyclicals. This brings us back to the CRB/bond ratio. A rising ratio favors economically sensitive cyclical stocks. A falling CRB/bond ratio favors the more defensive consumer staples. These trends were clearly evident during 1997 and 1998.

CRB/BOND RATIO COLLAPSES DURING 1997

Figure 4.7 shows that during the summer of 1997, the CRB/bond ratio started to tumble (reflecting higher bond prices and lower commodities). It con-

FIGURE 4.7   The CRB/bond ratio started tumbling during the second half of 1997.

tinued to tumble until the end of 1998. Bonds do better than commodities due to fears of economic weakness. (Bonds do better than stocks due to the same fear.) By October 1997, the stock market had fallen sharply, which heightened fears of economic damage. At the same time, the CRB/bond ratio fell to the lowest level in nearly two years. These trends caused a rotation out of cyclicals and into consumer stocks that lasted until the end of 1998.

RELATIVE STRENGTH ANALYSIS

The indexes that are used to measure these two market sectors are the Morgan Stanley Consumer Index (CMR) and the Morgan Stanley Cyclical Index (CYC). A visual comparison of these two indexes shows that consumer stocks rose from the middle of 1997 to the end of 1998, while cyclical stocks fell. A better way to compare their performance, however, is with ratio, or relative strength, analysis. Normally, when we measure the relative strength of any market group (or stock), we do so against a stock market benchmark like the S&P 500 Index. In this case, the Morgan Stanley Consumer and Cyclical Indexes are each divided by the S&P 500. These ratios are then compared. A

FIGURE 4.8   The Consumer/S&P 500 ratio rose during 1998, reflecting strength in defensive stocks.

FIGURE 4.9   The falling ratio during 1998 showed weak performance by economically-sensitive stocks.

rising ratio means that the market sector is outperforming the S&P 500, which is a sign of relative strength. A falling ratio is a sign of relative weakness.

The Consumer/S&P 500 ratio bottomed during October 1997 and rose until October 1998, as shown in Figure 4.8. The Cyclical/S&P 500 ratio peaked during October 1997 and plunged until the end of 1998 (see Figure 4.9). From the fourth quarter of 1997 to the fourth quarter of 1998, the ratio charts made it clear that the defensive consumer stocks were the place to be; the more economically sensitive cyclical stocks were not. This superior performance of consumer stocks over cyclical stocks continued until the CRB/bond ratio turned up at the start of 1999.

PLOTTING A RATIO OF TWO COMPETING SECTORS

A second way to compare two market sectors is to divide one by the other. When an investor is faced with two competing assets, it is usually better to go with the stronger of the two. A ratio that divides the Consumer Index by the Cyclical Index in 1997 and 1998 shows a dramatic upturn in October 1997 that lasted until the end of 1998 (see Figure 4.10). Investors would have done

FIGURE 4.10 The rising ratio showed stronger performance in defensive stocks during 1998.

much better by concentrating on consumer stocks and avoiding cyclicals. They could have come to this conclusion by plotting the CRB/bond ratio. By the start of 1999, the CRB/bond ratio started to turn higher. At the same time, money flowed out of consumer stocks and back into the more commodity-related cyclicals. As a rule of thumb, consumer staples are closely tied to bond prices; cyclical stocks are closely tied to commodity prices.

INTERMARKET LESSONS OF 1997 AND 1998

Much was learned about intermarket relationships during the years of 1997 and 1998. Those two years demonstrated the need to monitor global markets—not just in stocks, but in currencies as well. The collapse in a relatively obscure Asian currency started a ripple effect that eventually had a dramatic impact on the U.S. bond and stock markets. The most obvious impact was a flight out of stocks and into bonds that lasted for 18 months. Within the stock market, sector rotation trends were influenced. Funds rotated into more defensive consumer staples at the expense of economically sensitive cyclical stocks. Another effect of the Asian contagion was the collapse in commodity markets, which intensified fears of global deflation.

Perhaps the most important lesson of all was that deflationary trends coming from Asia caused a major change in the relationship between bonds and stocks. Rising bond prices no longer helped stock prices. Instead, a rising bond market came at the expense of stocks. This change would become even more pronounced during the major bear market in stocks that started a couple of years later. In the next chapter, we will see that 1999 reversed many of the trends of 1998. Although these intermarket trend reversals in 1999 helped stocks initially, they also contributed to the bursting of the stock market bubble in 2000.

CHAPTER 5

1999 Intermarket Trends Leading to Market Top

1999 SEES REVERSAL OF 1998 TRENDS

The global deflation fear that gripped the financial markets in 1998 caused a flight out of commodities and stocks and into the bond market. Figure 5.1 shows the decoupling of bonds and stocks that took place in 1998 because of

FIGURE 5.1 Shows decoupling of bonds and stocks during 1998.

FIGURE 5.2 During 1999, stocks rose while bonds fell.

this deflation threat. In 1999, these trends were reversed. The stock market soared to a new record high while bond prices suffered one of their worst years in history (see Figure 5.2). Part of the reason for the fall in bond prices was a sharp rise in the price of oil at the start of 1999, which pushed interest rates higher around the globe as inflation fears resurfaced. A recovery in Asian stock markets also contributed to global demand for industrial commodities like aluminum and copper. The rise in commodity prices prompted the Federal Reserve to start raising interest rates in the middle of the year, a move which contributed to a major top in the stock market the following year.

Initially, the negative impact of rising interest rates was seen in two places. One was in the deterioration in market breadth measures like the NYSE Advance–Decline line, which fell throughout the entire year. The other was in the area of sector rotation. Rising interest rates in 1999 had an especially negative impact on those stock market groups that are considered to be *rate sensitive*. At the same time, inflationary stock groups had a relatively good year. The market trends in 1999 also demonstrated the increasingly prominent role of global influences in intermarket work. A collapse in Asian markets had pushed commodity prices sharply lower throughout 1997 and

1998. A rebound in these same markets in 1999 pushed commodity prices higher and resulted in heavy losses in global bond markets. While the rotation out of bonds helped stocks initially in 1999, the longer-lasting effects were more damaging. Our discussion of intermarket trends in 1999 approaches the subject on three levels. The first is the *macro* relationships between commodities, bonds, and stocks. The second is the impact that these macro intermarket forces had on sector rotations within the stock market. The third deals with global influences.

COMMODITIES JUMP AT START OF 1999

The direction of commodity prices in 1999 played a key role in the direction of interest rates. It was no coincidence that 1999 saw the biggest upturn in commodity prices in years and one of the biggest downturns in bond prices. As a result of rising commodity prices, the Fed started raising rates that summer. This action had a subtle but negative effect on the stock market, particularly on *old economy* stocks that are traditionally more affected by interest rate direction. *New economy* technology stocks proved relatively immune to rising rates in 1999—but not in 2000.

COMMODITIES AND RATES TREND TOGETHER

A comparison of commodity prices to the yield on the 10-year Treasury note (which has become the new benchmark for long-term U.S. Treasury rates) shows that they generally trend in the same direction. (Commodity prices move in the opposite direction of bond prices but in the same direction as bond yields.) In 1997 and 1998, as deflation fears surfaced, interest rates and commodity prices fell together. By the start of 1999, however, both were rising again. Bond yields actually troughed in October 1998 as the stock market bottomed and bond prices peaked. This move reflected a massive asset allocation switch out of bonds and back into stocks which lasted through the following year. Commodity prices started moving up at the start of 1999. Throughout the balance of that year, commodity prices and bond yields rose together. Figure 5.3 shows the Goldman Sachs Commodity Index and Treasury Bond yields breaking down trendlines at the start of 1999 as they bottomed together.

FIGURE 5.3   The GSCI and bond yields bottomed together at the start of 1999.

INDUSTRIAL COMMODITIES AND OIL BOTTOM

Two of the commodity groups that turned up first at the start of 1999 were oil and industrial metals. Because of its heavy weighting in crude oil (which tripled in price that year), the Goldman Sachs Commodity Index was among the first of the commodity indexes to turn up. Figure 5.4 shows the GSCI rising above its 200-day moving average during March 1999, which was a sign that its major trend had turned up again.

Industrial commodity prices also turned up as shown in Figure 5.5. The Goldman Sachs Industrial Metals Index broke a resistance line during the first quarter of 1999 and rallied sharply thereafter. (The rebound in industrial metals was the result of a rebound in the Pacific Rim.) The upturn in the CRB Index was delayed by weak agricultural markets during the first half of 1999. With two of the most interest-sensitive commodity groups rising together in 1999—oil and industrial metals—it was no surprise to see a corresponding rise in short- and long-term interest rates.

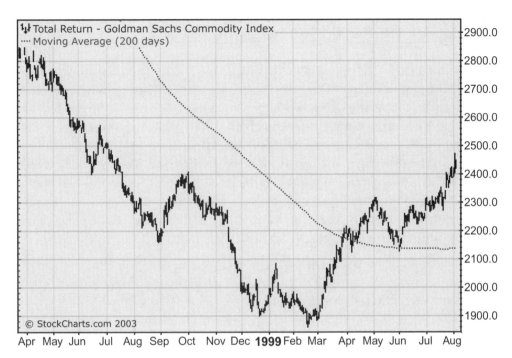

FIGURE 5.4 The GSCI rose about its 200-day average during March 1999.

FIGURE 5.5 Industrial Metals broke a resistance line during the first quarter of 1999.

THE IMPACT OF RISING RATES ON STOCKS

Rising interest rates usually have a negative influence on the stock market. This negative influence on the U.S. stock market was present in 1999, but in a subtle way. Although new economy technology stocks in the Nasdaq market rose sharply during the second half of 1999, old economy stocks (on the New York Stock Exchange) stopped rising right around the time that the Fed started tightening in the middle of the year. The New York Stock Exchange (NYSE) Composite Index peaked during July 1999 (just as the Fed started to raise short-term rates) and declined for the rest of that year. Although it retested its highs a year later, the summer of 1999 marked the beginning of the topping process in the NYSE Composite Index.

NYSE ADVANCE-DECLINE LINE FALLS IN 1999

A more dramatic demonstration of the impact of rising interest rates in 1999 was seen in the deterioration in the NYSE Advance-Decline line. (The AD line measures the difference between the number of advancing stocks and declining stocks on the NYSE. A falling line means that more stocks are declining than advancing, which is sign of stock market weakness.) The AD line actually peaked in 1998 and continued to fall throughout 1999. The NYSE AD line has a history of peaking ahead of the major stock market averages and is considered to be a leading indicator for the rest of the market. Historically, there has usually been a fairly close correlation between bond prices and the AD line. Over a third of the NYSE stocks are considered to be rate-sensitive and are usually the first to peak in a climate of rising rates. They in turn have a depressing effect on the NYSE AD line (see Figure 5.6).

The fall in the NYSE AD line in 1999 suggests that the broader stock market was more adversely affected by rising rates that most people realized. It also contradicted the view put forward by some market observers (especially in the media) that the stock market was largely unaffected by rising interest rates. This stock market deterioration in 1999 was masked by continuing strength in an increasingly smaller portion of the stock market that was concentrated in the Nasdaq market. In time, rising rates would take a toll there as well. On a *macro* intermarket level, 1999 saw a combination of rising commodity prices and rising interest rates, which has traditionally been a negative omen for stocks. Another sign of danger for the stock market was seen in the impact of rising commodity prices (mainly in oil) on various sectors within the stock market.

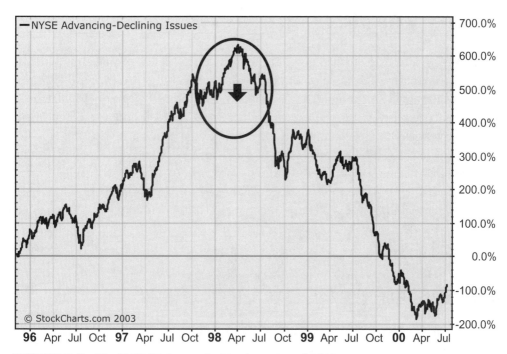

FIGURE 5.6 The NYSE AD line peaked in the spring of 1998.

INTERMARKET SECTOR EFFECT

Although intermarket trends say a lot about the direction of inflation and interest rates (and can have an important influence on asset allocation strategies), one of their most practical applications is in the area of sector and industry group rotation within the stock market. *Group rotation* refers to money flows from one stock market group to another. (There are 10 stock market *sectors*. Each sector is subdivided into *industry groups*. There are many more industry groups than sectors. The term *sector rotation* generally includes movements among sectors and industry groups.)

RISING CRUDE WAS GOOD FOR OIL SHARES

Crude oil prices tripled in 1999. Rising oil benefits some stock groups, but hurts others. The most obvious beneficiaries of higher oil prices are oil shares. It should come as no surprise, then, to find out that oil shares were the strongest part of the stock market in 1999. Figure 5.7 compares the AMEX Oil Index

FIGURE 5.7   Oil stocks and the XOI/S&P ratio turned up near the start of 1999.

(XOI) to a ratio of the XOI divided by the S&P 500. Both turned up near the start of 1999, indicating that oil shares were moving up on both an absolute and a relative basis. (There is, however, a warning in that.) The upturn in energy shares near the start of 1999 also confirmed the chartists' suspicion that oil prices were indeed headed higher, as there is usually a positive correlation between the direction of oil prices and oil shares. While oil shares benefited from rising oil prices, other groups suffered as a result.

TRANSPORTATION STOCKS FALL HARD

Transportation stocks (and airlines in particular) are especially sensitive to the direction of crude oil prices. So much of transportation companies' operating expenses are dependent on the cost of fuel. Within a couple of months of the upturn in oil prices at the start of 1999, transportation stocks started a major decline that lasted into the following spring. During this period, transports lost 40 percent of their value. Transportation stocks were not the only stock group hurt by rising oil prices in 1999. As rising oil prices led to rising interest rates, the market groups that are most sensitive to the direction of interest rates began to suffer—especially financial stocks.

FINANCIAL STOCKS LOSE FAVOR DURING 1999

We discussed the concept of ratio analysis and how it is used to measure the relative strength of a market group. (The group index is usually divided by a market benchmark like the S&P 500.) This technique was especially useful in 1999. Ratio analysis showed that oil stocks outperformed the S&P 500 that year, whereas transportation stocks underperformed. (It is always better to be in the group that is outperforming the S&P 500.) The ratio analysis technique showed that financial stocks were one of the year's weakest groups. A ratio of financial stocks divided by the S&P 500 shows that group underperforming the market all year (see Figure 5.8). This is consistent with the intermarket principle that financial stocks do not do well in a climate of rising interest rates. The falling relative strength ratio demonstrated how badly financial stocks did in 1999 relative to the rest of the market.

FIGURE 5.8   Financial stocks underperformed the S&P 500 during 1999 as interest rates rose.

This poor performance by rate-sensitive stocks in 1999 also confirmed the trend toward higher commodity prices and higher U.S. interest rates. The prior examples illustrate the importance of being in tune with intermarket trends from a sector rotation standpoint. They show that in a climate of rising oil prices and rising interest rates, oil stocks are generally a good place to be, while financial and transportation stocks are not. Although these examples may seem fairly obvious, there are more subtle intermarket principles that play on stock market groups.

OTHER SECTOR INFLUENCES

I explained that during a period of rising industrial commodity prices, basic material stocks (like aluminum and copper) usually do relatively well. At the same time, consumer staples usually do worse. Recall that in addition, a rising commodity/bond ratio favors inflation-type stocks. A rising commodity/bond ratio hurts rate-sensitive stock groups like banks, brokers, and consumer staples (including drugs). These trends were clearly evident in 1999. The commodity/bond ratio turned up. Figure 5.9 plots a ratio of the GSCI

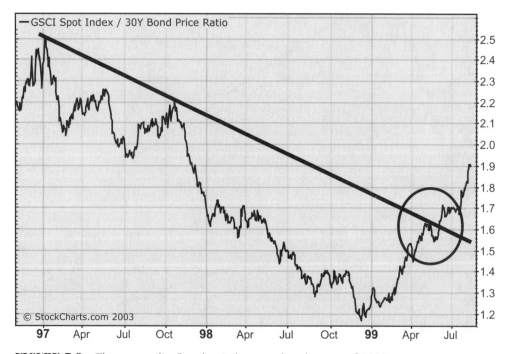

FIGURE 5.9   The commodity/bond ratio bottomed at the start of 1999.

divided by Treasury Bond prices. The commodity/bond ratio bottomed at the start of 1999. Its major down trendline was broken a few months later, which confirmed the important upside reversal.

Starting in the spring of 1999, economically sensitive cyclical stocks surged just as commodity prices started to rise (although the rise in cyclical shares was fairly dramatic, it proved to be relatively short-lived). Figure 5.10 plots two lines. The top line shows the Morgan Stanley Cyclical Index breaking a down trendline in April 1999. The lower line is a ratio of that index divided by the S&P 500. The ratio turned up as well that spring, meaning that cyclical shares were leading the market higher. At the same time, bank stocks turned down and continued falling through the balance of that year. Figure 5.11 plots a ratio of the Philadelphia Stock Exchange (PHLX) Bank Index (BKX) divided by the S&P 500. The falling ratio line shows the relative weakness of bank shares in 1999, and is reflective of the poor performance in the financial sector.

As cyclical stocks surged during April of that year, consumer staples lost favor. As part of the latter group, drug stocks fell both on an absolute and a relative basis. Figure 5.12 is a ratio of the AMEX Pharmaceutical Index (DRG) divided by the S&P 500 and shows a sharp drop during April. During that month, money going into the more inflation-sensitive cyclical shares

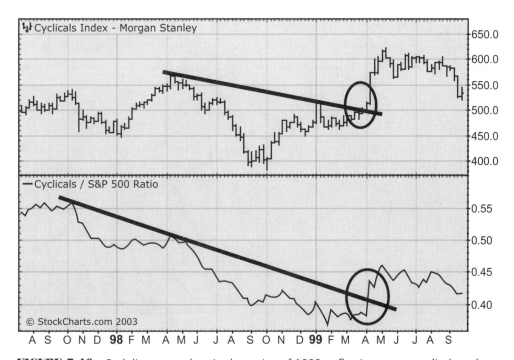

FIGURE 5.10   Both lines turned up in the spring of 1999, reflecting strong cyclical stocks.

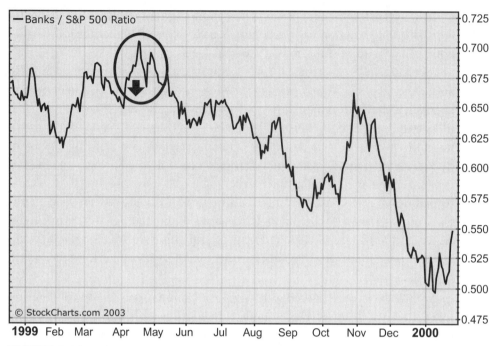

FIGURE 5.11   Money rotated out of bank stocks in April 1999.

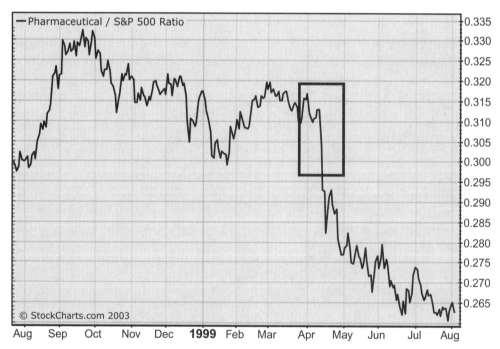

FIGURE 5.12   Drug stocks fell out of favor during April 1999.

rotated out of the more rate-sensitive stocks of banks and drugs (and consumer staples). The main reason for this rotation was that commodity prices were going up and bond prices were going down. (In Chapter 7, when we examine the bursting of the Nasdaq bubble in the spring of 2000, we will see a massive rotation back into these very same "defensive" groups like consumer staples, drugs, financials, and Treasury bonds.)

SECTOR ROTATION AND THE ECONOMY

Different market sectors do better at different stages of the business cycle. Near the end of an economic expansion, for example, energy stocks usually take over market leadership. This is primarily due to rising energy prices and the resulting buildup of inflation pressures. As happened in 1999, a rising inflation threat prompts the Federal Reserve to raise short-term interest rates. In time, rising rates have the effect of slowing the economy. This usually leads to an economic slowdown, which often turns into a recession. The surge in oil prices at the start of 1999 and the resulting jump in interest rates that year started in motion a series of events which led to a major market top one year later and a recession a year after that.

The stock market peaks in stages. Interest rate-sensitive stocks usually peak first owing to rising interest rates. Many of them started peaking in 1998. Energy stocks usually peak last. (Oil service stocks did not peak until 2000.) This usually signals the end of an economic expansion and the beginning of an economic contraction. One way to tell when the economy has crossed the threshold from *late expansion* to *early contraction* is when leadership switches from energy stocks to more defensive stock groups like consumer staples. This is exactly what happened in 2000. Later in the book, we will examine sector rotation within the business cycle in more depth. I introduce it here to explain why the surge in oil prices and oil shares in 1999 (and the resultant Fed tightening) were classic signs of a major market top in the making and the start of serious economic problems. These signs became even more obvious at the start of 2000.

GLOBAL INFLUENCES IN 1999

The last piece of the intermarket trilogy in 1999 has to do with global influences. The previous chapter showed the close correlation between a falling Hong Kong stock market in the middle of 1997 and the bearish effect that it had

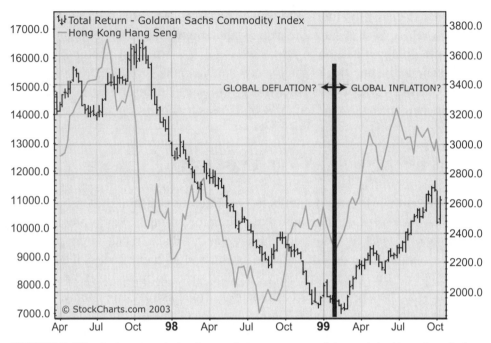

FIGURE 5.13 A close correlation is seen between commodities and the Hang Seng Index from 1997 to 1999.

on commodity prices (owing to deflation fears). Figure 5.13 shows the close correlation between the Hang Seng Index and commodity prices from the middle of 1997 through the middle of 1999. The Hang Seng Index peaked in July 1997. Commodity prices peaked three months later (although industrial metals peaked with the Hong Kong market over the summer). The Hang Seng Index bottomed during the third quarter of 1998. Commodity prices started bottoming shortly thereafter. By the start of 1999, the Hong Kong stock market and commodity prices were rising together. The deflationary fears coming from Asia in 1997 and throughout most of 1998 gave way to inflationary fears at the start of 1999. Falling Asian stocks pulled commodity prices down in 1997. By the start of 1999, rising Asian stocks were pulling commodity prices higher. (To carry the link with Asia a step further, the next chapter examines the close correlation between U.S. interest rates and the Japanese stock market, especially in the years after 1997.)

HONG KONG AND SEMICONDUCTORS

The direction of the Hong Kong stock market also has a strong influence on the direction of the semiconductor group. Figure 5.14 shows the close cor-

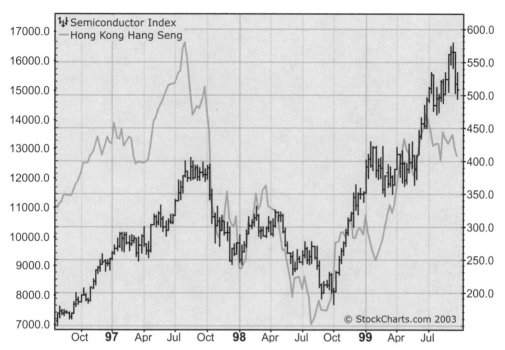

FIGURE 5.14   A close correlation is seen between the SOX Index and the Hong Kong stock market from 1997 to 1999.

relation between the Hang Seng Index and the Semiconductor (SOX) Index from 1997 to 1999. Both markets peaked together during the summer of 1997 and then bottomed together during the third quarter of 1998. The rally in Hong Kong in 1999 helped make the semiconductor group one of that year's strongest performers. Their strong linkage has to do with the fact that most of the world's semiconductors are produced in Asia. As a result, the health of the semiconductor sector is closely tied to the health of the Asian economy.

THE AUSTRALIAN DOLLAR AND COMMODITY PRICES

The Australian and Canadian currencies are closely tied to commodity prices (especially the Australian dollar). Both countries are big producers of natural resources. Figure 5.15 shows the strong link between the Australian dollar and the price of copper from 1997 to 1999. During the Asian crisis of 1997, the Australian dollar fell sharply along with copper (and commodity prices in general). The Australian dollar bottomed during the third quarter of 1998 just as the rest of the Pacific Rim was stabilizing. The rally

FIGURE 5.15 A stock link is seen between copper and the Australian Dollar from 1997 to 1999.

in the Australian dollar off that late 1998 bottom was an early sign of a bottom in commodity prices (like copper), which followed a few months later. (Chapter 10 discusses how a big commodity rally that started during 2002 helped make the Australian and Canadian dollars two of the world's strongest currencies.)

CHAPTER 6

Review
of Intermarket
Principles

INTRODUCTION

We have ended our coverage of the 1990s. But before examining the more difficult years after 2000, let us pause long enough to review just what intermarket analysis is. How does it add to traditional technical analysis? What are its applications to other areas of study including asset allocation, sector rotation, and even economic forecasting? It is also a good time to explain why technical analysis lends itself so well to this form of analysis, which requires the study of so many markets. This chapter also restates the basic principles on which intermarket analysis is based.

AN EVOLUTIONARY STEP IN TECHNICAL ANALYSIS

Over the past century, technical analysis was based primarily on *single market* analysis. This meant, for example, that stock market analysts looked only at stock market charts. Bond, commodity, and currency chartists looked only at charts of the market in which they were trading. Over the past decade, however, emphasis in the technical world has shifted away from single market work to a more intermarket approach. It is not unusual for technical analysts to supplement their stock market analysis with consideration of currency trends (to see where global money is flowing), commodity prices (to gauge inflationary trends), bond charts (to see which way interest rates are moving), and overseas markets (to measure the impact of global market trends). Those who fail to do so run the risk of seeing only a small part of the intermarket picture. In an increasingly interrelated financial world, the ability to study all markets gives intermarket technical analysts a huge advantage. With some understanding of how the markets interrelate, chartists have a decided edge over their economic and fundamental counterparts.

EMPHASIS ON SECTOR WORK

Although intermarket principles are invaluable in understanding how bonds, stocks, commodities, and currencies work off each other, it has also proven to be extremely helpful in understanding why certain sectors of the market do well at certain times and badly at others. An understanding of intermarket principles sheds new light on the application of sector rotation, which has become so important in recent years. It is no longer so much a question of whether or not to be *in* the market as much as it is *where* to be in the market. (Although a big bear market started in the stock market during the spring of 2000, money could still be made by rotating into defensive stock groups that started to rise as the rest of the market fell.) Being in the right sector at the right time (and out of the wrong sectors) has become one of the keys to stock market success. Fortunately, all kinds of charting tools exist to help investors do that.

ASSET ALLOCATION STRATEGIES

There are times when even sector work has its limitations, such as when stocks are in the midst of a major bear market. At such times, asset allocation strategies come into play. This might involve rotating out of stocks into bonds, raising one's cash exposure with a money market fund, or even buying gold shares. All of these strategies worked in the three years following the stock market top in 2000. Fortunately, there are charting tools to help investors with these decisions as well. These tools do, however, require some knowledge of intermarket principles.

THE BASIC PREMISE OF INTERMARKET ANALYSIS

The basic premise of intermarket analysis is that *all markets are related*. In other words, what happens in one market has an effect on another. On a macro level, the four interrelated markets are the commodity, currency, bond, and stock markets. Market analysts have long understood the impact of interest rates on stocks, for example. Rising interest rates have historically been bad for stocks, especially those in interest rate-sensitive market sectors. Interest rates are affected by the direction of commodity prices. Rising commodity prices are usually associated with rising inflation, which puts upward pressure on interest rates. Commodity prices and interest rates are influenced by the direction of a country's currency. (Because global commodities are quoted in U.S. dollars, the direction of the dollar has an influence on the direction of global commodity prices like gold.) A falling currency usually gives a boost to commodity prices quoted in that currency. This boost in commodity prices reawakens inflation fears and puts pressure on central bankers to raise interest rates, which has a negative impact on the stock market. Not all stocks, however, are affected equally. Some stocks get hurt in a climate of rising interest rates; others actually benefit.

GLOBAL MARKETS

Global markets play an increasingly important role in intermarket analysis. The bear market years of 1987, 1990, and 1994 showed that world stock markets usually fall together at such times. As evidenced by the Asian currency crisis that started in 1997, currency trends, commodity trends, and interest rate trends are global in scope and have a major impact on each other. The 1970s witnessed a bout of hyperinflation that was global. The 1980s and 1990s saw disinflationary trends that were evident worldwide. As a result, global commodities were generally weak during those two decades, while global bond and stock markets were strong. At the turn of the new millennium, deflationary trends that started in Asia affected world markets everywhere. During the three years following the bursting of the stock market bubble in 2000, the world's equity markets fell together in a dramatic demonstration of global linkages. As was demonstrated during the first and second Iraq wars in 1990–1991 and 2002–2003, a spike in the price of crude oil has a depressing effect on major stock markets and economies all over the planet.

GLOBAL SECTOR TRENDS

Global influences are also present on a sector-by-sector basis. When one sees sector strength or weakness, the trends are normally present on a worldwide basis. Because macro intermarket trends are usually global in scope, so is

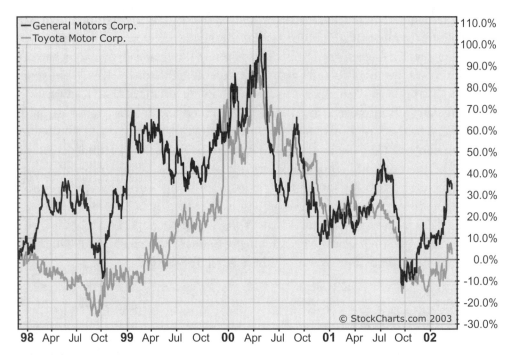

FIGURE 6.1   American and Japanese auto stocks trend in the same direction.

their impact on global market sectors and industry groups. Semiconductor stocks, for example, tend to rise and fall together all over the world; the same is true for other stock groups. When it is a good time to buy a Japanese auto stock, it is usually also a good time to buy auto stocks all over the world. They rise and fall together based on global economic trends. Figure 6.1 compares the price history of General Motors and Toyota over the last five years. It is hard to tell the two auto stocks apart even though one is an American car manufacturer and the other one Japanese. Figure 6.2 compares the price trends of Intel Corporation and Taiwan Semiconductor since 1998. The two semiconductor manufacturers move up and down together despite the fact that one is based in Taiwan and the other in Santa Clara, California. Sector and industry trends are global in nature and transcend national boundaries and geographic regions.

JAPAN'S EFFECT ON U.S. MARKETS

Even a market as far away as Japan affects market trends in the United States. One demonstration of that impact is seen by comparing the Japanese stock market with the yield on the U.S. 10-year Treasury note. This comparison shows

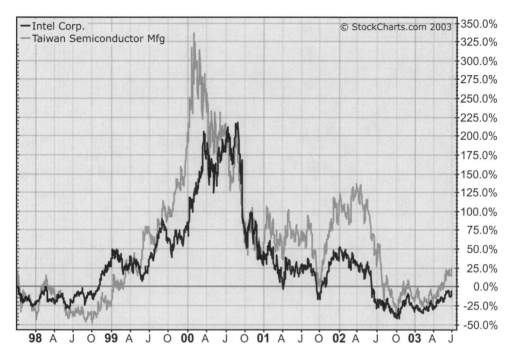

FIGURE 6.2   American and Taiwanese semiconductor stocks trend together.

a striking correlation over the past several years. (See Figure 6.3.) Although it may seem strange at first, the chart makes perfect sense. Japan has the second largest economy in the world. For most of the past decade, the Japanese economy has been in a deflationary recession (or depression), which in turn has contributed largely to the global downtrend in long-term interest rates.

Global interest rates peaked at the start of the 1980s and fell for the next two decades as disinflationary forces reigned. The Japanese market peaked at the start of the 1990s and fell for the following decade. The fall in the world's second largest stock market may have provided the first warning of the start of a deflationary trend. This threat took on more meaning after the Asian currency crisis of 1997, which was the second deflationary warning. This may explain why the linkage between U.S. interest rates and Japan became especially close around 1997. Figure 6.3 shows that both markets peaked together in 1996 and fell together through the Asian crisis years of 1997 and 1998. The Nikkei 225 and 10-year T-note yield bottomed together in the autumn of 1998 and rose together throughout 1999. (The previous chapter discusses how the recovery in Asia in 1999 helped boost industrial commodity prices, but pushed global interest rates higher.)

The two markets fell together again at the start of 2000. Within three years, both markets had fallen to the lowest levels in decades. One of the

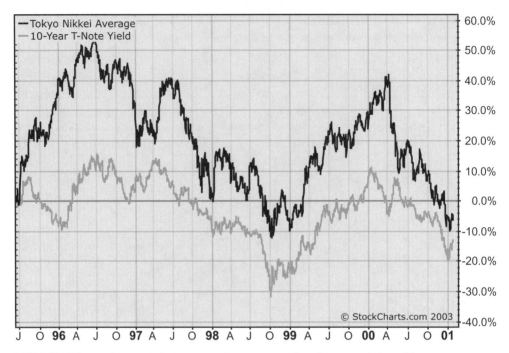

FIGURE 6.3 A close correlation exists between U.S. bond rates and the Nikkei.

main reasons for this remarkably close correlation between Japanese stocks and U.S Treasury note rates since 1997 is that the deflationary trend that started in Asia a decade before started to gain more attention after the Asian currency crisis. It also explains why it is important for American investors to understand trends in other global markets.

JAPAN EFFECT OVERRIDES THE FED

After the stock market bubble burst in the United States in 2000, the Federal Reserve lowered interest rates 12 times over eighteen months in an attempt to stop the bear market in stocks and stabilize the American economy. It did not work. Part of the reason it did not work was the influence of deflationary trends coming from Asia. By year 2002, even the Fed was using the D-word (deflation), although it was mainly in denial of its threat. That the Federal Reserve felt the need to make the denial at all suggested that it was indeed a threat. Intermarket chartists who studied the trends in Asia—and compared them to those in the United States—recognized this threat a few years earlier. (Later in the book, we will see that one of the tactics that the Fed used to combat the deflationary threat in the United States was to lower the dollar in an attempt to create a little price inflation.)

ECONOMIC LESSONS

The reaction of the economic community in 1999 and then again after 2000 was instructive—and demonstrates the need to study global forces. In 1999, rising commodity prices contributed to higher interest rates. Many U.S. economists spent most of 1999 questioning the rise in U.S. interest rates in the face of relatively low inflation. What they apparently failed to realize was that the upturn in U.S. interest rates in 1999 may have had more to do with a rebound in Asian markets and less to do with the U.S. economy. After 2000, economists also wondered why U.S. rates continued dropping in the face of so much stimulus from the Fed. After all, they argued, the United States was not in an outright deflation (which would have justified such low U.S. rates). Once again, American economists failed to look abroad. The deflationary trend in U.S. rates was largely the result of deflationary trends in the Far East. One did not have to be an economist to study price charts in commodity prices, bond yields, and the Japanese stock market, and to see that all three were falling together. As is usually the case, market trends anticipate economic trends.

THE TECHNICAL NATURE OF INTERMARKET ANALYSIS

It is difficult to separate market trends from economic trends. Economists have known for years that bond and stock markets anticipate economic trends (although it is amazing how often they ignore these market signs). This is where the technical analyst comes in. The technical analyst (who is probably more aptly called a *market analyst*) is mainly interested in market trends. If these market trends have some application to economic forces (and they do), so be it. But these economic trends usually show up in the financial markets first, where the intermarket chartist can easily spot them.

ADVANTAGES OF CHARTING—THE BIG VIEW

One of the main advantages that technical analysts have is the ability to plot several markets at the same time. They can easily chart the course of the dollar, oil, bonds, and the stock market. They can also chart the relative performance of stock market industry groups and sectors. It is also a simple task to chart and analyze the trends of major global stock markets. The ability to chart so many things at the same time gives the technical analyst a big edge in the area of intermarket analysis over those who lack this skill. Once the numerous markets are charted, the next logical step is to study their interrelationships.

Fundamental analysts, by contrast, tend to specialize in fewer market groups. The nature of fundamental analysis, with its emphasis on company and industry earnings, demands more specialization. Can you imagine an economist trying to master the intricacies of the Japanese economy as well as all of the world's major economies? The chartist has a unique advantage when it comes to grasping the big picture. More and more, some grasp of the big picture—both domestically and globally—is a necessary ingredient to having a thorough market view.

ECONOMIC FORECASTING

Awareness of the financial markets' intermarket condition also sheds light on why certain market sectors do better or worse at certain times. This insight, combined with relative strength (or ratio) charts, is invaluable in the implementation of sector rotation strategies. These sector rotations also shed light on the current state of the economy (as is depicted graphically in the next chapter concerning the events of 2000). Because financial markets act as leading indicators for economic trends, intermarket analysis elevates the usefulness of technical analysis to the realm of economic forecasting. The stock market top in the spring of 2000 correctly predicted the onset of a recession twelve months later, a warning that most economists and Wall Street security analysts chose to ignore. They ignored another traditional warning sign during the first quarter of 2000 that was clearly seen on the charts—an inverted yield curve occurred at the start of 2000 when short-term interest rates exceeded long-term rates, and warned of economic weakness.

MARKETS ANTICIPATE ECONOMIC TRENDS

One of the basic premises of technical analysis is that the markets *discount* economic and fundamental information. This simply means that the financial markets anticipate economic trends six to nine months into the future. The job of the chartist is to study the markets in an attempt to decipher their message about future trends, both in the markets and the economy. Nowhere is this more true than in the field of intermarket analysis. Financial markets always carry a message. The trick is knowing how to read the message (and then paying attention to it). It can best be done by tracking all of the markets—not just one or two—and taking all of their interrelationships into consideration. As is discussed in subsequent chapters, some knowledge of intermarket principles—along with some rudimentary chart-reading skills—could have saved a lot of people a lot of money in the bear market years that started with the new millennium.

THE ROLE OF THE DOLLAR

The three asset classes that get most of our attention in intermarket work are stocks, bonds, and commodities. These three markets normally peak and trough in a predictable order depending on the state of the economy. Near the end of an economic expansion, for example, commodity prices are usually strong, while bond prices are weak. Bonds peak before stocks do. Commodities usually peak last. During a recession, commodity prices fall while bond prices rise. Bonds bottom before stocks do. Commodities bottom last.

Currency markets play a role in the intermarket picture, but in a more indirect way. The influence of the dollar on bonds and stocks is usually filtered through its influence on commodity markets. If a falling dollar pushes commodity prices higher, it is usually bearish for bonds and, in time, stocks as well. Even so, the direction of the dollar and foreign currencies send important economic messages and have an influence on other markets.

GLOBAL IMPACT OF CURRENCY TRENDS

A falling dollar results in higher foreign currency values. Global investment funds tend to flow toward countries with stronger currencies. Stronger currencies are the result of higher interest rates, which reflect stronger economic conditions in a particular country. A weak currency sends the opposite message. A strong currency also increases the appeal of a country's bonds and stocks to foreigners. For an American investor, a weak dollar increases the appeal of foreign bonds and stocks. At the same time, a weak dollar diminishes the appeal of U.S. assets for foreign investors. Not all countries benefit equally, however, from rising currency trends. Countries that rely more heavily on exports (like Europe and Japan) may actually suffer when their currency rises too far too fast, because it hurts their export business. (In Germany, which has the biggest economy in Europe, exports account for a third of its gross domestic product.) As a result, the intermarket impact that the U.S. dollar has on American markets may not have exactly the same application in all foreign markets. Even within the U.S. market, there are qualifications that have to be made regarding the dollar. The direction of the U.S. dollar does not affect all American stocks equally.

DOLLAR IMPACT ON MULTINATIONALS

Large multinational stocks derive a big portion of their earnings from overseas sales. As a result, a rising dollar can have a negative impact on these foreign sales. By the same token, a falling dollar may actually help. This is true for two reasons. First, a falling dollar makes U.S. products more competitive in world markets, whereas a rising dollar makes them less competitive. Second, foreign sales by U.S. corporations have to be "exchanged" for U.S. dollars. If the euro, for example, is stronger than the dollar, the exchange out of euros and into dollars results in more dollars.

MCDONALDS AND PROCTER & GAMBLE PROFIT FROM WEAK DOLLAR

On April 23, 2003, the Dow rose 165 points to record its biggest one-day gain in three months. Two of the top Dow gainers were McDonalds and Procter & Gamble. The headline in *The New York Times* the next day read "Weak Dollar Value Helps McDonalds Return to Profit." The *Times* reported that much of the first-quarter gains reported by McDonalds came from a 2 percent increase in profit from the conversion of strong foreign currencies like the euro into the weaker dollar. Procter & Gamble, a multinational consumer products firm, gets half of its sales from overseas. Strong foreign currencies (combined with a weaker dollar) added 3 percent to that firm's first-quarter profit.

DOLLAR IMPACT ON DRUG STOCKS

Drug stocks provide another example of a multinational stock group that can be impacted by dollar trends. A falling dollar may help the bottom line of large multi-national pharmaceutical firms since so much of their revenue comes from foreign markets like Europe. This may also help explain why drug stocks usually hold up better than other stocks (on a relative basis)

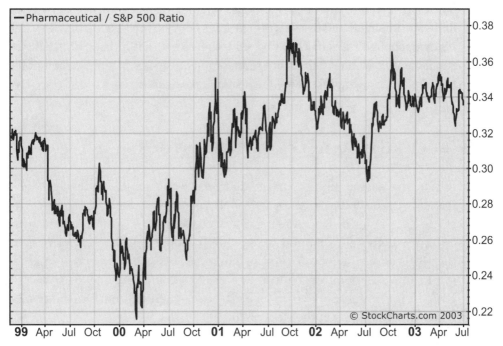

FIGURE 6.4   Drugs have outperformed the S&P since 2000. A falling dollar in 2002 also helped drugs.

when the dollar and the stock market are weak. Drug stocks are defensive in nature and show better relative strength when the stock market is weak. At the same time, a weaker dollar also increases the relative attractiveness of drug stocks because of their dependence on foreign sales.

Figure 6.4 plots a ratio of the AMEX Pharmaceutical Index (DRG) divided by the S&P 500 since 1999. The rise in the Drug Index (relative to the S&P 500) since the start of 2000 reflects the fact that the defensive drug stocks attract money when the stock market is weak and, as a result, outperform the general market. While the S&P 500 peaked during 2000, the Dollar Index did not start falling until 2002. This dollar weakness during the first half of 2002 may account for the boost that the drug stocks got from the middle of 2002 to the middle of 2003. A weak dollar and a weak stock market are usually a good combination for drug stocks.

SMALL STOCKS ARE DOMESTIC

The size of a stock may also determine how much it will be affected by dollar trends. Because most multinationals are large firms, they are more affected by dollar trends than smaller stocks. Smaller firms rely more heavily on domestic business and less on foreign sales, so they are less impacted by currency exchange rates. It could be said, therefore, that a rising dollar favors small-capitalization stocks more than large-cap stocks, while a falling dollar benefits large-cap stocks more than small-cap stocks.

WEAK DOLLAR ALSO HELPS SERVICE STOCKS

Although it is generally recognized that American manufacturers get a boost from a weaker dollar, it is not as widely recognized that American service stocks get a boost as well. American service companies (which include insurance, retailers, telecom, and worldwide package delivery services) spent the 1990s expanding into overseas markets. This put U.S. service-oriented stocks into position to benefit from a weaker dollar. Figure 6.5 shows that UPS (United Parcel Service) appears to have benefited from a weaker dollar which started falling at the start of 2002.

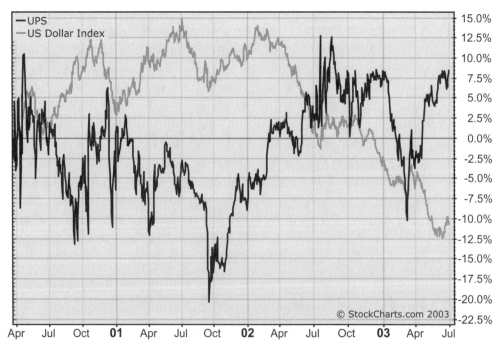

FIGURE 6.5   UPS benefited from a weak dollar after 2001. A falling dollar helps service companies.

RECAP OF INTERMARKET PRINCIPLES

Before we end our discussion of the profitable 1990s and being to examine the more difficult years after 2000, let's review the main intermarket principles covered in the preceding chapters. These are the intermarket relationships that ruled the markets over the last 30 years of the twentieth century. Some of them started changing in the late 1990s. Several intermarket changes were very dramatic after 2000.

- Basic intermarket principles
  - All markets are linked, domestically and globally
  - No market moves in isolation
  - Analysis of one market should include all the others

- Market Groups
  - The four market groups are stocks, bonds, commodities, and currencies

- Market Relationships
  - The dollar and commodities trend in opposite directions (Figure 6.6)
  - Bond prices and commodities trend in opposite directions (Figure 6.7)
  - Bonds and stocks normally trend in the same direction (Figure 6.8)

FIGURE 6.6   The dollar and commodities trend in opposite directions.

FIGURE 6.7   Bond prices and commodities trend in opposite directions.

FIGURE 6.8   Bonds and stocks normally trend in the same direction.

- ○ Bonds peak and trough ahead of stocks
- ○ During deflation, bond prices rise while stocks fall
- ○ A rising dollar is good for U.S. bonds and stocks
- ○ A weak dollar favors large multinational stocks

- • Effects of commodity/bond ratio
  - ○ A rising commodity/bond ratio favors inflation-type stocks including gold, energy, and basic material stocks like aluminum, copper, paper and forest products
  - ○ A falling commodity/bond ratio favors interest rate-sensitive stocks including consumer staples, drugs, financials and utilities

CHAPTER 7

The Nasdaq Bubble Bursts in 2000

AN HISTORIC YEAR

The preceding chapter discussed how 1999 experienced a rising inflation threat from rising oil and industrial material prices. This pushed interest rates higher, which began to have a negative impact on those sectors of the stock market that tend to be "early peakers." Interest rate-sensitive stocks are an example. Old economy stocks, which are sensitive to interest rate direction, had already started to weaken (which was reflected mainly in a falling NYSE Advance–Decline line). By contrast, new economy stocks shrugged off the threat of rising rates during the second half of 1999. Something happened at the start of year 2000, however, as a direct result of the dangerous intermarket trends that existed the previous year. The Fed had started raising short-term interest rates during the middle of 1999. By the first quarter of 2000, this tightening by the Fed had led to a condition known as an *inverted yield curve*.

INVERTED YIELD CURVE IMPLIES ECONOMIC WEAKNESS

An inverted yield curve, like the one that occurred near the start of 2000, is the graphical depiction of short-term interest rates that have risen above long-term rates. This usually occurs after a round of Fed tightening and, in the past, has been an early warning of economic weakness. The recessions of 1990, 1982, 1980, 1974, and 1970 were all preceded by inverted yield curves. In a normal yield curve, long-term rates are higher than short-term rates. When the Fed tightens monetary policy to fight off an inflation threat, it raises short-

97

term rates. The danger point for the economy (and the stock market) occurs when the Fed pushes short-term rates over long-term rates. This point was reached at the start of 2000. When an inverted yield curve develops, the stocks that become most vulnerable are those with the highest price/earnings ratios. At the start of the new millennium, those overvalued stocks happened to be in the dot-com world of Internet and technology stocks that resided in the Nasdaq market. By that spring, the bubble had finally burst in the Nasdaq market, and the longest bull market in history had become history. While this proved disastrous for the Nasdaq market, it actually launched bull runs in defensive market sectors that do better in the early stages of an economic slowdown like consumer staples, financials, utilities, and REITs. All of the intermarket trends—the good ones and the bad ones—were clearly visible on market charts as 2000 started. These trends gave ample warning that not only the stock market was in trouble—the entire economy was as well.

THE WARNING SIGNS WERE THERE ON THE CHARTS

Let us study the year 2000 in some depth. It was such an historic year and there were so many intermarket lessons to be learned. Another reason to study that year so closely was that it demonstrated the danger in relying too heavily on economic and fundamental analysis, to the exclusion of price charts and technical market analysis. One of the basic premises of technical work is that the markets are leading indicators of economic and fundamental trends. This means that the stock market usually peaks six to nine months ahead of the economy. Those who ignored the bearish technical signs on the stock market charts paid a heavy price—or at least their clients did. Some of these bearish signs came from traditional technical indicators like a falling NYSE Advance–Decline line and the breaking of chart support levels by the major stock indexes. Earlier warnings had come from dangerous intermarket trends that started the year before. Warnings came from sector rotations out of *late expansion* stocks into *early contraction* stocks. Another warning came from classic economic indicators like the inverted yield curve. The Wall Street community either missed the classic warning signs or chose to ignore them.

SEEING THINGS AS THEY HAPPEN

One of the traps that a financial writer can fall into is to analyze history with the benefit of hindsight. It is always a temptation to go into the past to choose the right chart to prove one's point or to reinterpret events after the fact. The best way to avoid this is to show charts that were visible at the time the historic market turns were taking place, and then quote from market analysis made at that time with these same charts. That is what is done in this chapter. Most of the charts shown in this chapter are taken from market messages published on the *MurphyMorris.com* website on January 30, 2000 along with the commentary that accompanied them. In some cases, the verbatim quote is given and, in others, the commentary is paraphrased. The main reason for doing it in such a way is to show that the intermarket principles explained throughout this book, combined with traditional technical analysis, were seen while they were happening—not just with the benefit of hindsight. This chapter also describes how market events of 2000 "bridged the gap" between technical market analysis and economic analysis. The next two paragraphs are taken from a market message published at the end of January 2000.

JANUARY 30, 2000: YIELD CURVE INVERSION

There was a lot of talk in the media this week about the inversion of the yield curve. They kept describing the market action as confusing. We don't agree. Here's how it works. In the late stages of an economic expansion, early signs of inflation begin to crop up—usually in the form of rising commodity prices. That puts upward pressure on bond yields. At some point, the Fed starts to raise interest rates to slow down the economy. That causes short-term rates to rise faster than long-term rates. The danger point arrives when short-term rates move above long-term rates (which happened this past week) . . . While an inverted yield curve helps bonds, it's negative for stocks.

Figure 7.1 shows the yield curve as it appeared on January 28, 2000. The downward slope meant that short-term rates were higher than long-term rates.

1969 ALL OVER AGAIN?

In the past, inverted yield curves have usually marked the end of economic expansions and the end of bull markets in stocks. The current economic expansion is now in its 106th month—which matches the previous record that lasted from 1961 to 1969. An inverted yield curve during 1969 signaled the end of that record expansion and the onset of

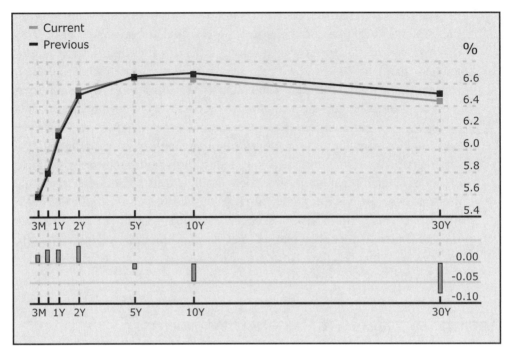

FIGURE 7.1   An inverted yield curve existed on January 28, 2000.

a recession the following year (1970). 1969 also marked the highpoint for the Dow (1000) which wasn't exceeded for another thirteen years (until 1982).

JANUARY LOWS BROKEN

During the second half of January, the Dow and the S&P 500 broke their January lows. They also fell beneath their 200-day moving averages, which is usually a serious warning of a major market decline. Figure 7.2 (which was posted on January 20, 2000) shows the Dow falling under chart support and its 200-day moving average. At the same time, the NYSE Advance–Decline line fell to the lowest levels in three years. The so-called January Barometer was on the verge of giving a negative signal for the year. (The January Barometer is based on the idea that as January goes, so goes the rest of the year.) As was noted at the time, January 2000 was not just a bad January. It was the worst January for the Nasdaq since 1990 and the worst for the S&P 500 in 30

FIGURE 7.2   The Dow Industrials fell under chart support and the 200-day average in 2000.

years. The negative implications of all of these technical intermarket warnings—not to mention the inverted yield curve—seemed pretty clear at the time. As a result, the January 30 website update ended with the following paragraph.

CASH IS GOOD

If the inverted yield curve is truly signaling economic weakness later this year, that will probably have a negative impact on stocks. As the Fed raises short-term rates, the primary beneficiaries are usually money market funds, which get higher yields as a result. Recent developments suggest . . . that it's time to take a much more defensive posture in the stock market which favors bonds, consumer staples, drugs, financials, and utilities. The best place to be, however, is probably a money market fund. We think it's time to take some money out of the stock market and raise your cash levels.

APRIL 15, 2000: NASDAQ BREAKS
MOVING AVERAGE LINE–NYSE FAILURE

By mid-April 2000, the Nasdaq had suffered its first Friday close beneath its 40-week (or 200-day) moving average since August of 1998. It had already lost 34 percent from its peak, which exceeded its 1998 drop of 30 percent. These are the types of numbers that worry chartists who see ominous warnings in drops of that sort. Meanwhile, the NYSE Composite Index had been in a *trading range* since the previous July when the Fed started tightening. The NYSE had failed a "retest" of that old high and had fallen under its 200-day moving average. With all major stock averages beneath their 200-day moving averages, the risk level in the entire market had taken a turn for the worse. Figure 7.3 (which was posted on April 15, 2000) shows the NYSE failing a test of the highs that had been hit the previous summer; it also shows the NYSE falling below its 200-day moving average. The caption on the chart describes the situation as "at best, still a trading range. . . . At worst, a possible top."

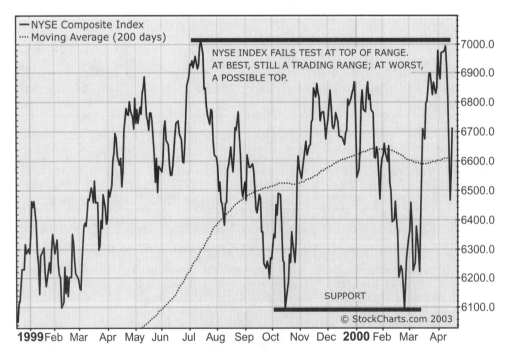

FIGURE 7.3   The NYSE failed a test of the highs hit during the summer of 1999.

REITS HOLD UP

Real estate funds (or REITs) were the top-performing stock group during the first half of April (as the Nasdaq was tumbling). Investors often turn to real estate funds for possible bear market insurance. REITs have three things going for them. The first is that there are high dividend yields (often in excess of 7 percent), which have more appeal in a falling stock market. Second, REITs show a low correlation with the stock market. As a result, they provide diversification value when the market is in trouble. Third, REITs historically have a negative correlation to technology stocks. As such, they usually rise when the techs fall. This is exactly what they did during the spring of 2000.

REITS SHOW GOOD RELATIVE STRENGTH

A relative strength ratio of the Morgan Stanley REIT Index (RMS) divided by the S&P 500 turned up during April (just as the Nasdaq was peaking), as shown in Figure 7.4. The relative strength line rose to a six-month high that

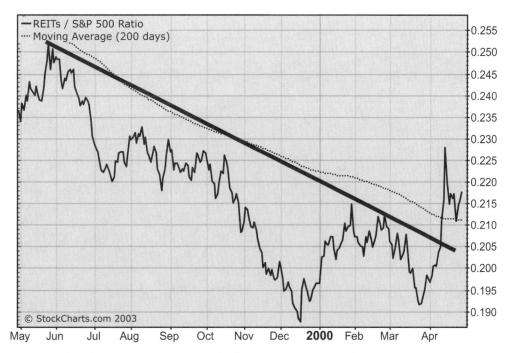

FIGURE 7.4 The REIT/S&P ratio turned up in April 2000 as the Nasdaq was peaking.

month and also broke a yearlong down trendline. In addition, the ratio line exceeded its 200-day average for the first time in two years. In addition to rising relative performance, REIT prices were rising as well.

REIT INDEX TURNS UP

REITs fell into a bear trend that began at the start of 1998 and ended during the fourth quarter of the same year. Near the end of 1999—a little over a year later—they "retested" their 1998 lows and started to bounce. During April 2000, the REIT Index broke its two-year down trendline. It also achieved a *bullish breakout* by exceeding its January high. Real estate mutual funds turned up as well. Figure 7.5 shows the Cohen & Steers Realty Fund turning up during March and breaking a down trendline during April. (A real estate mutual fund is the easiest way for an individual investor to participate in a REIT sector rally. Mutual funds can be charted just like anything else.)

FIGURE 7.5 Example of a REIT mutual fund turning up in the spring of 2000.

APRIL 21, 2000: MARKET'S ECONOMIC MESSAGE— ECONOMIC SLOWING

Intermarket work bridges the gap between traditional technical market analysis and economic trends. Although it may seem strange to have a technical analyst use the preceding headline, this is exactly what happened on April 21, 2000. Although economic analysis is not our primary goal, the markets often tell us a lot about the future course of the economy. The April 21 market comment that year was devoted to a discussion of what the markets were telling us about the economy.

From a more practical side, the market's message about the direction of the economy also gave clues as to what sectors of the market should start to do better given the likely position in the economic cycle. These economic conclusions also influence asset allocation decisions. Bonds usually do better than stocks during an economic contraction. This is exactly what happened in 2000 and for several years thereafter. When bonds are strong, rate-sensitive stock sectors do better. This also happened in 2000. The next four paragraphs are based on the April 2000 message.

COPPER AND LONG RATES PEAK TOGETHER AT START OF 2000

Certain key commodities help gauge the strength of the economy (and the direction of interest rates). The previous year saw a rise in industrial commodity prices and the upward pressure they put on interest rates. This picture reversed by the spring of 2000. Copper, which had been rising throughout 1999, peaked in January of 2000 and fell beneath its 200-day moving average during April. Figure 7.6 (posted on April 21, 2000) shows copper breaking an up trendline during February 2000 and, more importantly, its 200-day moving average during April. Since copper is a barometer of economic strength, its fall at the start of 2000 was a warning sign that the economy was weakening.

At the same time that copper was peaking, the yield on the 10-year T-note started dropping as well. Figure 7.7 shows the 10-year T-note yield peaking in January 2000 and breaking its 200-day average during April. At the time, these two factors were interpreted as early signs that the inverted yield curve that had occurred in January was indeed starting to slow the economy. Evidence of this was also seen in how the various stock market sectors were behaving.

FIGURE 7.6   Copper broke a support line and its 200-day average during April 2000.

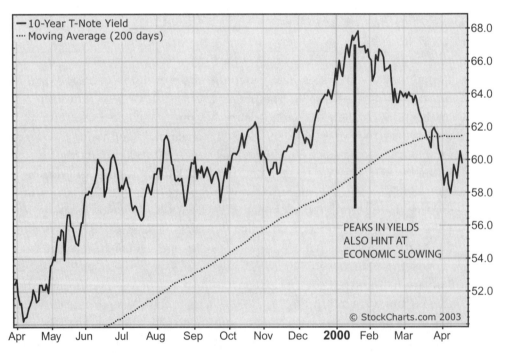

FIGURE 7.7   The 10-Year T-Note yield peaked during January 2000.

ECONOMIC WEAKNESS FAVORS CONSUMER STAPLES

Certain market sectors do better at different stages in the economic cycle. In the early contraction phase, the best-performing sector is consumer staples. Once the contraction takes hold, other groups like utilities and financials start to do better. The April 21, 2000, website message contained the following conclusion: "Our reading of the market suggests we're somewhere in between the 'late expansion' and 'early contraction' phase of the economic cycle."

CONSUMER STAPLES START TO OUTPERFORM

A relative strength ratio of the Morgan Stanley Consumer Index divided by the Dow (posted in April 2000) showed consumer stocks starting to outperform the Dow for the first time in a long time (see Figure 7.8). Consumer staples are defensive in nature, and include industry groups like beverage, food, drug, tobacco, and household products. The reasoning is that people

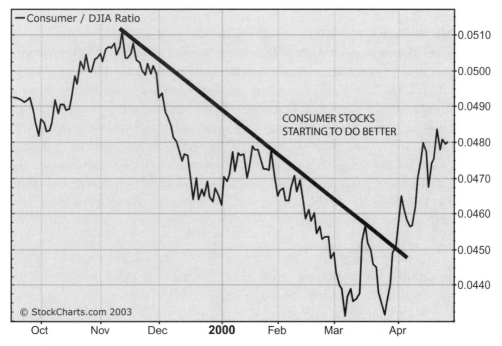

FIGURE 7.8   The Consumer/Dow ratio turned up during April 2000.

still have to use these products in good times and bad. Relative strength in this group often hints at economic slowing. The April 21 commentary ended with the following paragraph.

THINGS COULD NOT BE BETTER

Wall Street economists keep telling us things couldn't be better. If things can't get any better, doesn't that mean they can only get worse? Historically, the markets usually turn down long before the economy does. That's why the markets are considered to be leading indicators of the economy. And the market's message is that the economy is starting to slow. In time, that will hurt corporate earnings and the stock market. At such times, it's usually better to be in defensive sectors of the market (including money market funds). Last week, we commented on the upturn in REITs—a traditional defensive haven. Consumer staples also look like a good defensive choice.

AUGUST 11, 2000: SHIFT TO VALUE

The collapse in the Nasdaq market in the spring of 2000 caused several rotations to take place within the stock market that year. As previously described, there was a rotation out of technology and into consumer staples and REITs. Bonds also turned up as stocks in general started to weaken. Another major shift that took place that year was a move out of *growth* stocks into *value* stocks. This trend was described in a market message published on August 11, 2000. The first paragraph ended with the following observation: "Leadership in the market appears to have shifted back to old economy stocks (represented by the Dow) and away from the new economy stocks (represented by the Nasdaq)." The following paragraph was included in that same market message.

Another sign that investors are bracing for a weaker economy during 2000 is the shift back to value . . . For the past three years, value has underperformed growth. However, the S&P Value/Growth ratio formed two bottoms (in March and July) and is trending higher, as shown in Figure 7.9. Value stocks (with low price/earning ratios) usually do better than growth stocks (with high p/e ratios) in a weakening economy.

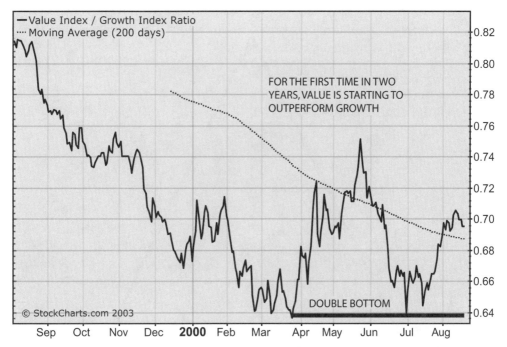

FIGURE 7.9   Value stocks started outperforming growth stocks during 2000.

> *It just so happens that most of the value stocks reside in the old econ-*
> *omy, while most of the growth stocks are in the Nasdaq.*

This switch from growth to value continued into the spring of the following year. However, it was just another manifestation of the same message—economic slowing and a faltering stock market. As suggested earlier,
different sectors outperform at various stages in the economic cycle. It is
time to show you where that information comes from.

SECTOR ROTATION WITHIN THE ECONOMIC CYCLE

Figure 7.10 is a diagram of how market sectors perform at various stages of
the economic cycle. The diagram was created by Sam Stovall and published in
the *Standard & Poor's Guide to Sector Investing*. There are five stages in one
complete economic cycle—three during an economic expansion and two during an economic contraction. The left side of the diagram shows which sectors
do best during an economic expansion. "Early Expansion" is characterized by

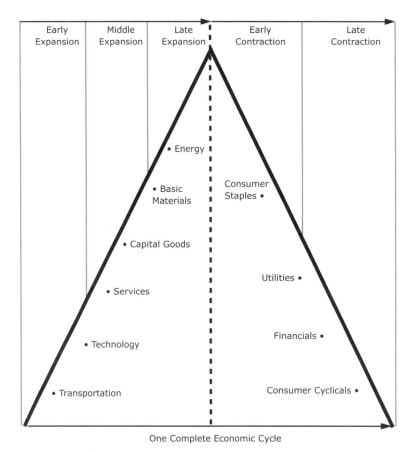

FIGURE 7.10   How market sectors perform during the business cycle.
(*Standard & Poor's Guide to Sector Investing,* McGraw Hill,
1995.)

relative strength in Transportation and Technology. (One of the reasons that
Transportation stocks lead an economic recovery is due to falling energy
prices, a move which occurs during a recession. The diagram also explains
why leadership in the technology sector is usually a good sign for the economy
and the stock market.) "Late Expansion" shows Energy to be the top-performing sector. The next two stages show sector leadership as the economy starts
to slow. "Early Contraction" shows Consumer Staples to be the leading market
group. "Late Contraction" shows rotation toward Utilities, Financials, and Consumer Cyclicals.

In our analysis of 1999 intermarket trends, we stated that Energy leadership (arising from rising oil prices) was a bad sign for the economy. The
reason for this can be seen in the diagram. Energy dominance usually takes
place in the "Late Expansion" phase of the economic cycle and is usually a

prelude to a peak in the economy. This is partly due to the simple fact that sharply higher oil prices are bad for the economy, and oil shares rise with energy prices. In addition, the Fed usually responds to higher oil prices by raising interest rates, which usually leads to economic slowing. Both events took place in 1999 and the early part of 2000.

WHY IT IS BAD WHEN ENERGY AND CONSUMER STAPLES ARE STRONG

One way we can tell when rising energy prices are starting to slow the economy is when market leadership starts to shift from Energy to Consumer Staples. Since that shift takes place gradually, the real danger sign becomes evident when Energy and Consumer Staples are the strongest two sectors in the stock market. This was the case during the first half of 2000.

Figure 7.11 shows the performance of four market sectors—Energy, Staples, Cyclicals, and Basic Industry—at the halfway mark of 2000 (all four sectors are plotted around the S&P 500, which is the flat line in the middle of the chart). It can be seen that Energy and Staples are the two strongest

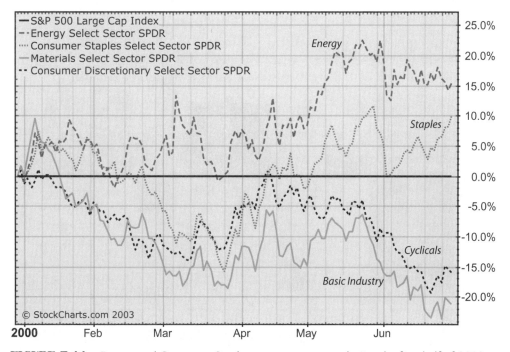

FIGURE 7.11 Energy and Consumer Staples were top sectors during the first half of 2000.

groups. This is consistent with market leadership in the early stages of an economic slowdown. At the same time, the two economically sensitive groups— Basic Materials and Cyclicals—are the weakest. This also makes sense in a weakening economy. As the economy starts to slow more, the rotation works its way down the right side of Stovall's diagram to Utilities and Financials. Let's see what the diagram was showing during the fourth quarter of 2000.

NOVEMBER 10, 2000: IT'S THE ECONOMY

Figure 7.12 shows another type of sector performance chart that was published on November 10, 2000 on the *MurphyMorris.com* website in an attempt to see whether the market sectors were following their normal economic rotation in a slowing economy. Sure enough, they were. Figure 7.12 uses a bar chart format to compare the performance of the 10 S&P market sectors. It shows how closely the sectors followed Stovall's economic cycle diagram. The four top performers during the first 10 months of 2000 were Energy (17 percent), Consumer Staples (18 percent), Utilities (21 percent), and Financials (20 percent). The three weakest sectors were the economically sensitive Basic Industries (–25 percent), Cyclicals (–22 percent) and

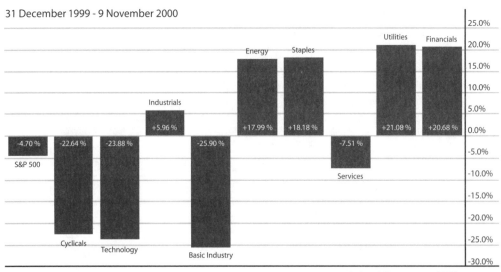

© StockCharts.com 2003

FIGURE 7.12   Energy, Staples, Utilities and Financials were top sectors in the first ten months of 2000.

Technology (–23 percent). All of these trends were consistent with a slowing economy.

TWOFOLD USE OF SECTOR ROTATION DIAGRAM

The use of the sector rotation diagram is twofold. By knowing which sectors are in leadership, it is possible to make a judgment about the state of the economic cycle. The message in 2000 was one of economic slowing. The second and more valuable use is in the implementation of sector rotation strategies. In 1999, for example, Energy stocks were the preferred sector in which to be. In 2000, however, the diagram would have suggested gradual rotation into Consumer Staples, Utilities, and Financials. All three rose in 2000. From an asset allocation standpoint, economic slowing favors bonds over stocks. Economic slowing is also bad for commodities. During that fateful year, stocks and commodities peaked while bonds started an impressive bull run. It was all there on the charts. All one needed to know was how to read them.

THE LESSONS OF 2000

If ever a year demonstrated how technical, intermarket, and economic analysis work together, 2000 was that year. Traditional technical indicators (like the NYSE Advance–Decline line) had started breaking down over a year earlier. Stock market indexes started to crack during January 2000. Most stock technical indicators were giving "sell signals" during the spring of 2000. Intermarket warning signs had been flashing during the second half of 1999 in the form of rising commodity prices and rising interest rates. The result was a round of Fed tightening that eventually resulted in an inverted yield curve, which has led to every recession since 1970. Sector rotation strategies followed the sequence that normally takes places at the end of an economic expansion. 2000 was a textbook example of a stock market top and an economic top in the making. Yet, incredibly, most Wall Street professionals did not see it coming—or pretended not to. This leads us to perhaps the biggest lesson of 2000, which is the need to use charts. Because, as the old-timers used to tell us, "Charts don't lie."

CHAPTER 8

Intermarket Picture in Spring 2003

FLIGHT TO GOLD

By the middle of 2002, the bear market in stocks was in its second year with no end in sight. Stocks were not the only asset class in a bear trend. Stocks had peaked during 2000. By the start of 2001, commodity prices had also peaked and entered a major decline of their own. Bond prices had been rising since the start of 2000. All three markets appeared to be following their deflationary script described in previous chapters. (During a deflation, bond prices rise while stocks and commodities fall.) The bond market was not the only place in which to make money, however. Gold (and gold stocks) were rising for the first time in years. Part of the move into gold was a flight from a falling stock market. A large part of it, however, was also tied to a fall in the U.S. dollar. The dollar had been in a bull market since 1995. By the end of 2000, the dollar stopped going up and started moving sideways.

By the spring of 2002, however, the dollar rolled over and entered a new downtrend. One of the key intermarket principles is that a falling dollar is bullish for gold. The dollar breakdown gave a big boost to gold and gold-related shares. Another intermarket principle is that gold usually trends in the opposite direction of the stock market. The combination of a falling stock market—and a falling dollar—lit a fire under gold (and gold stocks). A more subtle intermarket influence was also present in the relationship between gold bullion and gold stocks. Gold stocks turned up before bullion did. In time, gold followed. However, as is usually the case, stocks tied to a certain commodity (like gold) usually turn up before the commodity does. Rising gold stocks acted as a leading indicator for bullion.

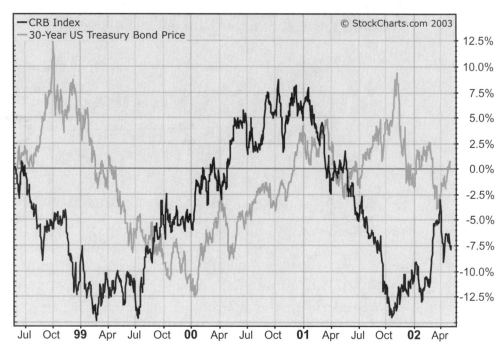

FIGURE 8.1   Bond prices and the CRB rose together during 2000, but diverged during 2001. Bonds rose while commodities fell.

BONDS AND COMMODITIES TREND IN OPPOSITE DIRECTIONS

During 1999, commodity prices rose while bond prices fell. At the start of 2000, however, bond prices started rising and remained strong for the next two years. (The main reason for the strength in bonds during 2000 was a massive flight out of equities after the Nasdaq peaked that spring.) Commodity prices, which had been rising at the start of 2000, continued rising until the end of that year. After that, they collapsed. Bonds and commodities rose together during 2000. By the start of 2001, they had resumed their normal relationship, which is to trend in opposite directions. During 2001, bond prices rose while commodities fell as shown in Figure 8.1.

SEPTEMBER 11 REVERSALS

A comparison of the CRB Index and bond prices from the middle of 2001 to the middle of 2002 shows an almost perfect inverse relationship (see Figure 8.2). A dramatic demonstration of their inverse link was seen in the months sur-

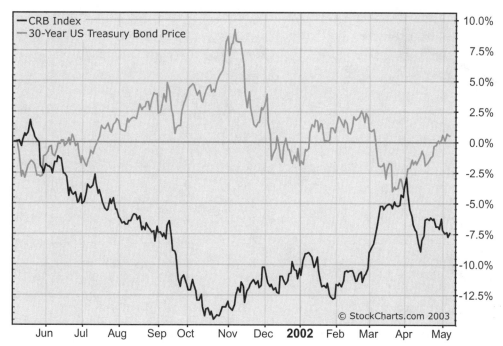

FIGURE 8.2   Bonds prices and the CRB traded inversely from the spring of 2001 to the spring of 2002.

rounding the attack on the World Trade Center on September 11, 2001. In the months leading up to September 11, bond prices had been rising while commodity prices had been falling. After that day, both markets changed direction within a week of each other but continued moving in opposite directions. The CRB Index bottomed on October 24; bond prices peaked on November 1. The stock market played an important role in both reversals.

COMMODITIES FOLLOW THE LEAD OF STOCKS

The CRB Index and the S&P 500 rose together during 1999 and part of 2000, before falling together throughout most of 2001 (although stocks peaked before commodities). They bottomed together after September 11 (see Figure 8.3). Although it is true that stock and commodity prices often trend in opposite directions, it is also true that they sometimes trend together. It depends on the position of the business cycle. At the end of an economic expansion, commodity prices rise along with stocks and eventually contribute to the stock market peak. Commodity prices can then keep rising after stocks peak (which they did during the second half of 2000). During a recession, commodity prices fall along with stocks. Commodities can keep falling long after stocks

FIGURE 8.3   Commodities bottomed after stocks in 1999 and peaked after stocks at the start of 2001.

have bottomed. (We'll discuss why that happens in a later chapter.) In both instances, however, stocks usually change direction before commodities.

In 1999, rising commodity prices lifted inflation expectations, which contributed to the stock market peak in 2000. In 1999, both markets rose together. While the Nasdaq market peaked during the spring of 2000, the S&P 500 did not peak until autumn (around Labor Day). The CRB Index continued rising for another three months before finally turning down at the start of 2001. This action is consistent with the order usually seen at stock market peaks: stocks peak first and commodities second. In 2001, stocks and commodities fell together—until September 11.

STOCKS LEAD COMMODITIES HIGHER

Prior to September 2001, stocks and commodities were both dropping. After the September 11 attacks, the stock market remained closed for a week. When trading resumed on September 17, the stock market initially fell for several days. Within a week, however, the market rallied sharply in an intermediate recovery that lasted into the following spring. Commodities followed stocks higher, as shown in Figure 8.4.

FIGURE 8.4 Commodities and stocks traded in tandem from the spring of 2001 to the spring of 2002. Both turned up after September 11.

A comparison of stocks and commodities after September 11 is instructional on two counts. One is that both markets rallied. Another is that commodities bottomed a month after stocks did. In other words, they followed their normal rotational pattern of commodities following stock prices. The Dow Jones Industrial Average bottomed on September 24, 2001. The CRB Index bottomed on October 24. The rebound in stock prices after September 11, and the resulting bounce in commodity prices, also explains the drop in bond prices that took place around the same time. Bonds had been rising, while stocks and commodities had been falling. These roles reversed, at least for awhile (see Figure 8.5). (The unusually close link between stocks and commodities and the inverse relationship of both to bonds were the result of deflationary pressures. In such an environment, stocks and commodities fall together, while bond prices rise.)

BOND AND STOCK PRICES TREND IN OPPOSITE DIRECTIONS

As previously mentioned, the inverse relationship between bonds and stocks represents the biggest change in traditional intermarket relation-

FIGURE 8.5 The T-Bond peak after September 2001 followed bottoms in the CRB and the S&P 500.

ships. History has shown that bond and stock prices rise and fall together, except at major turning points. At major tops, bonds turn down before stocks. At major bottoms, bonds turn up before stocks. This is why rising bond prices are normally bullish for stocks. When deflation is a threat, however, this decoupling can last for several years. In such an instance, rising bond prices are actually bad for stocks. By the middle of 2001, bond and stock prices had been traveling in opposite directions for more than three years. Bonds had been going up and stocks had been going down—until September 11 (see Figure 8.6).

SEPTEMBER 11 REVERSES TRENDS

Stocks bottomed during the last week of September 2001. Bonds peaked on the first day of November (about five weeks later). Stocks continued to rise—while bonds fell—into the spring of the following year. After that, bonds resumed their long-term uptrend; stocks eventually fell to new bear market lows. Throughout these traumatic months, the inverse relationship between bonds and stocks held fast (see Figure 8.7).

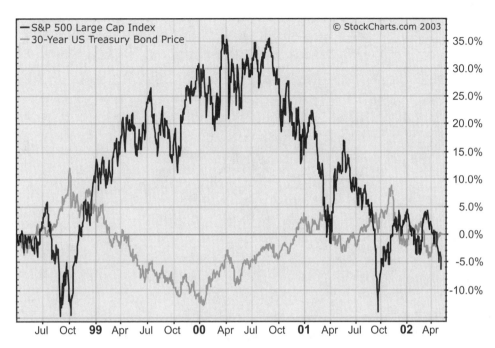

FIGURE 8.6 Bonds and stocks traded in opposite directions from 1998 to 2002. Starting in 2000, bonds rose while stocks fell.

FIGURE 8.7 Bonds and stocks changed direction after September 11, 2001 but continued to trend in opposite directions.

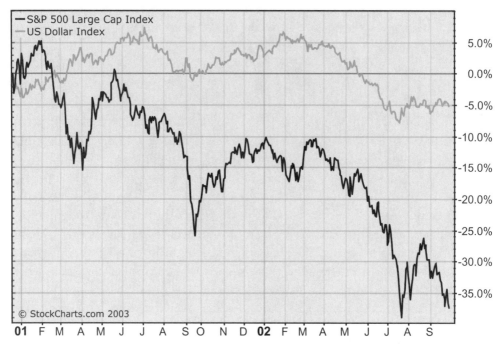

FIGURE 8.8   The dollar and stocks started falling together at the start of 2002.

The dollar was tracking the stock market closely in 2001. Both had been falling together in the months prior to September 11. Both bottomed together that month and stayed in sync on the upside until the following spring. The dollar actually bottomed on September 20, 2001, four days before stocks did, as shown in Figure 8.8. Stocks then resumed their bearish trend, while the dollar started a bear market of its own. There is one market that really shines when stocks and the dollar are in bear markets together—and that market is gold.

FALLING STOCKS ARE GOOD FOR GOLD

Gold peaked in 1980 over $700 and had been falling for 20 years. The stock market bottomed during 1982 and rose for the next two decades, which is consistent with the intermarket principle that gold and the stock market usually trend in opposite directions. The S&P 500 peaked near the end of August 2000. Gold stocks bottomed within two months (in November 2000) and started an impressive bull run. (Gold bullion did not turn up until April of the following year. It is normal for the shares to turn up before the commodity.) A new bear market in stocks helped usher in a new bull market first in the gold shares and then in gold itself (see Figure 8.9).

At that point in time, some skeptics questioned the staying power of the rise in gold shares on the grounds that gold was an *inflation hedge* and there was more deflation than inflation. However, gold shares have histori- cally done well during both inflations and deflations. The inflationary period of the 1970s saw strong gold shares (and a soaring gold market). Although gold bullion was set at a fixed price during the deflationary years from 1929 to 1932, the price of Homestake Mining (a gold stock) gained 300 percent while the stock market lost close to 90 percent of its value. (The 1929–1932 deflation also saw rising bond prices with falling stocks and commodities, much like the recent situation.) Gold is considered an alternative to paper assets. No one needed the insurance of gold during the big bull market in stocks. It is no accident, then, that the end of the 20-year bull market in stocks coincided almost exactly with the ending of the 20-year bear market in gold. Gold had another thing going for it besides a falling stock market, and that was a falling dollar.

FIGURE 8.9   A new bear market in the S&P 500 helped usher in a new bull market in gold shares and gold bullion.

MAY 22, 2002: MAJOR DOLLAR TOP IN THE MAKING

This headline is taken from a Market Message posted on the *MurphyMorris.com* website on May 22, 2002. A number of technical indicators were shown to make the point that the dollar looked to be making a major top. The last sentence in the opening paragraph concluded: "All are bearish indications for the greenback." From the fourth quarter of 2000 to the first quarter of 2002, the Dollar Index had formed three major peaks. (The technical name for that type of pattern is a *head and shoulders* top.) In April 2002, the Dollar Index broke a trendline drawn under the two troughs formed during January and September 2001. This was the chart signal that the topping pattern had been completed for the dollar; it indicated the start of a major decline (see Figure 8.10).

FALLING DOLLAR IS BULLISH FOR GOLD

Historically, the primary beneficiary of a falling dollar is the gold market and gold mining shares. There usually exists an inverse relationship between the

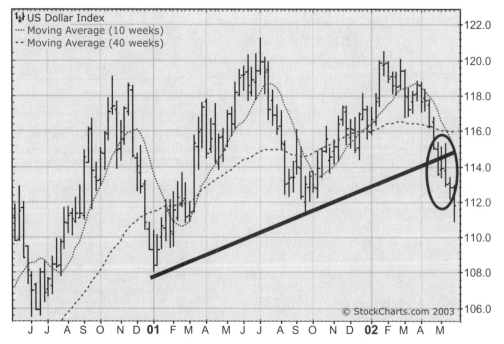

FIGURE 8.10   The U.S. Dollar Index broke a support line in April 2002, which completed a major top formation.

US Dollar Index
Gold - Continuous Contract

© StockCharts.com 2003

FIGURE 8.11 The drops in the dollar during 2001 and 2002 contributed to an upturn in gold bullion.

dollar and gold, meaning that they trend in opposite directions. If gold bullion was about to rise in the spring of 2002, it was normal to expect that gold shares would rise even faster. The following statement was made in May 2002: "And since gold stocks usually rise faster than the price of bullion—gold shares remain our favorite play."

A chart comparing the dollar to gold prices from 2000 to 2002 shows their inverse link (see Figure 8.11). The gold market had started rallying during the spring of 2001 after the dollar had formed the first of its three peaks a few months earlier. Six months into 2001, the dollar formed the second of its three peaks, coinciding with another rally in gold. The third and final dollar peak took place in February 2002. This gave the new uptrend in gold an even bigger boost. By the spring of 2002, the dollar was in a major decline and gold had climbed back over $300 for the first time in two years.

GOLD STOCKS SHINE

Gold stocks bottomed several months ahead of bullion. The actual bottom in the Gold Index (XAU) took place during the fourth quarter of 2000, just as the dollar was forming the first of its three peaks. By the time the dollar had completed its third peak during the spring of 2002, the Gold Index had already risen to the highest level since the fourth quarter of 1999. (Chart 8.12). Gold and gold shares had done exactly what an intermarket chartist would have expected them to do at that point. The combination of a major decline in the dollar and a major top in the stock market had historically proven to be bullish for the gold sector. Figure 8.12 shows the new uptrend in gold shares being helped by a weaker dollar.

Some traders took the view that gold was not much of an investment because it had done so poorly for 20 years. However, this was one of the most compelling reasons why gold (and its shares) had become such a good investment. The two-decade bull market in stocks had ended. What better time to buy gold? Consider the alternatives. Stocks were in a major decline. Interest rates had fallen to the lowest level in 40 years, making fixed income investments less attractive. Twelve Fed easings since the start of 2001 had pushed U.S. short-term rates to the lowest level among the major industrialized countries with the exception of Japan (whose rates were at zero). Money market funds were paying little more than 1 percent. With U.S. rates so much lower

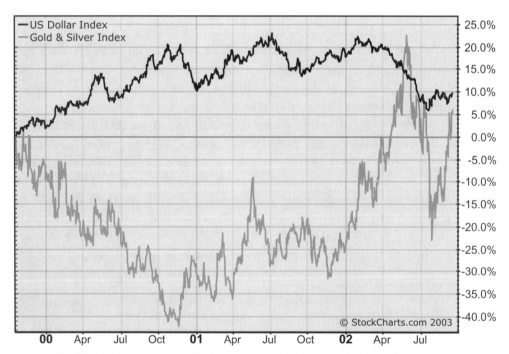

FIGURE 8.12 The bottom in gold shares coincided with a top in the dollar.

than they were in other countries, the dollar had nowhere to go but down. This made U.S. bonds and stocks even less attractive to foreign investors. A climate of falling stock prices, a falling U.S. dollar, and historically low interest rates do not leave people with a lot of investment alternatives. This is the exact type of intermarket climate that drives money to gold.

ONE YEAR LATER: THE FED DISCOVERS DEFLATION

Intermarket trends since the Asian currency crisis in the middle of 1997 had been hinting at a growing deflationary threat. In fact, the only intermarket model that made any sense after 1997 was based on deflation. The markets, which are discounting mechanisms, had already been trading for several years based on the assumption that the deflation threat was for real. Meanwhile, the economic community (including the Fed) kept referring to falling inflation and falling interest rates as good things. It took more than five years after the 1997 Asian crisis (and the worst bear market in stocks since the deflationary 1930s) for it to happen. In the spring of 2003, however, the Fed finally expressed some concern about the threat from falling prices.

On Tuesday, May 6, 2003, the Federal Reserve announced its decision to leave short-term rates unchanged at the 1.25 percent level. This was expected. What was unexpected was the statement released the same day that "the probability of an unwelcome substantial fall in inflation, though minor, exceeds that of a pickup in inflation from its already low level." Although it did not actually use the D-word, the Fed signaled that it was ready to lower interest rates again to ward off the threat of falling prices (which is deflation). This statement marked a major shift in Fed thinking, albeit a late one. It also marked the first time since World War II that a Fed Board had announced that deflation was a greater threat than inflation. The Fed started lowering rates in January 2001 just after the record expansion of the 1990s had ended and a new recession was starting. By May 2003, it had lowered rates 12 times to the lowest level since 1961. The fact that the most aggressive easing in 40 years could not stop the persistent drop in inflation should have sent off warning alarms in the investment world much earlier than it did.

Deflationary warning signs had already started to show up the previous year. In December 2002, a negative Producer Price Index (PPI) number of –0.3 percent was reported for that month. Core wholesale prices (as measured by the PPI) fell 0.4 percent for the year, which was the first time in 28 years that the United States had experienced an annual decline in wholesale prices. Economists took comfort in a small jump in the Consumer Price Index. What kept the CPI from falling throughout 2002 was a 3.2 percent rise in the prices of consumer services. The prices of consumer goods in 2002 actually fell 1.5 percent. The combined drop in the cost of goods during November and December of 2002 was the biggest decline on record going back to 1958. While economists were looking at inflation in medical costs and college tuition, American companies were being bled by deflation in manufactured goods.

By the spring of 2003, the Fed's preferred measure of inflation—the price index of personal consumption excluding food and energy—had fallen to 1 percent. This was the lowest level of this measure in 40 years. Within 2 weeks of the Fed's expression of concern about a "substantial fall in inflation," it was reported that April 2003 PPI numbers had fallen by 1.9 percent, which was the biggest monthly decline on record. A lot of that had to with the big drop in energy prices after the start of the Iraq war. The core PPI number (excluding food and energy) fell 0.9 percent, however, which was the biggest drop in nine years. A day later it was reported that the Consumer Price Index (CPI) fell 0.3 percent in April. Its annual increase of 1.5 percent was the smallest since 1966.

From October 2002 to April 2003, the CPI core inflation rate was an even smaller annual rate of 0.9 percent. Suddenly, the desired goal of zero inflation had gotten dangerously close to slipping into an undesirable state of deflation. Later in May 2003, a special International Monetary Fund task force warned of a high and increasing risk of deflation in Germany, Taiwan, and Hong Kong—and of worsening deflation in Japan.

Low inflation means that prices of goods and services are rising at a relatively slower rate. Deflation means that prices are actually falling. In such a climate, companies are not able to raise prices. As a result, they are forced to cut operating costs, translating into less hiring and more unemployment. Deflation is much more difficult to stop than inflation, especially with short-term interest rates already at 1.25 percent. With rates so close to zero, the Fed loses one of its main weapons against economic weakness and deflation: the ability to lower interest rates. This brings us back to the dollar.

LETTING THE DOLLAR FALL

The reaction of the financial markets to the Fed's sudden fear of deflation (combined with deflationary CPI and PPI numbers) in May 2003 was predictable. The yield on the 10-year Treasury note fell to the lowest level in 45 years. The dollar fell to a four-year low against the euro, a five-year low against the Canadian dollar, and a three-year low against the Australian dollar. (Money flows out of low-yielding currencies and into higher-yielding currencies. In May 2003, the U.S. two-year Treasury note yielded 1.5 percent. By comparison, the two-year note was yielding 4.61 percent in Australia, 3.69 percent in Canada, and 2.4 percent in Germany.)

Although the Fed could not lower rates much more, there was something else they could lower: the dollar. A falling dollar is one of the best cures for falling prices; it is usually considered to be inflationary. Some observers suspected that the Fed (and the U.S. Treasury) had been allowing the dollar to fall since the start of 2002 in an attempt to create a little inflation. This suspicion was confirmed a couple of weeks after the Fed issued its deflation warning when Treasury Secretary John Snow hinted that the U.S. government had abandoned its eight-year policy of verbally supporting a strong dollar. Mr. Snow commented that the U.S. Government no longer measured the value of the dollar by its market value against the other major currencies. Traders took this as a sign that the government wanted the dollar to fall in order to *reflate* (or reinflate) the economy. One place that this strategy worked was in the commodity pits. Immediately after Mr. Snow's comment, traders sold the dollar and bought gold. By that time, however, commodity prices had already been rising for over a year, thanks to the falling dollar. The plunge in yields in May 2003 proved to be short-lived. Within three months, higher commodity prices started pulling long-term rates higher and T-bond prices lower.

CHAPTER 9

Falling Dollar During 2002 Boosts Commodities

COMMODITIES INFLATE

The previous chapter mentioned the Fed's sudden concern about deflation in May, 2003, and the U.S. government's abandonment of its strong dollar policy. The plan was to sacrifice the dollar in an attempt to boost prices. By the time the Fed noticed that prices were falling, commodity markets had already been rallying for over a year. A lot of that had to do with the falling dollar. The rise in commodities, however, did not have the normal impact on bonds. As mentioned earlier, one of the major intermarket relationships that had changed since 1998 was the link between bonds and stocks. During the second half of 2002, another key intermarket relationship changed: the link between bonds and commodities.

Rising commodity prices during the second half of 2002 should have produced lower bond prices and higher bond yields. They did not. One possible explanation for the decoupling of bond yields and commodity prices is the presence of global deflationary trends. U.S. rates are linked to global rates, which tend to rise and fall together. With Japan still mired in a deflationary decline, global interest rates continued to drop together. This global deflationary influence helps explain why bond yields did not follow commodity prices to a higher level during the second half of 2002. Falling stock prices also kept a lid on interest rates. A closer examination of the individual commodity markets that led the CRB Index higher in 2002 also provides a clue to the lack of response on the part of the bond market.

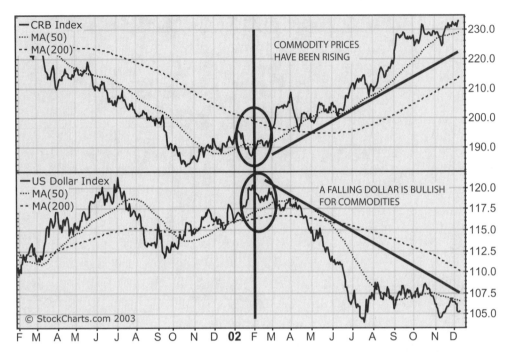

FIGURE 9.1   Throughout 2002, the falling dollar coincided with rising commodity prices.

DOLLAR PEAK COINCIDES WITH COMMODITY BOTTOM

The U.S. dollar hit its final peak during the first quarter of 2002. From that point on, it dropped sharply for the balance of that year. The CRB Index (which represents a basket of commodity markets) turned up at the exact point that the dollar peaked. For the rest of 2002, commodity prices continued an uninterrupted advance. This action is consistent with the intermarket principle that a falling dollar usually results in higher commodity prices (see Figure 9.1). In the previous chapter, we discussed the rally in the gold market as a result of the falling dollar. The fact is that the commodity rally spread to most commodity markets, not just gold.

BONDS AND COMMODITIES DECOUPLE

Such a strong rally in commodities should have put downward pressure on the bond market in 2002. This did not happen. During the first half of 2002, bond and commodity prices maintained their normal inverse relationship. Commodities bounced while bonds pulled back. Starting at mid-year, how-

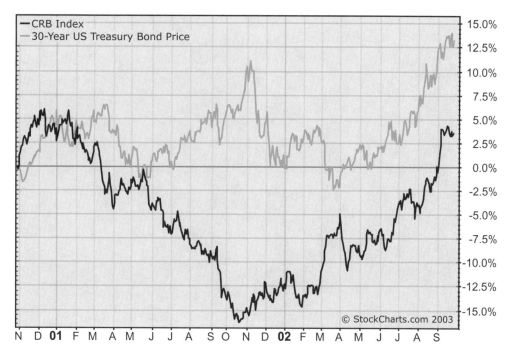

FIGURE 9.2   Bond and commodity prices trended in opposite directions until the middle of 2002.

ever, commodities turned sharply higher. This would normally have produced lower bond prices. Surprisingly, bond prices started rallying right along with commodities, as shown in Figure 9.2. Part of the explanation for the rise in bond prices comes from the fact that the stock market resumed its bear trend in the spring and summer of 2002; bonds rallied as a result. It seems that the bond market was more closely correlated with stocks during 2002 that it was with commodities. Part of the reason why bond traders ignored the commodity rally also lies in which commodity markets did the rallying.

WAR PREMIUM PUSHES OIL HIGHER

The direction of crude oil prices has an important influence on the direction of the CRB Index. A comparison of the two markets shows a close positive correlation from 2000 through 2002. Oil had peaked during the second half of 2000, then dropped until the end of 2001. The CRB Index peaked shortly after oil and also dropped throughout 2001. Both markets turned up again at the start of 2002 (aided by a falling dollar) as shown in Figure 9.3. Although the

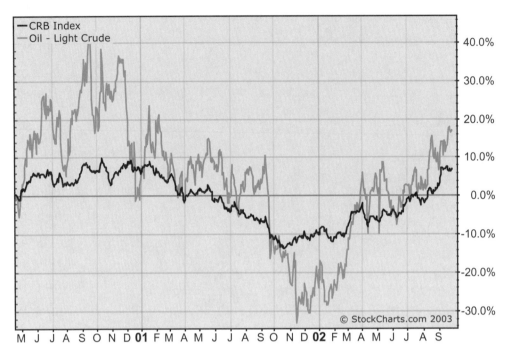

FIGURE 9.3   One of the reasons the CRB rose during 2002 was the war premium built into oil prices.

price of crude rallied throughout 2002, it was suspected at the time that an unrealistic and unsustainable *war premium* was being built into its price in anticipation of another war with Iraq. In other words, the oil rally was somewhat artificial and probably temporary. (This proved to be the case early in 2003 when crude prices tumbled more than 33 percent shortly after the Iraq war started.) It is also true that rising oil represents a tax on the economy and has the unfortunate result of slowing prospects for economic growth. Slower economic growth results in lower interest rates and higher bond prices. Instead of sending off inflation alarms in 2002 and causing lower bond prices, rising energy prices may have had the opposite effect.

COMMODITY DIVERGENCE: WEATHER VERSUS THE ECONOMY

The biggest gains in the commodity markets during the third quarter of 2002 actually came from the grain markets. Drought conditions in the U.S. Midwest caused agricultural markets to soar. This in turn gave a big boost to the CRB Index. At the same time, however, industrial metal prices were actually drop-

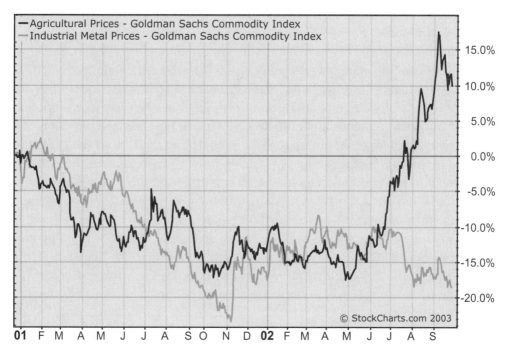

FIGURE 9.4   During the second half of 2002, weather problems pushed agricultural prices higher while industrial metals fell.

ping. The commodity markets were sending a mixed message, one which was not lost on the bond bulls. Bond prices—and interest rates—react to the economic message being sent by commodity markets. A *commodity divergence* existed during the second half of 2002. Agricultural markets, which react to weather conditions, were rising. Industrial metals, which react to economic conditions, were not. As a rule, grain markets have much less of an influence on interest rates than the price of copper. All it would have taken to stop the grain rally was a little more rain. It would have taken a much stronger economy, however, to push industrial metal prices higher. Part of the explanation as to why bond bulls were not concerned about a rising CRB Index in 2002 was based on the belief that the rally in the CRB Index was giving a false signal of economic strength. History seems to support this view (see Figure 9.4).

INDUSTRIAL METALS AND INTEREST RATES TREND TOGETHER

Industrial metals and bond yields peaked together at the start of 2000, signaling an economic downturn and a stock market peak. For the next three years, both markets fell together, as shown in Figure 9.5. In an earlier chapter, we discussed the fact that industrial metals (like aluminum and copper) are considered to be barometers of global economic strength or weakness. Rising industrial metals are associated with stronger economic conditions, as are higher interest rates. Falling industrial metals are associated with weaker economic conditions and lower interest rates. There is a tendency for industrial metals and interest rates to trend in the same direction. Both rebounded together during the fourth quarter of 2001 (after the September 11 tragedy). By the spring of 2002, however, industrial metals and interest rates started falling again, as did the stock market. Interestingly, all three—industrial metals, bond yields, and the stock market—bottomed together in October of 2002. It appears that bond traders were more concerned with the weak economic signals sent by falling industrial metals and falling stock prices in 2002 than they were with the lack of rain in the Midwest. (By the summer of 2003, industrial metals had become the strongest commodity group and began to exert upward pressure on long-term interest rates.)

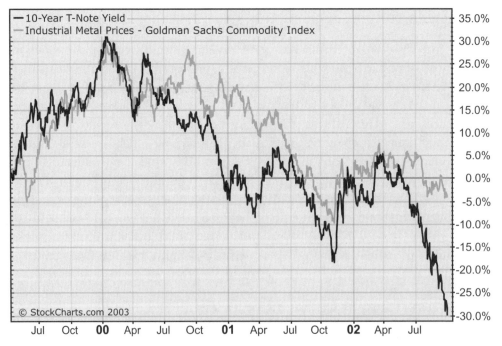

FIGURE 9.5   Both lines peaked together at the start of 2000 and fell together through 2002.

COMMODITY PRICES AND BOND YIELDS NORMALLY TREND TOGETHER

Any chart comparison of bond yields and commodity prices shows that they normally trend in the same direction. Bond yields and the CRB Index peaked together in 1996 and dropped until the end of 1998. (Much of the decline from the middle of 1997 to the fourth quarter of 1998 resulted from deflationary fears in the aftermath of the Asian currency crisis.) The CRB Index and bond yields rose together throughout 1999, which ultimately led to the stock market peak in 2000. Bond yields and commodities diverged in 2000; this happened as interest rates fell and commodities rose. This divergence was apparently caused by a massive flight to bonds following the Nasdaq market collapse. By 2001, bond yields and commodity prices were back in sync as they fell together. It was not until the middle of 2002 that they started to diverge again (see Figure 9.6). This book has already offered some possible explanations for the bond-commodity decoupling during the second half of 2002, due to the nature of the commodity rally and the fact that stocks were falling sharply. There may also have been a global explanation for the continuing drop in bond yields.

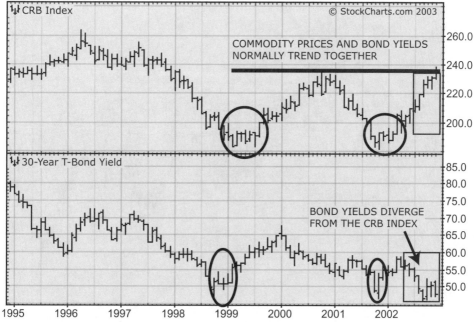

FIGURE 9.6 After trending together since 1995, bond yields and the CRB started to diverge in mid-2002.

ASIAN DEFLATION PULLS U.S. RATES LOWER

Since 2000, a remarkably close correlation has existed between the yield on the 10-year U.S. Treasury note and the Japanese stock market. Japan was the world's second largest economy and had fallen into a deflationary spiral of falling prices. (After the Asian currency crisis of 1997, these deflationary tendencies spread to the rest of Asia and eventually the rest of the world.) Because global markets are so closely linked, the deflationary trends exported from Asia had the effect of pulling down interest rates all over the world. This included U.S. rates. After falling together throughout 2000 and most of 2001, the Japanese market bounced—along with U.S. bond yields—after September 11, 2001, and continued to rise together into the spring of 2002. During the April–May 2002 period, both markets started dropping again (as did the U.S. stock market). By August 2002, the Nikkei had fallen to a 20-year low, while U.S. bond yields had dropped to the lowest level in 40 years, as shown in Figure 9.7. It could be argued that global deflationary trends coming from Japan continued to pull U.S. interest rates lower during the second half of 2002 and offset the impact of rising commodity prices.

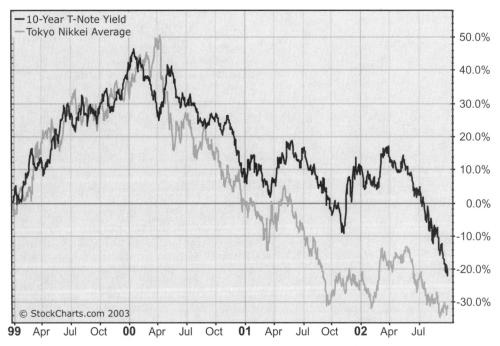

FIGURE 9.7   Asian deflation caused U.S. rates and Japanese stocks to fall together starting in 2000.

GLOBAL BEAR

Global linkages play an increasingly important role in the intermarket chain. Global interest rates rise and fall together. The same is true with stock markets. It should come as no surprise, then, to find out that the bear market which gripped the U.S. stock market in 2000 was global in scope. In other words, all of the world's major stock markets fell together. No part of the world escaped unscathed—not Asia, not Europe, and certainly not the United States. The fact that world stock markets were so closely correlated to the downside for three years is another dramatic example of how world markets are linked (see Figure 9.8).

The fact that global markets tend to fall together also bolsters the argument against global diversification during a big bear market. The idea of putting some of one's funds overseas to escape a falling U.S. stock market does not work during a global bear market. It also shows why it is so important for us as investors to know what is going on outside our own borders. U.S. markets are very much affected by global trends. If global stocks are falling, this usually means that global economies are weakening as well. If

FIGURE 9.8 World markets were closely correlated to the downside from 2000 to 2002 in a dramatic example of global linkages.

global economies are weak, who is going to buy American goods? If the American economy is weak, who is going to buy the goods of foreign countries who depend on exports to survive? In addition, the fact that global stock markets fell along with global interest rates also suggests that something drove all of them lower. Japan seems to be the logical candidate.

JAPAN PULLING WORLD MARKETS LOWER

As previously stated, there is a close correlation between the Japanese stock market and U.S. bond rates. This was done to make the point that deflation in Japan was primarily responsible for pulling U.S. rates lower (not to mention global rates). The same comparison can be made with global stock markets. A comparison of the Japanese stock market with an index of global stock markets also shows a remarkable correlation (see Figure 9.9). Here again, both peaked at the start of 2000 and fell together for the next three years. Throughout this three-year decline, even the intermediate peaks and troughs are closely matched. Both indexes bottomed during the fourth quarter of 2001 and rallied into the following spring. At that point, all rolled

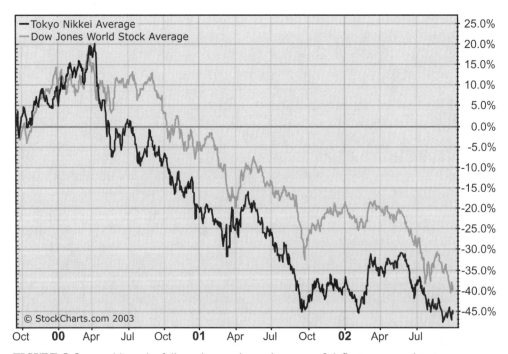

FIGURE 9.9 World stocks followed Japan lower because of deflationary tendencies.

over to the downside together. (By the end of 2002 most global stock markets started to stabilize and rallied together throughout most of 2003.)

DEFLATION SCENARIO: U.S. STOCKS AND RATES FALL TOGETHER

This brings us back to the U.S. bond and stock markets. There is a reason why we discussed global trends before returning to our study of U.S. markets. It was to simply make the point that the unusual relationship between U.S. bonds and stocks since 2000 seems puzzling only when looked at simply in U.S. domestic terms. A comparison of stock prices and U.S. interest rates since 2000 shows them falling together (see Figure 9.10). When markets do not follow their usual intermarket pattern, it is because something unusual is happening. At some point, the intelligent analyst has to start looking for reasons. Major decouplings of bonds and stocks normally take place in a deflationary environment. The last example of this happening was during the 1930s.

American economists, and Wall Street in general, held to the mantra that the United States was not actually in a deflation and all the market needed

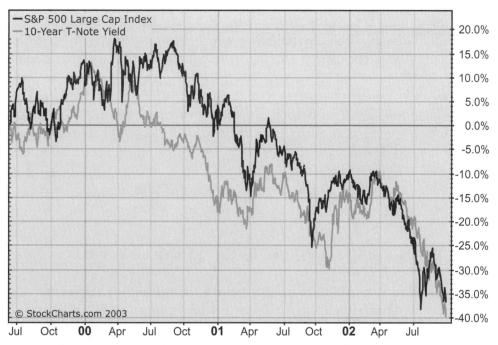

FIGURE 9.10   The deflation scenario explains why bond yields and stocks fell together from 2000 to 2002.

was another Fed easing. Japan was already in a deflation, however. The Japanese had lowered interest rates to zero with no apparent effect on their stock market or their economy. The Fed had lowered rates 12 times to the point where they were getting dangerously close to zero. U.S. bond yields had fallen to the lowest level in over 40 years. The Japanese stock market had fallen to the lowest level in 12 years. Japanese consumer prices had been below zero for 3 years. By the spring of 2003, U.S. core consumer prices were down to 1.5 percent—the lowest level in 40 years. All of these comparisons strongly suggest that the deflationary trend that started in Japan was largely responsible for the major decoupling of U.S. bonds and stocks over the past three years, as well as most of the other changes in the traditional intermarket model. The markets anticipate the future. Although the U.S. markets had not actually fallen into a deflation, the markets clearly saw trends moving in that direction. Anticipating trends are what the markets—and charts—are all about.

COMMODITIES GAIN FROM BATTLE AGAINST DEFLATION

Let us end this chapter where we began—with rising commodity prices. A falling dollar is normally considered to be inflationary. The collapsing dollar since the start of 2002 had already started to push commodity prices sharply higher. By the end of 2002, the CRB Index had risen to the highest level in five years. This rise in 2002 might be interpreted as an early sign that the falling dollar was already starting to have the desired effect of creating some commodity inflation. This is good news for commodity traders. If the government is willing to let the dollar drop, it can only boost commodity markets. If the Fed is preoccupied with deflation, it will be reluctant to raise interest rates. This is also bullish for commodity prices. Ironically, this makes commodity markets the biggest gainers from the Fed's battle against deflation.

DOLLAR TOP LEADS TO NEW BULL MARKET IN GOLD

One of the major tasks of chart reading is to determine if a trend change is only a relatively minor one, or if it represents a major shift in the direction of any market. One of the ways to incorporate intermarket analysis into the picture is to compare the chart action of two related markets. First, one simply compares their direction to see if they are following the normal pattern.

FIGURE 9.11 By the end of 2002, the Dollar Index was breaking a seven-year support line.

Recall that a falling dollar is bullish for gold. If gold is starting to rise, the first thing to do is to determine if the dollar is starting to drop. The next thing to do is to look at the separate charts of each market to determine the importance of their respective trend changes. A minor trend change in one may not justify a major trend change in the other. Their trend signals should be of similar magnitude.

The U.S. dollar had been dropping throughout 2002. At the same time, gold prices had been rising. By December of 2002, however, the Dollar Index was breaking a rising seven-year-old trendline, as shown in Figure 9.11. In chart work, this is a serious breakdown and is indicative of the start of a major decline in the U.S. currency. At the same time that the dollar was breaking down, the price of gold was *breaking out* of a sideways bottoming pattern that had been forming for five years (see Figure 9.12). Gold had just risen over the $325 level, which had been the peak toward the end of 1999. The upside breakout signaled the start of major bull market in gold. This is an example of how to blend traditional chart work with intermarket principles. Both gold and the dollar were experiencing major trend changes at the same point in time. And both were moving in opposite directions.

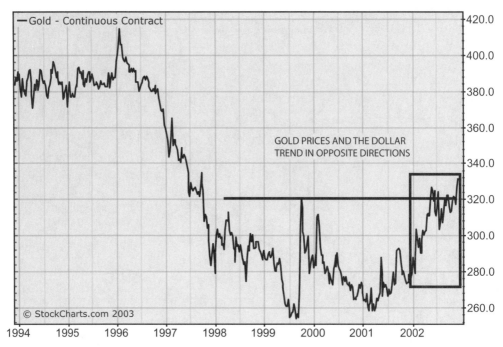

FIGURE 9.12   Gold prices were breaking out of a five-year bottoming formation at the end of 2002. The falling dollar helped.

SWING BACK TO HARD ASSETS?

Long-term charts suggest that hard assets may be starting a period of out-performance over paper assets. The 1970s were the last period to witness investor preference for commodities (hard assets) over bonds and stocks (paper assets). Since 1980, commodity markets had been in decline while bonds and stocks had been in major bull markets. Over the last two disinflationary decades, paper assets trounced hard assets. This may be changing, however. As is discussed in the next chapter, a generational shift may be taking place away from paper assets and back to commodity-type investments.

CHAPTER 10

Shifting from Paper to Hard Assets

GOLD COMES BACK INTO FAVOR

Gold is often used as a proxy for the entire commodity sector. This is probably due to its long history as a store of value and the fact that it is the most recognizable of all the commodity markets (with the possible exception of oil). Radio and television business shows always quote the price of gold, but not necessarily the price of cotton or soybeans. It is also relatively easy for investors to take advantage of gold trends by either buying individual gold shares or putting money into a precious metals mutual fund. Historically, the trend of gold is tied to trends in the general commodity price level.

Gold surged over $700 during the 1970s when commodity markets as a group were in major uptrends. Gold peaked in 1980 just as the commodity bubble was bursting. It then declined for the next 20 years as commodity prices fell out of favor. Gold also has a history of leading turns in the general commodity price level. As a result, what gold does has a major bearing on the direction of commodity prices and the public's perception of the attractiveness of commodities as an investment alternative to bonds and stocks. In addition, for the first time in 20 years, gold and commodities have been attracting attention—at the expense of bonds and stocks.

GOLD BREAKS 15-YEAR RESISTANCE LINE

Long-term charts are the most useful for spotting major trend changes. This is true for all markets. When prices break trendlines that have been in exis-

145

FIGURE 10.1 Gold breaks a 15-year resistance line.

tence for several years, it is usually an indication that something important is happening. The previous chapter talked about how the breaking of a seven-year up trendline by the U.S. dollar near the end of 2002 coincided with a bullish breakout in gold prices. However, this was only part of the intermarket story. As 2003 was starting, the price of gold had risen to the highest level in over five years. Even more impressive was the fact that bullion had risen above a fifteen-year trendline extending all the way back to 1987, as shown in Figure 10.1. It was another important chart sign that this latest rally in gold had staying power behind it and was more than just another bear market rally in a long-term downtrend. Something else happened that gave more credibility to the upturn in gold: Stocks were peaking.

GOLD TURNS UP AS STOCKS TURN DOWN

As mentioned earlier, there is a historical tendency for gold prices to trend in the opposite direction of stocks. Gold is considered to be a hedge against a falling stock market. It does not matter if the threat to stocks is coming from inflation or deflation. The fact is that gold is tied to the stock market—

but as an alternative investment. Gold prices peaked in 1980 and were in a bear market for nearly 20 years. Stocks bottomed during 1982 and were in a bull market for the same 20 years. In other words, the 20-year bull market in stocks coincided with a 20-year bear market in gold. It was no accident that both of those long-term trends started changing direction between 1999 and 2001.

Any comparison of the two markets will show that the bull market in stocks ended just as the new bull market in gold was starting. Most impressive of all was the fact that the gold market broke its 20-year down trendline at the same time that stocks broke their 20-year up trendline (see Figure 10.2). Taken one at a time, these trend changes looked important. Taken together, they reinforced each other's trend reversals. Using traditional charting tools, it could be seen that each market had experienced a major change in trend. From an intermarket perspective, it could also be seen that both trend reversals took place at the same time. Most importantly, they were still traveling in opposite directions. What was bad for one market (stocks) was good for the other (gold). Because gold is a harbinger of trends for other commodity markets, its major bullish turnaround after 2000 also signaled an

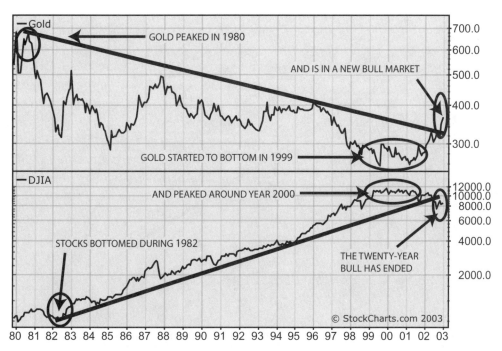

FIGURE 10.2 Gold entered a new bull market during 2002 just as the Dow was ending its twenty-year uptrend.

upturn in commodity prices. This indicated a major change in the relationship between stocks and commodities.

COMMODITIES OUTPERFORM STOCKS FOR FIRST TIME IN 20 YEARS

Gold was not the only commodity that was rising during 2002. As we showed
in the previous chapter, the CRB Index (which includes 17 commodity markets) rose to the highest level in five years before the end of the year. This
made the commodity markets the strongest market group during 2002. One
of the best ways to compare two asset classes is by using relative strength, or
ratio, analysis. The ratio divides one market by another. If the ratio line is
falling, it means the numerator is the weaker of the two markets. If the ratio
line is rising, the numerator is the stronger market (see Figure 10.3).

A ratio of the CRB Index divided by the Dow Jones Industrial Average for
the last twenty years presents a striking picture. (Be sure to use a *logarithmic* price scale for long-term chart comparisons as opposed to the more tra-

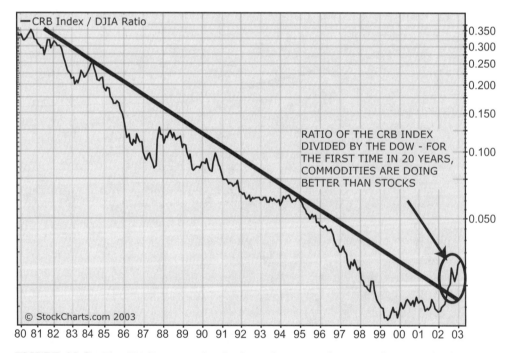

FIGURE 10.3   The CRB/Dow ratio has broken a long term down trendline. For the first time
in twenty years, commodities are doing better than stocks.

ditional *arithmetic* scale. The log scale measures *percentage* changes instead of *absolute* changes. Long-term trendline analysis is thus more valid when applied to a log scale.) The CRB Index/Dow ratio peaked in 1980 and dropped throughout the next two decades. It started leveling off between 1999 and 2001. During the first half of 2002, however, the ratio line broke the 20-year down trendline drawn over the highs of the prior two decades. This upturn in the CRB/Dow ratio marked a major change in their relationship to each other. For 20 years, stocks had been the stronger asset class. Now, for the first time in two decades, commodities had become the stronger one. The breaking of the 20-year down trendline in the CRB/Dow ratio appeared to be signaling a *generational* asset allocation shift out of paper assets (like stocks) and into hard assets (like commodities). (There is more on the use of relative strength, or ratio, analysis and its implications for asset allocation strategies in the next chapter.)

WHY 2003 WAS NOT A REPLAY OF 1991

At the start of 2003, the conventional wisdom on Wall Street and in the financial media was that the steep advance in gold was due primarily to the impending war with Iraq. The same thing had happened during Desert Storm in 1990–1991. In the six months before the earlier conflict, gold rallied while stocks fell. As soon as the war was resolved, gold prices collapsed and stocks turned back up again. A lot of people expected a replay of those trends during the first quarter of 2003 as the second Iraq conflict drew closer. An examination of long-term charts, however, revealed major differences in the two markets in the periods surrounding the two Iraq conflicts (see Figure 10.4).

In 1990, gold was in the midst of a long-term bear market. The rally that took place during the second half of that year was nothing more than a bear market bounce. After it ended, gold resumed its downtrend. The situation in stocks was exactly the opposite. In 1990, the stock market was only halfway through a long-term bull market. The decline during the second half of that year was a relatively minor interruption in the stock market's long advance. Once the war was resolved at the start of 1991, the stock market rose to record highs and resumed its long-term bull market. The situation in both markets in 2003 was quite different. Gold had already broken a 20-year resistance line and was now in a major bull market. Stocks had broken a 20-year support line and were now in a major bear market. The situations in both markets were exactly the opposite of what they were in 1990 and 1991. Gold was now in a secular bull market, while stocks were in a secular bear market.

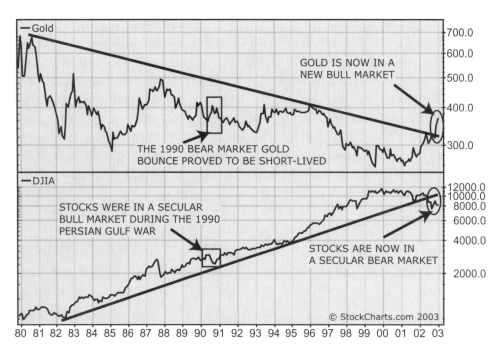

FIGURE 10.4 Why the 2003 Iraq war wasn't a replay of 1991. In 2003, gold is in a bull market while stocks are in a secular bear. Those situations were reversed during the Persian Gulf War in 1991.

CYCLICAL TRENDS VERSUS SECULAR

In order to understand the true meaning of these long-term trend changes, it is necessary to understand the difference between a *cyclical* trend and a *secular* trend. The best way to understand this is to study a 20-year chart of the stock market using a logarithmic scale. A 20-year chart of the S&P 500 shows an uptrend starting in 1982 and ending in 2002. A rising trendline can be drawn under the intervening lows that remained unbroken for 20 years (see Figure 10.5).

A *secular* bull market is very long-term in nature and can last for decades. The bull market in stocks from 1982 to 2002 was just such a bull market. There were three intervening bear markets, however, during this secular uptrend. These bear markets occurred during 1987, 1990, and 1994. The relatively small declines are referred to as *cyclical* bear markets. They are generally relatively shallow and do not do any damage to the secular uptrend. A cyclical bear market can be thought of as an interruption in a long-term bull

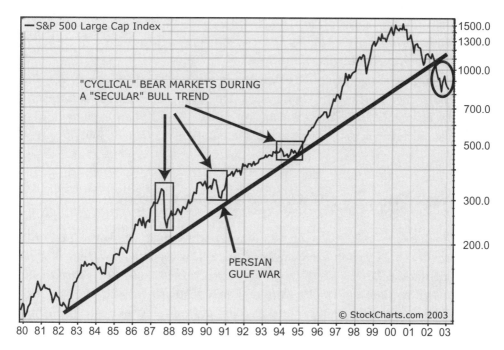

FIGURE 10.5 Cyclical bear markets took place in 1987, 1990, and 1994 during the secular bull market in stocks. Stocks are now in a secular bear.

market. During 2002, however, the S&P 500 broke its 20-year rising trendline and entered a secular bear market, one which would be much different from the three prior bear markets. It would be much steeper and last a lot longer. (The last two secular bear markets took place during the 1970s and the 1930s.) Bull markets can take place during a secular bear market. However, such bull markets are cyclical in nature. As a result, they tend to be shallower and shorter than cyclical bull markets that take place during a secular bull market.

HISTORICAL RESEARCH ON CYCLICAL BULLS

In a June 16, 2003, interview in *Barron's* entitled "Bear's Pause," Ned Davis[1] discussed some of his research on the difference between cyclical and secular trends. Davis divided secular stock market trends lasting 16 to 20 years into three or four shorter cycles (which allows for the traditional four-year

---

[1]President of Ned Davis Research, Venice, Florida.

cycle). He found that cyclical bull markets in secular bear markets "didn't last as long as other cyclical bulls and they didn't go quite as high. . . ." He isolated seventeen cyclical bulls within secular bear markets and found that the S&P 500 gained an average of 50.6 percent and lasted 371 days on average. Davis also studied four cyclical bull moves that occurred within the Japanese secular bear since 1989. These Japanese cyclical rallies gained 48 percent, 34 percent, 56 percent, and 62 percent; these numbers averaged about 50 percent.

SECULAR BEAR IN STOCKS IS GOOD FOR GOLD

Which brings us back to the relationship between stocks and gold. For two decades, gold was in a secular bear market, while stocks were in a secular bull market. After 2002, the situation was reversed. Gold had entered a secular bull market and stocks were now in a secular bear market. This meant that the odds were pretty good that gold (and gold shares) would probably be a much better place to be than stocks for several years to come. The same was true for commodities. This realization has enormous implications in the asset allocation process. Most people take *asset allocation* to mean choosing from only bonds, stocks, and cash. There are compelling arguments, however, for treating commodities as a separate asset class as well, arguments which are presented in the next chapter. If the long-term charts shown in this chapter are telling the true story, commodities may be one of the strongest asset classes for several years to come.

RISING CURRENCY MARKETS

Commodities are not the only markets that benefit from a falling dollar. When the U.S. currency is in a major decline, foreign currencies move up. Just as a falling dollar produces higher gold prices, it has the same bullish impact on foreign currencies. That means that a bull market in gold should correspond with bull markets in other currency markets. This has been the case for the past two years. A chart comparison of the gold market to the euro, for example, shows them rising together, primarily as a result of the falling dollar. The euro starting moving up in earnest during the spring of 2002, just as gold was rising over $300. By the spring of 2003, the euro was hitting a four-year high as gold exceeded $375 (see Figure 10.6).

FIGURE 10.6 The gold market and the euro have been moving up together since 2001. Both uptrends are being caused by a weak dollar.

THE FALLING DOLLAR HURTS GLOBAL MARKETS

Over the previous year, the euro had gained 27 percent against the dollar. By contrast, the Japanese yen had risen only 8 percent. The smaller rise in the yen was due to intervention by Japanese central bankers to keep their currency from rising too fast. In a deflationary economy like Japan's that depends heavily on exports, a rising yen hurts exports and makes deflation worse by keeping prices down. By the spring of 2003, there were growing concerns that Germany (the biggest economy in Europe) might also be on the brink of a deflationary recession. With German first quarter economic growth close to zero, the rising euro was cutting into German exports.

A rising euro also had the unwelcome effect of pushing German prices lower, which was potentially deflationary. The rising euro was not so much signaling European economic strength as much as it was signaling American economic weakness. While the falling dollar was intended to help the U.S. economy, it was making things worse everywhere else. Although the falling U.S. dollar was intended to create a little inflation here at home, it was having the opposite effect of creating deflation in other countries by raising the value of their currencies.

CHINA NOT AFFECTED BY DOLLAR MOVES

One country that was not negatively impacted by the falling dollar was China. The Chinese currency was informally pegged to the dollar. As a result, the falling dollar did not hurt the competitive advantage of the Chinese as much as it hurt Japan and Europe. The continuing supply of Chinese goods on the world markets was another factor which contributed to the global deflationary trend. The global supply of goods was simply greater than the global demand for them. As a result, international pressure was put on the Chinese government in 2003 to revalue their currency in an attempt to level the playing field with other countries in Asia and Europe.

COMMODITY CURRENCIES RALLY

As previously discussed, there are two commodity-based currencies that are closely tied to the fortunes of commodity markets: the Australian and Canadian dollars. Both countries are big producers of commodities and natural resources. As a result, they do better when commodity prices are rising. In Chapter 5, we compared the Australian dollar to commodity prices to show them falling together in 1997 and 1998 (in the aftermath of the Asian currency crisis), then rising together in 1999. During the first half of 2002, commodity prices had rebounded from prior lows formed at the start of 1999 and started to move higher. Not surprisingly, the Australian and Canadian dollars began impressive bull runs of their own. Part of their rise was due to the fall in the U.S. dollar. But it also had a lot to do with rising commodity prices as shown in Figures 10.7 and 10.8. Relatively high interest rates in Australia and Canada resulted in high-yield currencies that attracted foreign capital. Their relatively high interest rates were due largely to rising commodity prices.

USING THE FUTURES MARKETS

When one talks about commodity markets and foreign currencies, the discussion is primarily about futures markets. Futures markets provide a built-in asset allocation model that encompasses bonds, stocks, commodities, and

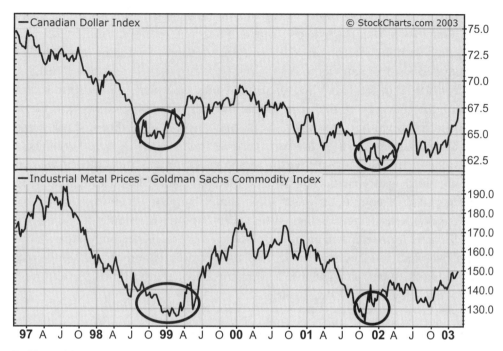

FIGURE 10.7   The Canadian dollar is closely linked to commodity prices.

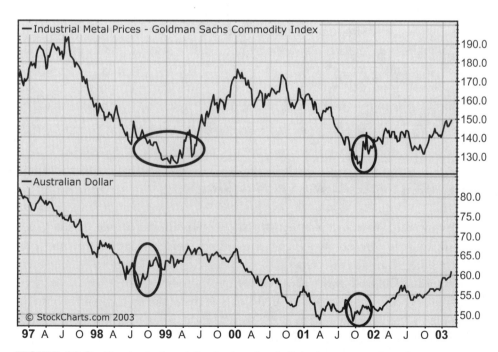

FIGURE 10.8   The Australian dollar is also closely linked to commodity prices.

currencies. Futures traders have an enormous edge in this regard, and have a number of ways to take advantage of intermarket opportunities. They can easily switch funds among the four futures groups. Switching from bonds to stocks—or from stocks to commodities or currencies—is a simple task. All of these markets have actively-traded futures contracts. Within the commodity markets, traders can buy individual commodities like gold or oil. Alternatively, they can buy and sell baskets of commodities. Futures contracts exist for the CRB Index and the Goldman Sachs Commodity Index.

Futures traders also have the advantage of trading from both the *long* and *short* side of markets. This means that they can profit from bull and bear markets. Of course, futures trading is a risky business and certainly is not for everyone. The next chapter, however, explores more fully a possible role for the futures markets in the asset allocation process without having to buy or sell individual commodity or futures contracts. I am referring here to managed futures accounts which are similar to stock mutual funds; the difference is that they deal in futures markets.

NOT A LOT OF ALTERNATIVES IN TRADITIONAL MARKETS

If the long-term charts are right, stocks should produce subpar returns for several years. With long-term interest rates at forty-year lows, upside potential in the bond market also appears limited. Historically low short-term interest rates make money market funds relatively unattractive. If investors are looking for growth over the next several years, they may have to start looking outside of the traditional bond and stock markets. Commodities and currencies are two areas where most of the growth potential may lie.

BUYING COMMODITY-RELATED STOCKS

It is possible to take advantage of rising commodities without having to actually buy the commodities themselves. Many stock market sectors and industry groups are tied to commodity markets. Gold stocks are an excellent case in point. The best way to participate in a bull market in gold is to buy gold shares (or a gold mutual fund). Not only is it simpler to buy gold shares than bullion, gold shares tend to rise faster than the price of gold. When the price of bullion is rising, unhedged gold stocks also rise faster than gold-mining companies that hedge their gold production. [The AMEX Gold Bugs Index (HUI) includes only unhedged gold stocks.] Energy stocks (or energy sector funds) are an excellent way to participate in rising oil or natural gas prices.

Basic material stocks (like aluminum and copper) benefit when these same commodities are rising. Forest product stocks benefit from rising lumber prices, which were also showing signs of bottoming by the summer of 2003. Rising agricultural prices increase the demand for farm equipment like large tractors. Some food stocks may also benefit from rising livestock and poultry prices. Investors can benefit from rising prices in commodities by buying individual common stocks related to these markets. The availability of sector mutual funds and Exchange Traded Funds (ETFs) also makes it much easier for investors to take advantage of strong commodity markets by putting funds in stock sectors that are tied to these markets.

CHAPTER 11

Futures Markets and Asset Allocation

RELATIVE STRENGTH ANALYSIS AMONG ASSET CLASSES

The previous chapter used relative strength analysis to compare the commodity and stock markets. The CRB Index was starting to outperform stock prices for the first time in 20 years in what was described as a *generational* shift from paper to hard assets. This chapter expands on the use of ratio analysis to show how to measure the relative strength between bonds, stocks, and commodities in order to determine which of the three asset classes is doing the best at any given time. The idea is to concentrate one's capital in the classes that are doing the best and to avoid the ones that are doing the worst. Fortunately, ratio charts make it relatively easy to compare the strength or weakness of the three market groups. Ratio charts can help warn of impending trend changes and can be an important supplement to traditional chart analysis. One need not be a charting expert to learn how to spot such trend changes. Market developments since 2000 provide several striking examples of why it is important to know which markets are going up—and which ones are going down.

BONDS VERSUS STOCKS

Bonds and stocks are always competing for investor money. When investors are optimistic about the stock market and the economy, they usually put more money into stocks and less into bonds. When they are more pessimistic about things, they usually commit more funds to bonds and less to stocks.

159

Ratio analysis provides a relatively simple way to see which asset is doing better at any given time—bonds or stocks.

Figure 11.1 is a ratio of Treasury bond prices divided by the S&P 500 since 1994. From 1994 to the end of 1999, the ratio line is falling meaning that bonds were underperforming stocks. During those six years, an investor would have done better by concentrating on stocks and placing less emphasis on bond investments. Near the end of 2000, however, the bond/stock ratio broke the down trendline that had existed since 1994, and signaled a shift in the relationship between the two markets. Bonds became the stronger market, which called for some asset allocation switching out of stocks and into bonds. An investor using this relatively simple chart could have side-stepped much of the bear market in stocks that started in 2000 and could have profited from rising bond prices. Many financial advisors recommend a relatively static bond-stock mix in one's portfolio to achieve balance and diversification. As Figure 11.1 shows, however, asset allocation weightings need to change along with changing market trends. Ratio charts make this task much easier.

Figure 11.2 plots the bond/stock ratio from the start of 2000 to the summer of 2003. The rising ratio line during these three years clearly favored bonds over stocks. To the upper right, however, it can be seen that the ratio

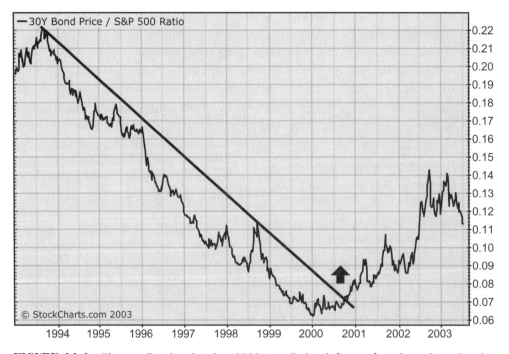

FIGURE 11.1   The trendline break in late 2000 signalled a shift out of stocks and into bonds.

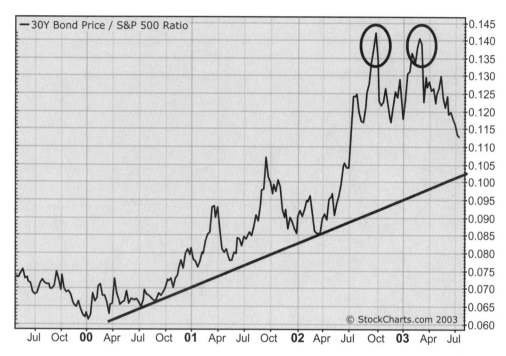

FIGURE 11.2 The "double top" starting in October 2000 signalled a shift out of bonds and into stocks.

line has formed a possible *double top* starting in October 2002. Such a pattern is marked by two prominent tops and often signals that an existing trend may be ending. The two tops on the ratio chart were formed in October 2002 and March 2003. The decline in the bond/stock ratio starting in the fourth quarter of 2002 showed that money was starting to switch out of bonds and back into stocks. The summer 2003 break of the lows formed in the ratio line during the fourth quarter of 2002 confirmed that stocks had become the stronger market.

COMMODITIES VERSUS BONDS

Ratio analysis can also be applied to the bond and commodity markets to see which is in a position of relative strength. Figure 11.3 plots the CRB/T-bond ratio from 1990 into the spring of 2003. Two things are evident on the chart. The first is that the ratio started rising in 2002 as commodity prices started rising faster than bond prices (partially as the result of the falling dollar). However, the ratio did not break the down trendline drawn along the peaks

FIGURE 11.3 The 2002 rise in the ratio stopped at the long-term trendline.

of the prior 12 years. An upside break of the trendline would signal a major shift in the relationship between the two markets in favor of commodities over bonds. In the third quarter of 2003, a drop in bond prices and rally in commodities pushed the ratio to the highest level in two years.

Figure 11.4 plots the CRB Index alone and shows another crucial trend-line. The chart shows the CRB Index soaring to a five-year high in 2002 in what could be the early signs of a major bottom. Notice, however, that the CRB rally stopped right at the resistance line drawn over the highs of 1988 and 1996. This is another critical trendline. So far, it has contained the CRB rally. Any upside break of the line, however, would be an extremely bullish sign for commodity markets.

THE DOW/GOLD RATIO

Another popular intermarket ratio that can be monitored over time is the Dow Jones Industrial Average relative to gold. The Dow/gold ratio peaked at 28 during 1966 and fell steadily throughout the inflationary 1970s. Needless to say, gold (and commodities) were a better investment than stocks during those years. The Dow/gold ratio bottomed during 1980 and rose steadily until

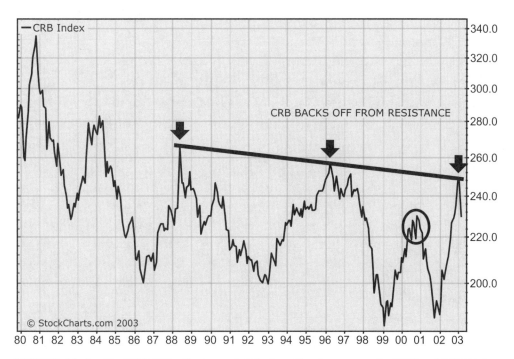

FIGURE 11.4 The 2002 CRB rally stopped at the trendline drawn over the 1988 and 1996 highs.

1999 when it hit a record high of 44. During those twenty years, stocks were a much better investment than gold (or commodities).

Figure 11.5 shows the Dow/gold ratio peaking in the middle of 1999. More importantly, the ratio broke its rising trendline during the first half of 2001 and fell for the next two years. The breaking of that support line signaled the need for a shift out of stocks and into gold (or gold-mining shares). The drop in the ratio to the low 20s at the start of 2003 was the lowest reading in more than five years. It also brought the Dow/gold ratio back to the same level recorded in the early 1970s, just as gold was starting a long period of outperformance over the Dow. The previous chapter showed a ratio of the CRB Index divided by the Dow breaking a twenty-year down trendline. This suggests a major change in the relationship between these two markets in favor of commodities. Gold and commodities generally trend in the same direction.

INCLUDING COMMODITIES AND CURRENCIES

The previous chapter also discussed the potential for major bull markets occurring in the commodity and currency markets over the next several years. It was explained that rising commodity markets (especially gold) usually

FIGURE 11.5   The Dow/gold ratio peaked in mid-1999, signalling a shift out of stocks and into gold.

coincide with rising foreign currencies as a direct result of a falling U.S. dollar. Commodities and currencies, however, lie within the world of futures trading. This chapter argues for the treatment of commodities and currency markets as separate asset classes—along with bonds and stocks. It also discusses the benefits of using managed futures accounts along with bonds and stocks in traditional portfolios to achieve better diversification. If it can be shown that commodity markets do relatively well when bonds and stocks are doing badly, why would a portfolio manager not consider holding positions in commodity markets both as a diversification tool and to profit from rising commodity prices?

Market history teaches us that bonds and stocks are positively correlated most of the time. They tend to rise and fall together. Bonds and stocks usually fall together in the early stages of an economic contraction and at the start of bear markets. (The exception to this rule occurs in a deflationary environment when bond prices rise and stocks fall, which describes the situation after 2000.) How is portfolio diversification achieved by limiting one's choices to two assets that usually fall together at the same time? It seems to make more sense to include in one's portfolio a separate asset class that often rises when bonds and stocks are falling.

Commodity prices usually continue to rise after bonds and stocks have peaked, especially if the peak in bonds and stocks was caused by rising inflation. Coming out of a deflationary environment, central bank attempts to reinflate global economies can also translate into higher commodity prices. The same can be said for foreign currency markets. Real diversification can only be achieved by including markets that are poorly correlated—not just ones that usually rise and fall together.

CAN FUTURES PLAY A ROLE IN ASSET ALLOCATION?

With the development of financial futures over the past 30 years, futures traders have the opportunity to participate in all financial markets. Traditional commodity markets, representing the oldest part of the futures world, are traded on various commodity exchanges. Energy and metals markets are traded in New York, while most agricultural markets are traded in Chicago. The existence of futures contracts on the Reuters CRB Index and the Goldman Sachs Commodity Index offers a basket approach to trading traditional commodity markets.[1] Interest-rate futures provide exposure to Treasury notes and bonds as well as short-term debt instruments. Stock index futures facilitate a basket approach to trading stock market trends. The U.S. Dollar Index is traded against a basket of foreign currencies. Individual foreign currencies can also be bought and sold on futures exchanges. All four market groups are represented in the futures markets—commodities, currencies, interest rates, and stocks. Futures contracts also exist on foreign bond and stock markets to add an international dimension to one's trading.

BUILT-IN ASSET ALLOCATION MODEL

In many ways, the futures markets provide an excellent asset allocation forum. Futures traders can easily switch funds among the four financial markets to take advantage of both short- and long-term market trends. They can *buy* positions in bond and stock index futures when those financial markets are outperforming the commodity and currency markets. They can reverse the process just as easily when the financial markets start to slip and commodities and currencies begin to outperform them. During periods of rising inflation, they can supplement bullish positions in commodities with bullish

---

[1] A third futures contract is also traded on the Dow Jones–AIG Commodity Index.

positions in the euro or commodity-based currencies like the Australian and Canadian dollars. Alternately, they can simply short the dollar. (When shorting a market, a trader sells it at a higher price and hopes to buy it back at a lower price.)

CHARTS COMPARING FUTURES MARKETS— GOING LONG OR SHORT

Figure 11.6 shows four markets—the S&P 500, The Dollar Index, the euro, and the CRB Index—in 2002. All four markets can be traded via the futures markets. The chart demonstrates the kind of flexibility available to futures traders. The two best performing markets were the CRB Index (+24 percent) and the euro (+17 percent). The Dollar Index, which is the dollar versus a basket of foreign currencies, fell 12 percent. The S&P 500 was the weakest of the four markets, losing 22 percent. [Treasury Bonds did better than stocks and the dollar (gaining 10 percent), but underperformed the CRB Index and the euro.] The futures trader had several ways to capitalize on these trends in 2002.

FIGURE 11.6   Of the four futures markets shown, the CRB and the euro were the strongest in 2002.

The best choice was to buy futures contracts in the CRB Index and/or the euro. The futures trader could have avoided positions in the S&P 500 and the dollar, since both were in downtrends. Or, as a more aggressive alternative, the trader could have *shorted* stocks and the dollar, profiting from their price declines. (A short position makes money when a market is falling.) In other words, the futures trader could have been *long* the CRB Index and the euro, while being *short* the dollar and the S&P 500. (To be long a market means to buy it in hopes the price will rise). In futures trading, going short a market is just as easy as buying the market. (Before selling a stock short, the trader has to first borrow the stock. That is not the case in futures trading.) Add in the fact that the futures markets cover all four financial markets—commodities, currencies, bonds, and stocks—and you have a lot of potentially profitable intermarket trading opportunities. This combination of trading opportunities is what adds to the appeal of managed futures accounts.

USING MANAGED FUTURES ACCOUNTS

The idea of incorporating futures markets into traditional portfolios is not new. Two decades ago some money managers began considering the potential benefits of allocating a portion of their assets to *managed futures accounts* to achieve diversification and some protection against inflation. (Managed futures accounts refer to professionally managed futures funds.) Serious attention started to focus on this area with the work of Professor John Lintner of Harvard University. In the spring of 1983, Lintner presented a paper at the annual conference of the Financial Analysts Federation in Toronto, Canada. The paper was entitled "The Proposed Role of Managed Commodity-Financial Futures Accounts (and/or Funds) in Portfolios of Stocks and Bonds," and it drew attention to the idea of including managed futures accounts as a portion of the traditional portfolio of bonds and stocks. Since then, other researchers have updated Lintner's results with similar conclusions: futures portfolios have higher returns and higher risks. However, since returns on futures portfolios tend to be poorly correlated with returns on bonds and stocks, significant improvements in reward/risk ratios can be achieved by some inclusion of managed futures. (The research done by Dr. Lintner and others was based on the track records of Commodity Trading Advisors and managed futures funds.) Lintner's paper contained the following statement:

Indeed, the improvements from holding efficiently selected portfolios of managed accounts or funds are so large—and the correlations between the returns on the futures portfolios and those on the stock and bond portfolios are so surprisingly low (sometimes even negative)—that the return/risk tradeoffs provided by augmented portfolios, consisting partly of funds invested with appropriate groups of futures managers (or funds) combined with funds invested in portfolios of stocks alone (or in mixed portfolios of stocks and bonds), clearly dominate the tradeoffs available from portfolios of stocks alone (or from portfolios of stocks and bonds). . . . The combined portfolios of stocks (or stocks and bonds) after including judicious investments in appropriately selected . . . managed futures accounts (or funds) show substantially less risk at every possible level of expected return than portfolios of stocks (or stocks and bonds) alone.

FUTURES PORTFOLIOS CORRELATE POORLY WITH BONDS AND STOCKS

There are two major reasons why futures managed accounts are poorly correlated with bonds and stocks. The first lies in the diversity of the futures market. Futures fund managers deal in all sectors of the futures markets. Their trading results are not dependent on just bonds and stocks. Most futures fund managers are trend followers. During financial bull markets, they buy interest rate futures and stock index futures and benefit accordingly. During downturns in bonds and stocks, however, their losses in the financial area will be largely offset by profits in commodities and foreign currencies, which tend to rise at such times. They have built-in diversification by participating in four different sectors, which are usually negatively correlated.

The second reason has to do with short selling. Futures managers are not tied to the *long* side of any markets. (Going *long* a futures market means to buy a futures contract in hopes of selling it later at a higher price.) They can benefit from bear markets in bonds and stocks by *shorting* futures in those two areas. (A short seller sells a futures contract at a higher price in hopes of buying it back at a lower price. The intention is to "sell high and buy low" and profit from the difference.) In such an environment, managers can hold short positions in the financial markets and long positions in commodities and/or currencies. In this way, they can do very well during periods when financial markets are experiencing downturns, especially if inflation is the major culprit, or when central bankers are trying to create a little inflation to fight deflationary tendencies. Let us narrow our focus and concentrate on only one portion of the futures portfolio: the traditional commodity markets.

COMMODITY FUTURES AS AN ASSET CLASS

A basket approach to the traditional commodity markets has been made possible by the creation of futures contracts on a couple of widely-followed commodity indexes—namely the CRB Index and the Goldman Sachs Commodity Index. These indexes are comprised of nonfinancial markets. In other words, they do not include bonds, stocks, or currency markets. They are made up of tangible commodities that can be grown, mined, or refined. These are primarily agricultural, energy, and metals markets. The question addressed here is the possible benefit of incorporating a *commodity* basket approach into the traditional portfolio along with bonds and stocks. Research into this area was published as far back as 1990.

PUSHING THE EFFICIENT FRONTIER

The following study is based on statistics published by the New York Futures Exchange in a work entitled "Commodity Futures As An Asset Class." The *efficient frontier* is a curve on a graph that plots portfolio risk (standard deviation) on the horizontal axis and expected return on the vertical axis. The efficient frontier slopes upward and to the right, reflecting the higher risk associated with higher returns. The study first developed a set of optimized portfolios utilizing only stocks and bonds. By solving for the higher expected return for each level of risk, an efficient frontier was created. After determining optimal portfolios using only bonds and stocks, commodity futures were added at three different levels of commitment. The result was four portfolios—one with no commodities, and three other portfolios with commodity commitments of 10 percent, 20 percent, and 30 percent.

Figure 11.7 shows the effects of introducing the CRB Index at those three levels of involvement. (The commodity portion is represented by a return on the CRB Index plus 90 percent of the return on Treasury Bills, since a CRB Index futures contract requires only a 10 percent margin deposit. This creates an *unleveraged* commodity portfolio that greatly reduces the risk associated with *highly leveraged* commodity trading.) Four lines are shown in Figure

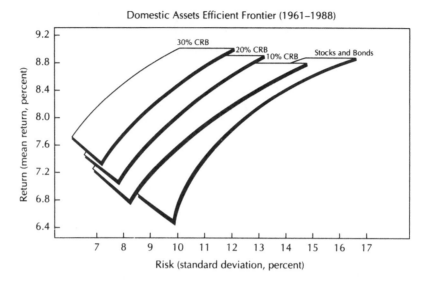

FIGURE 11.7   The efficient frontiers of four different portfolios. The line
to the far right includes just bonds and stocks. The lines
shift upward and to the left as commodities are added in
increments of 10 percent, 20 percent, and 30 percent. The
efficient frontier plots portfolio risk (standard deviation) on
the horizontal axis and expected return on the vertical axis.
(*Commodity Futures as an Asset Class,* prepared by Powers
Research Associates, L.P., published by New York Futures
Exchange, January 1990.)

11.7. The one to the far right is the *efficient frontier* for a portfolio of just
stocks and bonds. Moving to the left, the second line has a CRB exposure of
10 percent. The third line to the left commits 20 percent to commodities,
whereas the line to the far left places 30 percent of its portfolio in the CRB
Index. The chart demonstrates that increasing the level of funds committed to
the CRB Index has the beneficial effect of moving the efficient frontier
upward and to the left, meaning that, in the words of the report, "the portfolio
manager faces less risk for a given level of return when a basket of commodities is added to the asset mix." Statistics are also presented that measure the
change in the reward to risk ratios that take place as the result of including
commodities along with bonds and stocks. To quote directly from the report:

> *Note in all cases, the addition of commodity futures to the portfolio
> increased the ratio, i.e., lowered risk and increased return. The increase
> grows as more commodity futures replace other domestic assets . . . the
> more of your portfolio allocated to commodity futures (up to 30 per-
> cent) the better off you are.*

At the time this research was first published, bonds and stocks were still in the middle of major bull markets and commodities were a much weaker asset class. These roles now appear to have reversed. Since the start of 2002, commodity markets (represented by the CRB Index) have outperformed both bonds and stocks. If this trend continues, the earlier research arguing for inclusion of commodity markets in traditional portfolios may have a lot more relevance than when it was first published over a decade ago. In any case, it still leaves another rising asset class to be considered: foreign currencies.

TREATING CURRENCIES AS AN ASSET CLASS

On May 27, 2003, *The Wall Street Journal* carried a front page story entitled "Dollar's Fall Is UBS's Silver Lining." The main point of the story was how the decision by some Wall Street firms to make a commitment to currency trading had paid off during a year when the stock market yielded disappointing returns. The profits made by UBS Warburg—and some other Wall Street firms—came from rising customer volume in currency trading and profits derived by their own participation in the rising trend of the euro over the prior twelve months. The *Journal* article reported that roughly 70 percent of UBS's first-quarter profits were derived from currency and debt-trading operations. The article cited other firms like J.P. Morgan Chase and Goldman Sachs Group that benefited from *proprietary trading* in currency trends (taking positions to profit from currency moves); it went on to describe how Merrill Lynch had revealed plans to increase its focus on currency trading. When times are bad on Wall Street (which is during a long bear market in stocks), the need arises for *counter-cyclical* revenues. When the dollar is falling along with stocks, some of these revenues can be found in currency markets, either for hedging purposes or for profit.

Many institutions use currency markets to hedge foreign exposure. American firms holding foreign bonds and stocks can lose money if the dollar is strong. They can hedge that currency risk by buying the dollar (or shorting the foreign currency). Foreigners holding U.S. bonds and stocks can hedge their risk of a falling dollar by shorting the dollar. American firms can also augment their foreign holdings by buying currencies that are showing strong gains. In each instance, some market timing is needed to determine when a hedge is appropriate or to determine which currency markets hold the greatest profit potential. Much of the currency trading is done by large institutions like pension plans and hedge funds. However, as the *Jour-*

nal article observes, "a growing number of investors have begun to view foreign currencies as an asset class distinct from stocks, bonds, and commodities, and one that can provide diversification in a bear market." I could not have said it better myself.

THE IMPACT OF A FALLING DOLLAR

The impact of a falling dollar on global markets can be quite dramatic at times and shows why investors need to take steps to protect their portfolios accordingly. By the middle of 2003, the U.S. dollar had become one of the world's weakest currencies. This created potential problems (and opportunities) for global investors. A falling dollar has a strong impact on the competing results of investments in U.S. bonds and stocks versus those in foreign countries. During the first six months of 2003, for example, an index of world stock markets rose 7.47 percent in local currency terms. (This means that each country's stock market is quoted in its own local currency.) When quoted in dollar terms, however, the world's stock markets gained 10.86 percent. The better performance in dollar terms is simply the result of a weaker dollar.

The higher returns in dollar terms works to the benefit of American investors and encourages more foreign exposure. For foreign investors, however, the lower dollar discourages investments in U.S. stocks and bonds (unless those investments are hedged by selling the dollar short). The biggest discrepancies are seen in those countries whose currencies have outperformed the U.S. dollar by the widest margin. Two good examples during the first half of 2003 were the euro and the Canadian dollar.

In local currency terms, European stock markets gained 2.08 percent during the first half of 2003. In dollar terms, Europe's gains were a much bigger 10.34 percent. Even more dramatic differences were seen in countries like France and Germany. France's stock market gained 11.73 percent in dollar terms versus a small loss (–0.97 percent) in its local currency (the euro). Germany, which is the biggest economy in Europe, gained only 5 percent in terms of its local currency (the euro) versus an 18.5 percent gain in terms of the dollar. These differences are due to the strong gains by the euro against the U.S. dollar. Another strong currency in 2003 was the Canadian dollar. As a result, the Canadian stock market gained 24 percent during the first half of 2003 when quoted in U.S. dollar terms versus a much more modest gain of 6 percent in terms of the Canadian dollar. Clearly, the direction of currency markets has to be taken into consideration when investing in global markets.

GOLD MEASURED IN FOREIGN CURRENCIES

As previously discussed, there was a major upturn in the price of gold in terms of the U.S. dollar. A falling dollar is bullish for gold mainly because gold is priced in dollar terms. One of the ways to tell if the rise in gold is global in scope is to chart it in foreign currency terms. During the 1970s, when gold had its last bull run, the price of bullion rose not just in dollar terms but also when quoted in foreign currencies (see Figure 11.8). The same

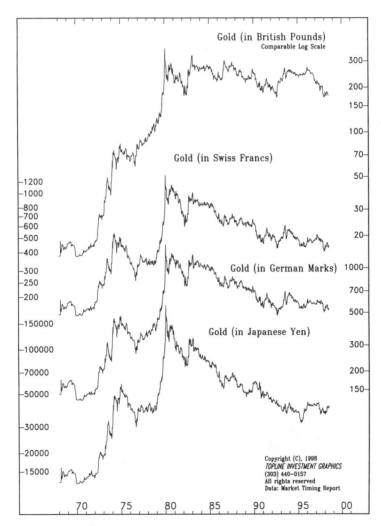

FIGURE 11.8   During the 1970s, gold rose not just in dollar terms but also when quoted in foreign currencies. That's a hallmark of a true bull market in gold.

has been true since the second half of 1999 when the price of gold hit bottom and started to rise. While it is true that a rising gold price usually accompanies rising foreign currencies (since the dollar is falling), it is important that the price of gold rises faster than foreign currency markets. This brings us back to ratio analysis.

GOLD/CURRENCY RATIOS ARE RISING

Figures 11.9 through 11.11 show a ratio of the dollar price of gold divided by the British pound, the Canadian dollar, and the Japanese yen. The fact that all three ratios have risen since the end of 1999 means that gold has risen faster than all three currencies. This is what should happen if the rally in gold is truly global. Figure 11.12 shows that gold has also outperformed the euro from the end of 1999. To the far right, it can be seen that gold dropped in euro terms from the spring of 2002 to the spring of 2003. However, the major trend over the entire three years has been upward.

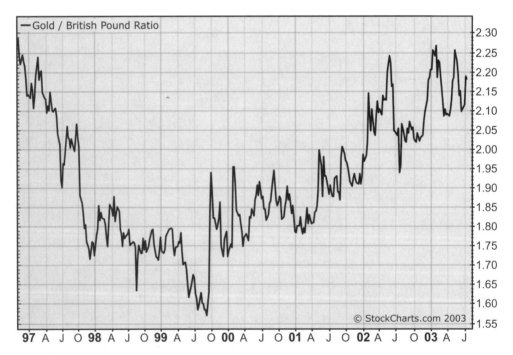

FIGURE 11.9   The rising ratio shows that gold has risen faster than the pound since late 1999.

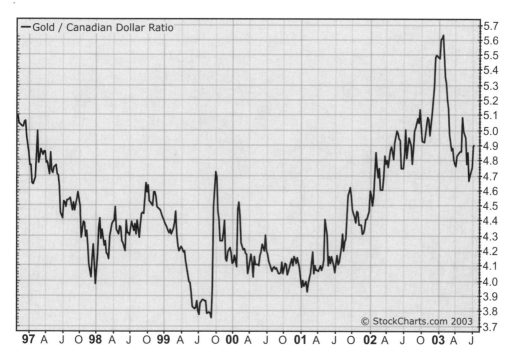

FIGURE 11.10   The rising ratio shows that gold has outperformed the Canadian dollar since late 1999.

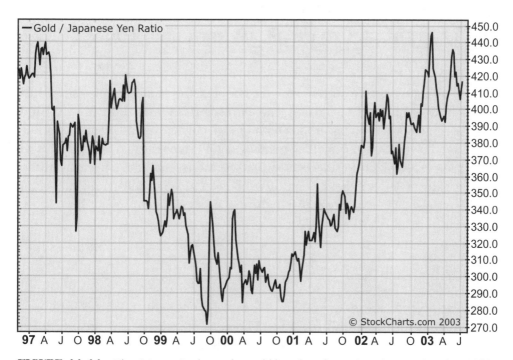

FIGURE 11.11   The rising ratio shows that gold has risen faster than the yen since late 1999.

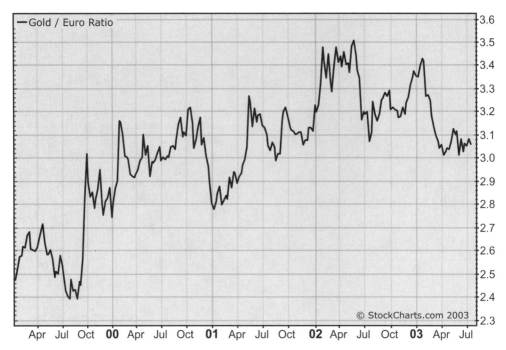

FIGURE 11.12   Gold has risen more than the euro since mid-1999.

GOLD IS STRONGER THAN ALL MAJOR CURRENCIES

Figure 11.13 overlays the price of gold (in dollar terms) versus the world's two biggest foreign currencies—the euro and the Japanese yen—since 1999. It shows all three lines rising. The euro has risen faster than the yen. However, gold has risen faster than both foreign currencies. The value of the euro and the yen have been falling relative to gold since the end of 1999. This has been especially true since 2001 when the returns on both currencies turned negative relative to gold. The British pound, Canadian dollar, and Swiss franc have also been falling relative to the dollar price of gold.

SUMMARY

This chapter utilizes ratio analysis to better monitor the relationship between commodities (the CRB Index) and bonds and stocks—and between bonds and stocks only. Ratio analysis provides a useful technical tool for spotting trend changes in these intermarket relationships. Trendline analysis can be

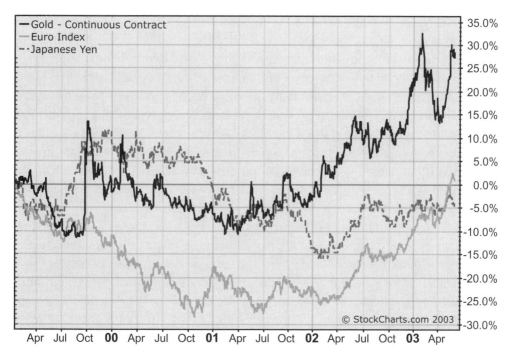

FIGURE 11.13 Gold has risen faster than both foreign currencies since 2000.

applied directly to the ratio lines themselves (as well as other technical indicators like moving averages). A rising bond/stock ratio favors investment in bonds over stocks. A falling bond/stock ratio favors stocks over bonds. A rising bond/stock ratio is usually associated with economic weakness, while a falling bond/stock ratio is associated with economic strength. A rising CRB/bond ratio (or a rising CRB/stock ratio) ratio favors investments in commodity markets over bonds and/or stocks.

The commodities included in the CRB Index should qualify as an asset class along with bonds and stocks. Because commodity markets are usually negatively correlated to bonds, and show little correlation to stocks, an *unleveraged* commodity portfolio (with 10 percent in commodity futures and 90 percent in Treasury Bills) could be used to diversify a portfolio of bonds and stocks. The risks usually associated with commodity trading are the result of low margin requirements and resulting high leverage. By using a conservative (unleveraged) approach of keeping the unused 90 percent of the futures funds in Treasury bills, much of the risk associated with commodity trading is reduced and its use by portfolio managers becomes more realistic.

Futures markets—including commodities, currencies, bonds, and stock index futures—provide a built-in model for asset allocation. Because their returns are poorly correlated with bond and stock market returns, professionally managed futures funds may qualify as a legitimate diversification instrument for portfolio managers. There are two separate approaches involved in the potential use of futures markets for diversification. One has to do with the use of professionally managed futures accounts, which invest in all four sectors of the futures markets (and also operate from both the *long* and the *short* side of those markets). In this way, the futures portfolio is treated as a separate entity. The term *futures* refers to all futures markets, of which commodities are only one portion. The second approach treats the commodity portion of the futures markets as a separate asset class and utilizes a basket approach to trading these commodities.

When commodity prices are rising, the U.S. dollar is usually falling. Foreign currency markets usually rise along with commodity markets. A case can be made for also including currencies as a separate asset class along with commodities. The impact of currency trends on global bond and stock returns should also be taken into consideration by global investors. Currency hedging can help alleviate some of the risks associated with investing in foreign markets. One of the side effects of a falling dollar is a rising gold market. A truly global bull market in gold, however, requires that bullion rise in value not just in dollar terms, but in foreign currency terms as well. Since the second half of 1999, when gold bottomed, the price of bullion has outpaced gains in all major foreign currencies. This has not happened since the 1970s, which was the last time that gold embarked on a major bull market.

CHAPTER 12

Intermarket Analysis and the Business Cycle

THE FOUR-YEAR BUSINESS CYCLE

Over the past two centuries, the American economy has gone through repeated up and down cycles. Sometimes these cycles have been dramatic, such as the Great Depression of the 1930s, the runaway inflationary spiral of the 1970s, and the deflation-inspired downturn since 2000. At other times, their impact has been so muted that their occurrence has gone virtually unnoticed. Most of these cycles fit somewhere in between these two extremes and have left a trail of fairly reliable business cycle patterns that have averaged about four years in length. This means that approximately every four years the economy has experienced a period of expansion, which is followed by a contraction or slowdown. Those slowdowns usually coincide with or follow downturns in the stock market. The tendency for the stock market to hit bottom every four years is referred to as the *presidential cycle* because American presidents are elected every four years.

The contraction phase often turns into a recession, which is a period of negative growth in the economy. The recession or slowdown inevitably leads to the next period of expansion. During an unusually long economic expansion, when no recession takes place, the economy may undergo a slowdown which allows the economy to "catch its breath" before continuing to its next growth phase. When this happens, the time between actual recessions can stretch out to eight years. The recessions of 1970 and 1974 were exactly four years apart. The next scheduled recession during 1978 did not occur on schedule. However, two recessions occurred in 1980 and 1982. Even though the 1980 recession was two years late, the 1982 recession occurred "on time": eight years after the 1974 recession.

Following the 1982 recession, it took eight years for the 1990 recession to arrive. After 1990, the U.S. economy entered the longest expansion on record (lasting just over 10 years), which exceeded the previous record expansion of the 1960s. When no recessions actually occur, the timing of stock market downturns is helpful since bear markets are usually associated with expectations for economic weakness. Based on the four-year business cycle, for example, the economy skipped scheduled recessions in 1986 and again in 1994. However, major downturns in the stock market occurred during 1987 and 1994, still adhering quite closely to the business cycle model.

Since 1948, the American economy has experienced nine recessions. Prior to 1990, when the last economic expansion started, postwar expansions averaged 45 months in length, while economic contractions averaged 11 months. By 2000, 10 years had elapsed since the last recession and six years since the last bear market in stocks. A recession and a bear market were long overdue. The bear market started during the spring of 2000. A recession started a year later during the spring of 2001.

THE BUSINESS CYCLE EXPLAINS INTERMARKET ROTATION

The business cycle has an important bearing on the financial markets. These periods of expansion and contraction provide an economic framework that helps explain the linkages that exist between the bond, stock, and commodity markets. In addition, the business cycle explains the chronological sequence that develops among these three financial markets. Near the end of an economic expansion, bonds usually turn down before stocks and commodities. During a recession or slowdown, bonds usually turn up before stocks and commodities. In both instances, commodities are usually the last market to change direction. A better understanding of the business cycle sheds light on the intermarket process and confirms that what is seen on the price charts makes sense from an economic perspective. At the same time, intermarket analysis can be used to help determine the current state of the business cycle. Although it is not our primary intention as investors, intermarket analysis can have a role in economic forecasting.

Some understanding of the business cycle (together with intermarket analysis of bonds, stocks, and commodities) impacts on the asset allocation process. Different phases of the business cycle favor different asset classes. The beginning of an economic expansion favors financial assets (bonds and stocks), while the latter part of an expansion favors commodities (or inflation hedges like gold and oil stocks). As a general rule, periods of economic strength favor stocks, while periods of weakness favor bonds.

In this chapter, the business cycle is used to help explain the chronological rotation that normally takes place between bonds, stocks, and commodities. Most of the commodity research presented in this chapter is based on the Journal of Commerce Index, which is comprised of industrial commodity prices. This is different from the CRB Index in that it does not include agricultural markets. This book presents research on the predictive ability of bonds, stocks, and commodities in anticipating turns in the economy. The threat of deflation has resurfaced for the first time since the 1930s; it is beneficial to look at the intermarket relationships that existed during that era.

THE CHRONOLOGICAL SEQUENCE OF BONDS, STOCKS, AND COMMODITIES

Figure 12.1 (taken from "InterMarket Review" written by Martin J. Pring) shows an idealized diagram of how the three financial markets interact with each other during a typical business cycle. The curving line shows the path of the economy during alternating periods of expansion and contraction. A rising line indicates expansion and a falling line, contraction. The horizontal line is the equilibrium level that separates positive and negative economic growth. When the curving line is above the horizontal line but declining, the

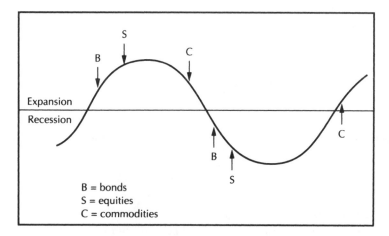

FIGURE 12.1　An idealized diagram of how bonds (B), stocks (S), and commodities (C) interact during a typical business cycle. (*InterMarket Review* by Martin J. Pring, *www.pring.com.*)

economy is slowing. When it dips below the horizontal line, the economy has slipped into recession. The arrows show the direction of the three financial markets—B for bonds, S for stocks, and C for commodities.

The diagram shows that as the expansion matures, bonds are the first of the three markets to turn down. This is due to increased inflation pressures (arising from rising commodity prices) and resulting upward pressure on interest rates. In time, higher interest rates put downward pressure on stocks, which turn down second. Because inflation pressures are strongest near the end of the expansion, commodities are the last of the three to turn down. Usually by this time, the economy has started to slow and is slipping into recession. A slowdown in the economy reduces demand for commodities. Inflation pressures begin to ease. Commodity prices start to drop. At this point, all three markets are dropping.

As the economy starts to weaken, interest rates begin to soften as well (usually in the early stages of a recession). As a result, bond prices begin to rally. For a time, bond prices rise while stock prices fall. After some time, stocks begin to turn up as well (usually after the midpoint of a recession). Only after bonds and stocks have been rallying for a time and the economy has started to expand will inflation pressures start to build, contributing to an upturn in gold and other commodities. (As already discussed, the upturn in commodities may also occur in a deflationary climate as the Fed tries to reflate a sagging economy.) After an economic expansion has been in place for some time, there can come a point where all three markets are rising together. This can continue until the inflationary impact of rising commodity prices causes bond prices to peak. At this point, bonds turn down and the whole process starts over again.

BONDS ARE THE FOCAL POINT

Bonds seem to be the focal point in the intermarket chain. Bonds are usually the first market to peak and the first to bottom. When bond prices are much weaker than stocks, it tells us that inflationary pressures are building, which can eventually hurt stocks. An unusually strong bond market relative to stocks (such as existed after 2000) can send the opposite signal, namely that deflationary forces are present, which may also hurt stocks. Bonds have a tendency to peak about midway through an economic expansion and hit bottom about midway through a contraction. The peak in bond prices during an economic expansion is a signal that a period of healthy *noninflationary* growth has turned into an unhealthy period of *inflationary* growth. This is usually the point where commodity markets are starting to accelerate on the upside and the bull market in stocks is living on borrowed time. In the unusual situation in which deflation is a threat, rising commodity prices and a weaker bond market may indicate that deflationary forces are abating and may be a positive sign for the stock market and the economy.

THE SIX STAGES OF THE BUSINESS CYCLE

Martin Pring divides the business cycle into six stages (see Figure 12.2). Stage 1 begins as the economy is slipping into a recession and ends with Stage 6, where the economic expansion has just about run its course. Each stage is characterized by a turn in one of the three asset classes—bonds, stocks, or commodities. The following list summarizes Pring's conclusions:

Stage 1 . . . Bonds turn up   (stocks and commodities falling)
Stage 2 . . . Stocks turn up   (bonds rising, commodities falling)
Stage 3 . . . Commodities turn up   (all three markets rising)
Stage 4 . . . Bonds turn down   (stocks and commodities rising)
Stage 5 . . . Stocks turn down   (bonds dropping, commodities rising)
Stage 6 . . . Commodities turn down   (all three markets dropping)

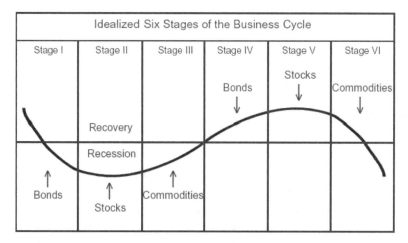

FIGURE 12.2 The six stages of a typical business cycle through recession and recovery. Each stage is characterized by a turn in one of the three sectors—bonds, stocks, and commodities. (*InterMarket Review* by Martin J. Pring, *www.pring.com.*)

The implications of the above sequence for asset allocators should be fairly obvious. As inflation and interest rates begin to drop during a slow-down (Stage 1), bonds (or interest-sensitive stocks) are the place to be. After bonds have bottomed and as the recession shows some signs of leveling off (Stage 2), stocks become attractive. As the economy begins to expand again (Stage 3), gold and gold-related assets should be considered as an early infla-tion hedge. As inflation pressures begin to pull other commodity prices higher, and interest rates begin to rise (Stage 4), commodities or other infla-tion hedges should be emphasized. Bonds and interest-sensitive stocks should be de-emphasized. As stocks begin a topping process (Stage 5), more assets should be funneled into commodities and other inflation hedges such as gold and oil shares. When all three asset groups are falling (Stage 6), "cash is king," as the saying goes.

The chronological sequence described in the preceding paragraphs does not imply that bonds, stocks, and commodities always follow this exact rota-tional sequence. There have been times when the markets have peaked and troughed out of sequence. Pring's diagram describes the ideal rotational sequence that usually takes place between the three markets; it gives us a useful roadmap to follow. When the markets are following the ideal pattern, the analyst knows what to expect next. When the markets are diverging from the normal rotation, the analyst is alerted to the fact that something is amiss and is warned to be more careful. While the intermarket analyst may not always understand exactly what the markets are doing, it can be helpful to know what they are *supposed* to be doing. The lessons of the markets since 2000 are an excellent example of why it is a good idea to be especially vigi-lant when something unusual is happening.

LESSONS OF 2000

After the stock market bubble burst in 2000, the Federal Reserve embarked on an aggressive series of interest rate cuts that should have stemmed the stock market's decline. By the end of 2001, the Fed had lowered rates 11 times. However, the usual beneficial impact of falling rates was not helping stocks. Bonds and stocks had completely decoupled. Something unusual was happening in this business cycle. As already stated, the un-usual ingredient was the threat of global deflation, something that had not been experienced since the 1930s. The fact that none of the current gene-ration of investors (or economists) had lived through the earlier deflationary cycle probably explains why so few of them recognized its dangerous symptoms.

BONDS AS A LEADING ECONOMIC INDICATOR

Bond prices have an impressive record as a leading indicator of the economy, although the lead time at peaks and troughs can be quite long. In *Leading Indicators for the 1990s* (Don Jones-Irwin, 1990), Geoffrey Moore (one of the nation's leading authorities on the business cycle) details the history of bonds as a long-leading indicator of business cycle peaks and troughs. By 1990, when Dr. Moore published his research, the U.S. economy had experienced eight business cycles starting in 1948. The Dow Jones 20 Bond Average led each of the business cycle peaks by an average of 27 months. At the eight business cycle troughs, the bond lead was seven months on average. From 1948 through 1990, bond prices led all business cycle turns by an average of 17 months.

STOCKS AND COMMODITIES AS LEADING INDICATORS

Stocks and commodities also qualify as leading indicators of the business cycle, although their warnings are much shorter than those of bonds. Research provided by Dr. Moore (in collaboration with Victor Zarnowitz and John P. Cullity) in the previously-cited work, *Leading Indicators for the 1990s*, provides us with lead and lag times for all three markets—bonds, stocks, and commodities—relative to turns in the business cycle. This supports the rotational process described in Figure 12.1.

In the eight business cycles from 1948 to 1990, the S&P 500 stock index led turns in the business cycle by an average of seven months, with a nine-month lead at peaks and a five-month lead at troughs. Commodity prices (represented by the Journal of Commerce Index) led business cycle turns by an average of six months, with an eight-month lead at peaks and a two-month lead at troughs.

Several conclusions can be drawn from these numbers. One is that technical analysis of bonds, stocks, and commodities can play a role in economic analysis. Technical analysis can be applied to all three markets. Another is that the rotational nature of the three markets (as pictured in Figure 12.1) is confirmed. Bonds turn first (17 months in advance), stocks second (seven months in advance) and commodities third (six months in advance). The rotational sequence of bonds, stocks, and commodities turning in the proper order is maintained at both peaks and troughs. In all three markets, the lead at peaks is much longer than at troughs. The lead time given at peaks by bonds can be extremely long (27 months on average) while commodities provide a very short warnings at troughs (two months on average). The lead time for commodities may vary depending on the commodity index being used. Dr. Moore uses the Journal of Commerce Index, which he helped create; it is an index comprised of industrial commodities. Martin Pring also expresses a preference for using industrial commodities. Their work places less importance on agricultural commodities, which are included in the CRB Index.

MORE ON THE JOC INDEX

The Journal of Commerce Index was introduced in Chapter 3. Its full name is the Journal of Commerce (JOC)—Economic Cycle Research Institute (ECRI) Industrial Price Index. The JOC Index is made up of 18 industrial commodity prices which include textiles, metals, petroleum products, and some miscellaneous prices that include plywood. The metals category includes aluminum, copper, lead, nickel, tin, steel, and zinc. Dr. Moore's pioneering work on the impact of the financial markets on the business cycle is carried on by the Economic Cycle Research Institute, currently located in New York City. Let us follow the intermarket script laid down by Dr. Moore in 1990 to see if the bond, stock, and commodity markets correctly anticipated the recession that started in the spring of 2001.

PREDICTING THE 2001 RECESSION

For this study, I refer to an article that I wrote for the *MurphyMorris.com* website on January 8, 2001 entitled "Market Suggests Recession Due." The stock market had peaked during the previous spring and commodity prices had started to fall. The intention of the this article was to try to use the financial markets to time the onset of a possible recession. To do this, I relied on the numbers published by Dr. Moore for bonds, stocks, and commodities. Here is what I wrote:

*Bonds usually peak an average of 27 months before the economy. Trea-
sury bond prices peaked in October of 1998. Counting forward from
that month suggests that a recession would be due to start in January
2001 (this month). . . . The S&P 500 usually peaks about nine months
before a recession. The S&P 500 peaked in March 2000—giving a possible target for the onset of a recession in December of 2000 (which was
last month). . . . The Journal of Commerce Index (which is the commodity benchmark used in Dr. Moore's research) peaks an average of
eight months before the economy. It hit two peaks last year—March and
September. That projects a possible recession anywhere from November
2000 to July 2001.*

Although the economy had already started to weaken when this article
was written at the start of 2001, the recession did not officially start until two
months later in March 2001 (determined by the National Bureau of Economic
Research). The three financial markets still did a credible job not only of
predicting the start of the 2001 recession, but also in following Dr. Moore's
published timetable. If we use the Fed's actions as an indication of when the
economy started its contraction, the recession date would be in January 2001
when they lowered rates for the first time.

THE THREE MARKETS FOLLOWED
THE PROPER ROTATION FOR TOPS

There are two lessons to be learned in studying this time period. One is simply the fact that the financial markets do lead turns in the economy—and
these turns can be timed with some degree of accuracy. The second is the
fact that all three markets turned in the proper rotational order. Bonds peaked
first during October 1998, the S&P 500 peaked second during March 2000,
and commodities peaked third. The commodity peak shows some variation
depending on which commodity index is used. The JOC Index showed two
peaks—one in March 2000 and a second one in September 2000. If the first
(March) peak is used, it would mean that stocks and commodities peaked
together. (There is some precedent for this as we will see shortly when dis-
cussing the 1920s.) If the second (September) peak is used, commodities
peaked six months after stocks. The CRB Index (which includes agricultural
markets) peaked in October 2000—seven months after the S&P 500 did (see
Figures 12.3 through 12.5).

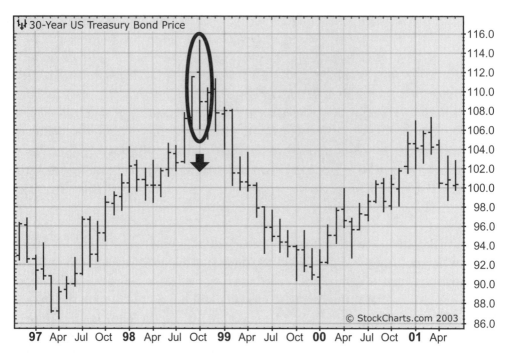

FIGURE 12.3   Bond prices peaked in October 1998, which projected a recession within 27 months.

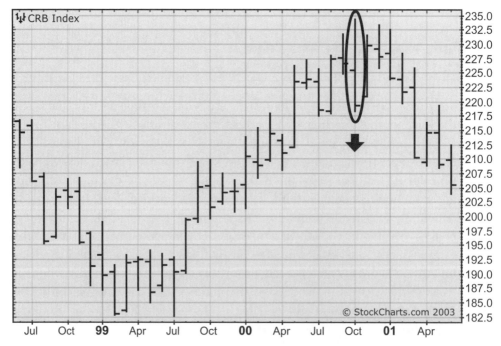

FIGURE 12.4   The CRB peaked in October 2000 six months after stocks and two years after bonds.

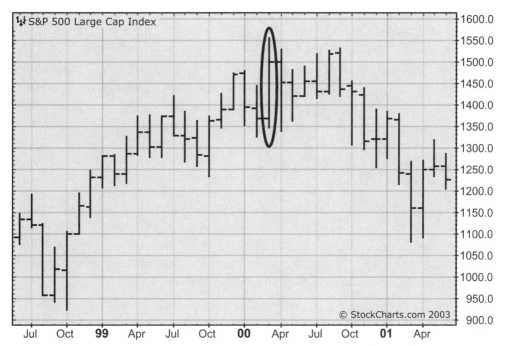

FIGURE 12.5 The S&P 500 hit its high in March 2000, predicting a recession within nine months.

MARKET ROTATIONS DURING THE 1920s AND 1930s

As accurate as Dr. Moore's numbers were in predicting the onset of the 2001 recession, intermarket rotations since 2000 have not followed the normal pattern seen in most post–World War II recessions. The main deviation from the postwar norm has been the major decoupling of bonds and stocks. As mentioned, the main reason for this changing relationship is the appearance of deflationary signs not seen since the 1930s. It begs the obvious question as to whether or not the three markets followed their normal rotation during that prior deflationary period. The fact that many recent trends have not been seen since the 1930s also invites comparisons to that earlier era in order to see what lessons can be learned about the current environment.

COMMODITIES PEAKED IN 1920

Any study of the events of the late 1920s and the early 1930s has to begin with the turn of events starting in 1920. The decade before the 1920s was dominated by the inflationary impact of World War I. In the five years prior to 1920, commodity prices had been rising while bond and stock prices had been weak. Things took a turn for the better starting in 1920. During that year, commodity prices peaked and fell sharply until 1921. From 1921 to 1929, commodity prices remained relatively flat. With commodities peaking in 1920, bonds should have bottomed—and they did.

BONDS BOTTOM DURING 1920

Bond prices bottomed during 1920 at the same time that commodity prices peaked. The peak in commodities meant that the inflationary spike caused by World War I had ended. After bottoming in 1920, bond prices continued rising until 1928. This major upturn in bond prices at the start of the 1920s should have signaled a bottom in stock prices—and it did.

STOCKS BOTTOM DURING 1921

Historically, bond prices have acted as a leading indicator for stocks; they tend to form major tops and bottoms ahead of stocks. The lead time can be as long as a year. This is exactly what happened at the start of the 1920s. Bonds bottomed in 1920 (as commodities peaked). The stock market bottomed in 1921, one year after bonds bottomed. The stock market then began a major climb that lasted into 1929. For most of the 1920s, weak commodity prices were accompanied by rising bond and stock prices. Until 1928, the three markets followed their normal disinflationary script. Starting in 1928, however, things took a turn for the worse. Not surprisingly, it started with bonds.

BONDS TURN DOWN IN 1928

One of the key intermarket principles is that bonds turn down first at major tops. During the first half of 1928, bond prices started to fall. By the start of 1929, bond prices had fallen to the lowest level in two years. For the first time since the start of the 1920s, bond prices were falling while stock prices were rising. This created a negative divergence between bond and stock prices and provided an early warning that the stock market advance had entered a dangerous stage. Just how dangerous became clear in 1929 when stock prices peaked. By the end of 1929, the stock market had started the biggest drop in its history. During the following three years, stocks lost almost 90 percent of their value. From an intermarket perspective, the actions of the two other markets—bonds and commodities—are very instructive.

BONDS AND STOCKS DECOUPLE IN 1929—COMMODITIES PLUNGE

From 1928 to 1929, bond prices were weak while stock prices rose. After the stock market peak during the second half of 1929, stock prices plunged while bond prices rose. This major decoupling of bonds and stocks lasted for the next two years. It was caused largely by the action in the third market: commodities. Starting in late 1929, commodity prices (which had remained relatively flat during the 1920s) began another major decline at the same time that stocks peaked. This plunge in commodity prices turned what had been a relatively benign decade of disinflation into a harmful deflationary era that lasted for several years. In a deflationary climate, stocks and commodities fall together—but bond prices rise. Did the three markets top in their normal sequence from 1928 to 1929? The answer is a qualified "yes." Bonds clearly peaked first; however, stocks and commodities peaked at the same time. The deflationary trends in the three markets at the end of the 1920s closely parallel their respective trends at the end of the 1990s.

STOCKS AND COMMODITIES BOTTOM TOGETHER IN EARLY 1930S

When deflation is the main threat, stocks and commodities become closely correlated. These two peaked together during 1929; they both bottomed three years later. The stock market bottomed around the middle of 1932. Commodities bottomed about half a year later. (It is interesting that even though both markets bottomed closely together, stocks followed their normal pattern of bottoming first.) Both then rose together for several years. In a deflationary climate such as existed during the early 1930s, rising commodity prices are considered a plus for stocks and the economy. A rising stock market suggests that economic trends have also seen their worst. (Industrial production, which had plunged during the years 1929–1932, bottomed along with stocks and commodities in the early 1930s—as did the Consumer and the

Producer Price Indexes, which had plunged into negative territory during those deflationary years.)

REFLATING DURING THE 1930s

There is another comparison that could be made between the battles against deflation during the 1930s and the one in 2002. It has to do with the dollar and gold. In Chapter 9, it was stated that a falling dollar in 2002 had given a big boost to commodity prices and gold in particular. It was thought that the Fed was using the weaker dollar to boost gold prices in an attempt to *reflate* the economy. A similar move was attempted during the 1930s. Prior to 1930, gold was convertible into dollars at a fixed rate of $20. In 1933, President Roosevelt halted the conversion of dollars into gold. At the start of 1934, the official price of gold was raised to $35 an ounce. The jump in the price of gold resulted in a devaluation of the U.S. dollar. It should be evident, then, that the idea of weakening the dollar and raising the price of gold to reflate a deflationary economy is not new. It was tried in the 1930s (see Figure 12.6).

FIGURE 12.6   The official price of gold was raised to $35 during the early 1930s in an attempt to reflate a deflationary economy.

BOND YIELDS SPIKE UP TEMPORARILY IN 1931

Bond yields experienced an upward spike from 2 percent to 6 percent in 1931, reaching their highest level in almost seven years. The spike proved short-lived, however. Yields declined in 1932 and hit new lows in 1934. They were to decline for another ten years until the mid-1940s. Because bond prices move inversely to yields, they did exactly the opposite. After rallying from the middle of 1929 through the first half of 1931 (while stocks fell), bond prices experienced a sharp decline that lasted into the end of that year. During the second half of 1931, all three markets (bonds, stocks, and commodities) fell together. At the start of 1932, however, all three markets turned higher—led by bonds. Bonds bottomed at the start of 1932, stocks bottomed at mid-year, and commodities bottomed at the end of year. (Here again, the three markets followed their normal rotational pattern of bonds turning up first, stocks second, and commodities last.) 1933 turned out to be a relatively strong year for stocks and commodities. However, bonds suffered from a rotation back into stocks that year as rising commodity prices signaled that deflationary forces were lifting, which favored stock investments over bonds. After stalling in 1933, however, bond prices resumed their advance in 1934 and rose into the 1940s.

STOCKS AND COMMODITIES COMPLETE BOTTOMS IN EARLY 1940s

The period from 1932 to 1942 is probably best described as a *bottoming* process for stocks and commodities. Both markets rose until 1937 and then declined into the early 1940s. Stocks and commodities retraced about half of their 1930s gains. In 1942, about midway through the Second World War, the S&P 500 (and commodities) turned up again and advanced throughout the rest of that decade. (It was not until 1954, however, that the stock market exceeded the 1929 highs that had been hit 25 years earlier.) In an effort to keep deflation at bay and to help stimulate the economy, the Federal Reserve tried hard to keep U.S. interest rates from rising during the 1940s. With short-term rates close to zero, they resorted to buying large amounts of long-term Treasury bonds from 1942 to 1951. By 1951, the economy was in recovery and long-term rates rose accordingly. (In the spring of 2003, with short-rates again close to zero, there was talk that the Fed might use the same 1940s strategy of buying Treasuries to keep long-term rates from rising in another attempt to fight deflation and stimulate the economy. By that summer, however, the Fed appeared to have abandoned that unconventional strategy.)

ROTATING ASSET CLASSES OVER DECADES

It is instructive to track the rotating leadership between bonds, stocks, and commodities over long periods of time. During the inflationary decade that includes World War I, commodities were the strongest of the three markets. During the disinflationary 1920s, the leadership passed to stocks. During the deflationary 1930s, bonds became the top performing asset. After World War II, stocks resumed a leadership role that lasted from the 1940s to the 1960s. The inflationary spiral of the 1970s put commodities on center stage again (partially due to the Vietnam War). After commodities peaked in 1980, stocks became the top performer for the next two decades (bonds also did well, but not as well as stocks). The deflationary cycle that started in the late 1990s shifted the leadership away from stocks and back to bonds. This had not happened in 70 years. History has a way of repeating itself. Sometimes, though, we have to go back a long way to study that history.

LESSONS OF LONG CYCLES

In looking over these long cycles of rotation between bonds, stocks, and commodities, there are lessons to be learned. The most obvious is that each asset class has its "day in the sun." Those "days" can last for years—even decades. Let's study the tricky relationship between stocks and commodities. In the early stages of a major long-term expansion (as was seen in the 1940s), rising commodity prices are positive for stocks. A *little* inflation is a good thing. It is when commodity prices jump to much higher levels (as they did in the 1970s) that a little inflation turns into a *big* inflation, which is bad for stocks. *Rising* commodity prices can be good for stocks; *soaring* commodity prices are bad. *Falling* commodity prices can also be good for stocks. Commodity prices peaked in 1920 and 1980 and, in each case, remained relatively flat for years afterward. Declining (or flat) commodity prices ushered in both eras of falling inflation (or disinflation) that carried stock prices higher during the 1920s and the two decades after 1980. *Collapsing* commodity prices are bad for stocks, however. In 1929 and 1998, a collapse in commodity prices to the lowest levels in decades turned a beneficial *disinflation* into a *deflation*, which is harmful to the economy and the stock market.

THE KONDRATIEFF WAVE

No treatment of long economic cycles can be complete without mentioning the Kondratieff Wave. This long cycle of economic activity, which lasts approximately 55 to 60 years, was discovered in the 1920s by Nikolai Kondratieff, a Russian economist. The wave appears to exert a major influence on stock and commodity prices as well as on interest rates. Kondratieff tracked his *long wave* from 1789 and showed three major peaks, the last one occurring in 1920. I described the Kondratieff Wave in my 1986 book, *Technical Analysis of the Futures Markets*, with the following quote: "The Kondratieff cycle has become a popular subject of discussion in recent years, primarily owing to the fact that its last top occurred in the 1920s, placing its next major top sometime in the 1980s." A decade after the writing of these words, the full implications of this top would be felt.

Figure 12.7 (courtesy of Topline Investment Graphics) shows the Kondratieff Wave back to 1789. It tracks four long waves during the past two hundred years. The four peaks occurred in 1816, 1864, 1920, and 1980. Each of these four economic expansions led to a burst of inflation (characterized by rising commodity prices and rising interest rates). Interestingly, all four of these inflations roughly coincided with major American wars (the War of 1812, the Civil War, World War I, and the Vietnam War). Each burst of inflation is followed by a peak in commodity prices. (The last two peaks occurred in 1920 and 1980.) After peaking, commodities usually plateau for a decade or longer. During this plateau period (which we call disinflation), stock prices do especially well. That occurred during the 1920s and the period from 1980 to 2000.

The danger point in the long cycle comes when commodity prices end their plateau period and start falling again. This is when deflationary forces start to exert their negative influence on the stock market and the economy. (This is what happened in 1929 and 1998.) The chart shows the major peaks in stocks that took place in 1835, 1874, 1929, and 2000. The average time between these peaks is 55 years (although the time between the 1929 and 2000 peaks is an unusually long 71 years). The chart also shows that interest rates follow the trend of inflation or deflation. The plunge in bond yields since 1980 is matched by a similar decline that lasted from 1920 to 1945. When the long cycle turns down (as it appears to have done around 2000), falling rates become a symptom of economic weakness and do not provide much help to the stock market.

One of the messages that comes from studying these long cycles is that the contraction part of the Kondratieff Wave can last for long periods of time—even as long as a decade or more. This possibility should dampen expectations of an early return to the "good old days" that characterized the last two decades of the twentieth century.

DIVIDING A LIFETIME CYCLE INTO FOUR SEASONS

The notations in Figure 12.7 are the work of Ian Gordon (Vice President of Canaccord Capital Corp., Vancouver, Canada) who has written a newsletter since 1998 entitled *The Long Wave Analyst*. Gordon divides the Long Wave into four parts, which he compares to the four seasons of the year. Each sea-

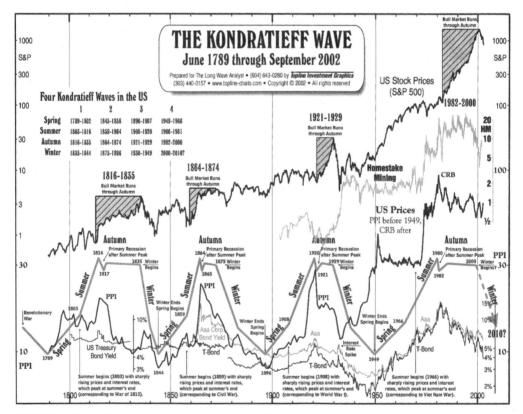

FIGURE 12.7   The Kondratieff Wave back to 1789 shows four long waves.

son lasts approximately a quarter of the wave's entire length (about 15 years). These seasons are superimposed over the Kondratieff Wave in Figure 12.7. The spring season (which Gordon puts at 1949 to 1966) is characterized by a strengthening economy and benign inflation when stocks do well. Summer (which he puts from 1966 to 1980) is an inflationary period and is marked by rising commodity, gold, and real estate values. Autumn (which Gordon says started in 1980) sees the greatest speculation in bonds, stocks, and real estate. This speculative era also sees a massive buildup of debt. Gordon puts the start of the Kondratieff winter in 2000. The main characteristic of the economic winter (marked by a collapse in commodity prices) is deflation, which is made worse by the need to repay all of the debt built up during the autumn period. Stock prices plunge (as do real estate values) during the winter season of the long cycle. The two best defenses are cash and gold.

Because its length is approximately 60 years, Gordon describes the Kondratieff Wave as a *lifetime cycle* because most people live through it only once. This explains why each generation is unprepared for its onset—and unfamiliar with its solutions. People have never seen it before. Because each bear market is a mirror image of the preceding bull market, the "hangover" after the speculative "party" can go on for a very long time. After all the debt has been repaid, and confidence slowly restored, the spring season starts the *long cycle* all over again.

CHAPTER 13

The Impact of the Business Cycle on Market Sectors

SECTOR ROTATION WITHIN THE BUSINESS CYCLE

The previous chapter showed how the business cycle has a major impact on the relationship between bonds, stocks, and commodities (and also how the position of these three markets tells us something about the position of the business cycle). This chapter shows how the business cycle impacts sector rotations within the stock market. There are two goals here. One is to show that different market sectors do better at different stages of the business cycle. By tracking the business cycle, one is able to anticipate which sectors will give the trader the "most bang for the buck" at any given time. The second goal is to show that sector rotations follow a repetitive pattern where money flows from one sector to another as the economy goes from expansion to contraction and back to expansion. By studying which sectors are leading the overall stock market at any given time, the trader can also make a more reasonable estimate as to where exactly the business cycle is. In this sense, the study of sector rotation can also play a role in economic forecasting.

SECTOR ROTATION IN 2000 FAVORED CONTRACTION

The subject of sector rotation within the business cycle was introduced in Chapter 7, which covered the stock market topping process during 2000. That chapter showed how sector rotations during that year signaled the end of the economic expansion of the 1990s and the start of an economic contraction. Figure 7.10 tracked the rotating leadership among market sectors through one complete economic cycle. Chapter 7 also discussed how Energy stock leadership (which occurred in 1999) usually takes place near the end of an economic expansion, and how rotation to Consumer Staples (which took place in the spring of 2000) signals the start of an economic contraction. Chapter 7 also shows that the four top sectors during the first 10 months of 2000 were Energy, Consumer Staples, Utilities, and Financials. The rotational leadership from the Energy sector into these three defensive sectors that started during the spring of 2000 followed the exact sequence that takes place when the economy moves from expansion to contraction. It took the economic world until the following spring to come to this realization, however.

ANOTHER VIEW OF THE ECONOMIC CYCLE

Figure 13.1 is another version of the sector rotation diagram shown earlier (and is also based on Sam Stovall's *Standard & Poor's Guide to Sector Investing*). Figure 13.1 plots one complete economic cycle in the form of a circle. Starting from the lower left, the economy moves from Late Contraction to Early Expansion to Middle Expansion to Late Expansion to Early Contraction. Each stage is marked by leadership in one or two stock market sectors.

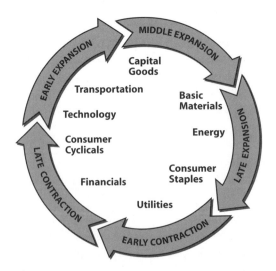

FIGURE 13.1   Technology and transportation leadership during 2003 fits Early Expansion phase.

The far right of Stovall's circle shows that the transition from the Late Expansion phase of the economic cycle to the Early Contraction phase is identified by rotation from Energy to Consumer Staples and Utilities. The transition to the Late Contraction phase shows that money then flows to Financials. All of these rotations took place in the proper order during 2000 and properly anticipated the downturn in the business cycle. Our attention in this chapter is on the possible transition taking place in 2003 from the Late Contraction to Early Expansion phase of the cycle.

SECTOR ROTATIONS DURING 2003 SUGGEST EARLY EXPANSION

Figure 13.1 indicates that the two sectors that show market dominance as the economic cycle moves from Late Contraction to Early Expansion are Consumer Cyclicals and Technology. The diagram tells us two things. If the economy is starting to strengthen in the spring of 2003, these are the two market sectors that should assume a leadership role in the stock market. This information tells traders where to concentrate their funds—if they believe that the economy is starting to improve. Approaching it from the other direction, signs of leadership in these two sectors (based on relative strength analysis) tell us that the economy is indeed strengthening. Fortunately, we have technical tools to help us to determine in which direction market leadership is heading.

SECTOR LEADERSHIP MOVES TO CONSUMERS AND TECHNOLOGY

Figure 13.2 is a bar chart that compares the relative performing of the nine Sector SPDRs (traded on the AMEX) during the first six months of 2003 compared to the S&P 500. Those sectors above the horizontal line (0.0 percent) are outperforming the S&P 500. This is what is desirable—relative strength and market leadership. The only four sectors that are doing better than the S&P 500 during the first half of 2003 are (starting from the right) Financials, Utilities, Technology, and Consumer Discretionary (which is also called Consumer Cyclicals). If one consults Stovall's circle, it is evident that these are supposed to be the top four sectors as the economy goes through the transition from Late Contraction to Early Expansion.

Another positive sign is that Consumer Staples are the weakest of the nine sectors thus far in 2003. It is normally a sign of increasing consumer con-

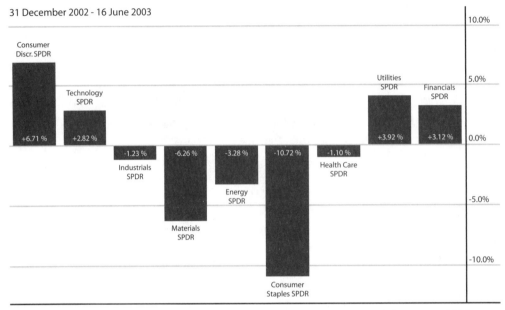

31 December 2002 - 16 June 2003

FIGURE 13.2   Leadership by financials, utilities, technology and consumer discretionary sectors during the first half of 2003 hints at a move into Early Expansion phase of the economic cycle.

fidence when the defensive Consumer Staples are lagging behind (as they are doing here). During the first half of 2000, Consumer Staples became the top-performing sector. This reflected a loss of confidence in the stock market and the economy in 2000. Their relative weakness in 2003 is sending a more confident message. (We will come back to this point later in the chapter when we compare the relative performance of Consumer Staples and economically sensitive Cyclical stocks in 2003.) Another sign of confidence is the fact that Consumer Discretionary stocks are in the top spot during the first half of 2003.

RELATIVE STRENGTH OF CONSUMER SPENDING

Figure 13.3 shows the Consumer Discretionary Select SDPR turning sharply higher in March 2003 (when the entire stock market started moving higher as well). As impressive as its rally was during the second quarter of 2003, the rising relative strength line along the bottom of the chart is even more impressive. This is a ratio (relative strength) line of the Consumer Discretionary SPDR divided by the S&P 500. The rising line shows the group outperforming the S&P 500 since its March bottom.

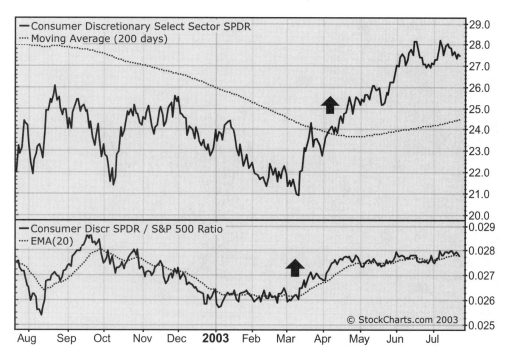

FIGURE 13.3   This sector bottomed during March 2003 and started to outperform the S&P 500.

The Consumer Discretionary group includes stocks that sell products (or offer services) that consumers do not necessarily *need* (like consumer staples), but that they *want*. The fact that consumers are willing to spend money on discretionary items shows increasing confidence in the economy. Stocks that are included in the group are auto-related, entertainment, home appliances, homebuilders, restaurants, and retailers. The retailing stocks play a prominent role in the group. An upturn in retail stocks is considered a sign of confidence.

RETAIL BUYING

Figure 13.4 shows the S&P Retailing Industry Group Index rallying sharply starting in March 2003. The chart also shows that the March 2003 bottom was a successful retest of the prior low of September 2001. The line along the bottom of the chart is a ratio of the Retail Industry Group Index divided by the S&P 500. The ratio line bottomed in September 2001 and again in January 2003. This meant that retail stocks were moving up faster than the rest of the stock market; another sign that consumers have turned more confident about

FIGURE 13.4 This sector bottomed during March 2003, but started to outperform the S&P in January.

the stock market and the economy. Consumer spending accounts for two-thirds of the economy.

Homebuilders have been one of the most resilient market groups throughout the bear market in stocks and the economic downturn after 2000. This probably has less to do with confidence in the economy than it does with record-low interest rates. Homebuilders are examined in more detail in the next chapter. After Consumer Cyclicals start doing better than the rest of the market, the next sector that should start to exert market leadership in the early stages of a new economic expansion is Technology.

TECHNOLOGY LEADERSHIP IS A GOOD SIGN

Figure 13.5 shows the percentage gains of the major stock market averages from October 2002 (when the stock market hit bottom) until June 16, 2003. The top percentage gainer during these eight months was the Nasdaq Composite Index which gained 37 percent. The small-cap Russell 2000 Index

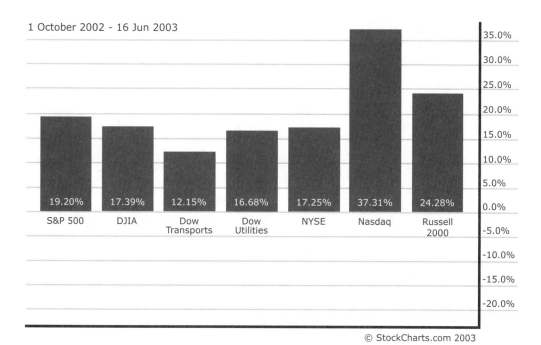

1 October 2002 - 16 Jun 2003

19.20%	17.39%	12.15%	16.68%	17.25%	37.31%	24.28%
S&P 500	DJIA	Dow Transports	Dow Utilities	NYSE	Nasdaq	Russell 2000

© StockCharts.com 2003

FIGURE 13.5 From October 2002 to June 2003, the Nasdaq and the Russell 2000 were top gainers.

gained 24 percent to take second place (more on that later). The S&P 500 and the Dow Industrials are the laggards, showing gains of only 19 percent and 17 percent, respectively. On relative strength grounds, the technology-dominated Nasdaq market was the clear leader. Historically, it is usually a good sign for the rest of the market when the Nasdaq is leading it higher.

NASDAQ LEADS MARKET HIGHER DURING 2003

Figure 13.6 is a ratio of the Nasdaq divided by the S&P 500. The ratio peaked during 2000 as the bubble in Nasdaq market burst. The ratio line shows a gradual leveling-off starting in October 2002 (which is where we obtained the previously-cited performance numbers). The rising ratio line since that bottom shows that the Nasdaq market was stronger than the S&P 500 over those eight months.

The Nasdaq is dominated by large technology stocks. One way to determine if the Nasdaq Composite rise is being led by technology stocks is to

FIGURE 13.6   The Nasdaq has been outperforming the S&P 500 since October 2002.

compare its performance to the Nasdaq 100 Index, which includes the largest nonfinancial stocks in the Nasdaq market (which are mainly in technology). During the eight months in question (from the October 2002 bottom to June 2003), the Nasdaq 100 gained 42 percent, which is 5 percent better than the Nasdaq Composite advance of 37 percent. The stronger performance by the Nasdaq 100 shows that the Technology sector was primarily responsible for the Nasdaq's ability to outperform the rest of the market from the fourth quarter of 2002 through the middle of 2003. Technology performance is what should happen as the economy moves into the Early Expansion phase of the cycle.

TRANSPORTATION LEADERSHIP

Moving up the left side of Stovall's circle further into the Early Expansion phase of the economic cycle, one finds Transportation. If the economy is going to produce goods, it has to also transport them. (The Dow Theory, which is the oldest technical theory of market behavior, states that for a true bull market (and an economic recovery) to occur, the Dow Industrials and the Dow Transports must move up together. While the Industrial companies manufacture the goods, the Transportation companies move them. One cannot exist without the other.) There is another element at work here in the economic cycle and it has to do with oil. As previously mentioned, rising oil prices during 1999 were especially damaging to Transportation stocks; they fell heavily that year. Rising oil prices (and a rising Energy Sector) in 1999 also contributed to the end of the economic expansion in 2000. After the economic slowdown, oil prices peaked and Energy stocks weakened. This usually gives a boost to Transportation stocks and is another sign that things are getting better.

Figure 13.7 shows the Dow Jones Transportation Average during the second quarter of 2003 exceeding the highs hit during the fourth quarter of 2002. This upside move coincided with a similar breakout in the Dow Jones Industrial Average, meaning that both key stock averages were moving up together by June 2003. This is what should happen if the stock market is bottoming and an economic recovery is starting. More importantly, the ratio

FIGURE 13.7   The Dow Transports have been stronger than the Dow Industrials during 2003.

line beneath the price chart shows the Transports moving up from the March 2003 low faster than the Industrials. If this relative strength continues, it would have two positive implications. The first is that the rising Transports, which are also considered to be cyclical in nature, are starting to show leadership just when they should in the early stages of a new economic expansion. The second is that stronger Transports are usually associated with weaker oil prices. Since rising oil prices contributed to the economic slowdown in 2000, weaker oil prices in 2003 should help to stimulate an economic rebound.

CYCLICALS STARTING TO OUTPERFORM STAPLES

Chapter 4 explained how economically sensitive cyclical stocks and the more defensive consumer staples compete for investor funds. In addition, it illustrated how the relationship between these two market sectors tells us something about consumer sentiment and the strength or weakness of the economy. When investors are more optimistic about the economy, they favor cyclical stocks. The very word *cyclical* implies that they are tied to the business cycle. As a result, cyclical stocks usually do better when the economy is on the upswing and worse when it is in decline. The opposite is the case with consumer staples. They lag behind when the economy is gaining momentum, but become safe havens when things start to look bad. This was the case in the spring of 2000 when "scared" money moved aggressively into these more defensive stocks. Figure 13.8 plots a ratio of the Morgan Stanley Cyclical Index divided by the S&P Consumer Staples Index. The direction of the ratio line tells us something about the direction of the economy—or at least what the markets expect for the economy.

The ratio peaked during the first half of 2000 as the stock market peaked. Money flowed out of economically sensitive cyclical stocks and into economically resistant consumer staples. It was a sign that investors were already starting to anticipate an economic slowdown. The situation in the middle of 2003 is exactly the opposite. The cyclical/staple ratio has been rising since October 2002. More importantly, it has broken the down trendline extending back to the early 2000 peak and has established a pattern of *higher highs* and *higher lows*. This new uptrend in the ratio line implies that cyclical stocks have gained dominance over consumer staples for the first time in three years. This type of sector rotation is another sign that the market has become more optimistic about the direction of the business cycle.

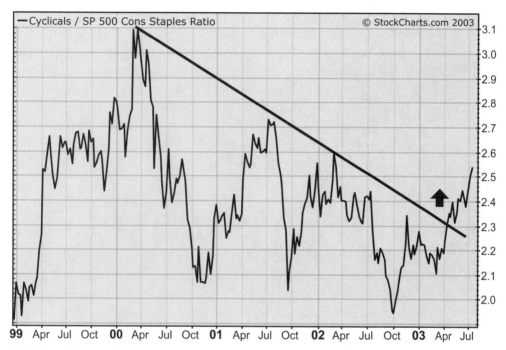

FIGURE 13.8 The break of the trendline in April 2003 signalled new leadership in cyclicals.

SMALLER STOCKS LEAD AT BOTTOMS

The performance numbers given earlier (from the October 2002 bottom to June 2003) showed the small-cap Russell 2000 Index outperforming both the Dow and the S&P 500 (Russell +24 percent, the S&P 500 +19 percent, the Dow +17 percent). This outperformance by smaller stocks also held up through the first six months of 2003. If the relatively strong performance by small-cap over large-cap stocks continues, it would bode well for both the stock market and the economy. Smaller stocks usually lead the stock market when the economy is coming out of recession. The historical track record is impressive. Six recessions took place between 1960 and 1991. Small stocks outperformed large stocks in the first year following each of these previous recessions.

Figure 13.9 plots a relative strength ratio of the small-cap Russell 2000 Index divided by the large-cap Russell 1000 Index. The ratio bottomed during October 2002 when the entire stock market bottomed. Since then, small caps have risen more than large caps, as evidenced by the rising ratio line. The breaking of the down trendline in April 2003 was another compelling chart sign of a new investor preference for smaller stocks.

FIGURE 13.9   The break of the trendline in April 2003 signalled new leadership in small caps.

SECTOR ROTATION MODEL

Figure 13.10 gives another visual representation of how sectors rotate throughout the business cycle. This theoretical model is also based on Sam Stovall's research. It presents the same data as Figure 13.1, but is shown in graph form. Notice that the Market Cycle precedes the Economic Cycle at peaks and troughs, further proof that the stock market turns before the economy and is a leading indicator for the economy. The Sector Rotation Model shows that Energy and Consumer Staples are strongest as the Economic Cycle weakens. The transition from Recession to Early Recovery sees market leadership coming from Cyclical and Technology stocks.

SECTOR ROTATION MODEL SUPPORTING DATA

More information goes along with the Sector Rotation Model shown in Figure 13.10. It has to do with economic/fundamental factors that accompany dif-

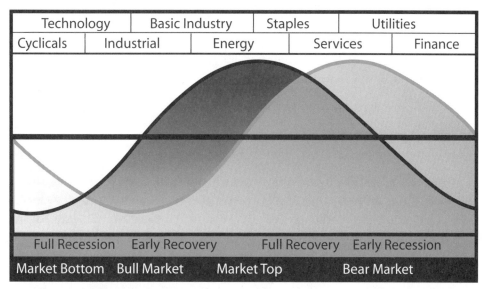

Technology	Basic Industry	Staples	Utilities
Cyclicals	Industrial	Energy	Services	Finance

Full Recession	Early Recovery	Full Recovery	Early Recession
Market Bottom	Bull Market	Market Top	Bear Market

Legend: ■ Market Cycle ■ Economic Cycle

FIGURE 13.10 A visual look at Sector Rotation throughout the business cycle.

ferent stages in the business cycle. These are less technical in nature but do serve to round out the type of chart analysis generally employed in intermarket work. The factors are: consumer expectations, industrial production, the direction of interest rates, and the slope of the yield curve. By keeping an eye on these factors, a chartist is able to better discern if they are meshing with relative strength performance charts. So far, the relative performance of the various market sectors has been used to determine the position of the business cycle. Let's see what these four factors should be doing as the economy goes through expansion to contraction and then back to expansion.

Cycle Stage:	Recession	Early Recovery	Recovery	Early Recession
Consumer Expectations:	Reviving	Rising	Declining	Falling Sharply
Industrial Production:	Bottoming	Rising	Flat	Falling
Interest Rates:	Falling	Bottoming	Rising	Peaking
Yield Curve:	Normal	Steep	Flattening	Inverted

Consumer Expectations are very important because consumer spending accounts for two-thirds of the economy. Rising Consumer Expectation in the Early Recovery phase of the economic cycle usually translates into higher consumer spending. When Consumer Expectations are falling sharply in early recession, consumer spending dries up, which contributes to the economic slowdown. Industrial Production (IP) is one of the most widely followed measures of economic activity. During a recession, with business and consumer spending on the decline, Industrial Production is falling. When IP starts to rise, it is an early sign that the economy is recovering.

INTEREST RATE TRENDS

The subject of how interest rates behave during periods of economic expansion and contraction has already been covered. It related to the discussions of how the bond market fits into the economic cycle. As a rule, interest rates rise during an economic recovery and fall during an economic contraction. As this model suggests, a rapid rise in interest rates usually occurs in the late stages of economic recovery (usually caused by Fed tightening), which contributes to the eventual recession. Conversely, rapidly falling interest rates during a recession (usually caused by Fed easing) contribute to the eventual economic recovery. Interest rates have a tendency to bottom during the early recovery phase. Thus the direction of interest rates is one way to measure the strength or weakness of the economy. The yield curve provides investors with another way.

THE YIELD CURVE

The *yield curve* measures the slope (or spread) between short-term rates and long-term rates. When the yield curve is normal, long-term rates are higher than short-term rates. The slope of the yield curve is caused mainly by movement in short-term rates. Short-term rates are the ones most directly impacted by Federal Reserve policy. The Fed controls the direction of short-term rates; inflationary (or deflationary) expectations control the direction of long-term rates. During an economic recovery, the yield curve has a tendency to flatten out. This means that short-term rates are rising faster than long-term rates and the spread between the two flattens. The crucial point comes when short-term rates exceed long-term rates. It is a dangerous situation called an *inverted yield curve* and is usually an early signal of an economic contraction. Chapter 7 showed how an inverted yield curve in January 2000 (resulting from rising oil prices and Fed tightening during 1999) was an early sign that the upward expansions in the stock market and the economy were nearing completion.

During a recession, the yield curve normalizes. This happens because the Fed lowers short-term rates (as they started doing at the beginning of 2001). Long-term rates fall as well, but they do so more slowly. A steep yield curve is usually a prerequisite for early recovery. A *flattening* yield curve is a sign of an economy that is in recovery. The flattening yield curve can occur in two ways. One way it can happen is if short-term rates start rising faster than long-term rates as the economy strengthens. Another way is if long-term rates start dropping faster than short-term rates.

YIELD CURVE FLATTENS DURING 2003

Figure 13.11 is a snapshot of the yield curve as of June 17, 2003. The black line shows that the yield curve has an upward slope, which means that it is positive (or normal). (The line starts with lower short-term rates to the left and moves upwards toward higher long-term rates to the right.) There is a "shadow" on the black line, which shows where it has been over the previous few weeks. The fact that the current yield curve (which is the black line) is at the lower end of the shadow means that it is moving lower (or flattening). This means that the spread between short and long-term rates is narrowing. The flattening yield curve during the spring of 2003 was primarily due to the fact that long-term rates started falling faster than short-term rates. The rate

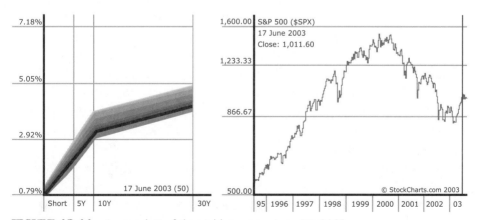

FIGURE 13.11   A snapshot of the yield curve on June 17, 2003.

on the three- and six-month T-bills had fallen below 1 percent. The 10-year Treasury note and the 30-year Treasury bond were yielding 3.3 percent and 4.4 percent, respectively.

During May 2003, the Fed announced that it would lower rates even more (and keep them low) in order to head off any threat from deflation. Since short-term rates could not drop much more, most of the downward movement was seen in the long end of the yield curve. The buying of T-bonds and notes was also influenced by the Fed's hinting that it might be willing to buy 10-year Treasury notes to keep long-term rates from rising. And with short-term rates nearing zero, money managers (and investors) were forced to move further out along the curve to find higher yields. As low as interest rates were, a 4 percent yield on the T-bond still seemed better than 1 percent on a T-bill.

The search for yield in the low interest rate environment that existed during the first half of 2003 also caused investors to move into investment-grade corporate bonds and high-yield (junk) bonds, which offered higher returns than Treasuries. The same motivation also caused fixed-income funds to flow into emerging-market bonds. These more aggressive moves indicated that investors were willing to assume more risk, signalling growing confidence in the economy.

ANOTHER VIEW OF THE YIELD CURVE

Figure 13.12 plots the ratio between the yield on the 3-month Treasury bill and the 10-year Treasury note. Plotted this way, the relationship between the two can be seen more easily. In 2000, the short-term rate moved over the long-term rate, (as a result of Fed tightening), causing the inverted yield curve that led to a weakening of the economy. Short-term rates started to fall at the start of 2001 when the Fed began an aggressive easing policy. The dramatic drop in short-term rates relative to long-term rates continued throughout 2001 (as the Fed lowered short-term rates 11 times). Short-term rates leveled off in 2002. The ratio fell to a new low during the summer of 2003 due to a jump in long-term rates.

On June 25, 2003, the Federal Reserve lowered the Fed funds rate a quarter point to 1.00 percent. This was the lowest level in 45 years. The immediate market reaction was not what the Fed had in mind. Within six weeks of the quarter-point rate cut, the yield on the 10-year Treasury note jumped from

FIGURE 13.12 The falling ratio shows a steepening yield curve from the start of 2001. That was the result of the Fed's lowering short-term rates thirteen times through the middle of 2003.

3.25 percent to 4.50 percent. Bond traders were hoping for a more aggressive half-point cut to emphasize the Fed's commitment to battle deflation. Many took the less aggressive move as a sign that the Fed's 13th easing since January 2001 might be its last. This caused heavy selling in the bond market. The jump in long-term rates also reflected the market's view that the Fed had abandoned its earlier plan to buy 10-year Treasury notes.

CHAPTER 14

Diversifying
with Real Estate

LOCATION IS EVERYTHING

They say that the three key words in real estate are "location, location, location." Since the big bear market in stocks began in 2000, real estate has been a good place for investors to locate their money. This has been true both in terms of home ownership and any stock related to homebuilding and real estate. This is not necessarily the norm, however. Real estate has usually been viewed as an inflation hedge. Real estate prices were usually tied to the cycle of inflation. The value of homes and real estate rose during periods of high inflation and fell during periods of low inflation. The price of a home peaked along with the inflationary bubble around 1980. Home prices then followed the inflation rate, dipping into the 1990s. More recently, however, their paths have diverged. Over the last five years, home prices have jumped 39 percent. Home values jumped 7.5 percent each year in 2001 and 2002 as the inflation rate dropped to 2 percent. Part of the reason for the aberrant behavior of real estate during this down cycle in the economy is the fact that interest rates have acted differently and have fallen to the lowest levels since the 1950s.

THIS CYCLE HAS BEEN DIFFERENT

There is no question that the latest downturn in the business cycle has been different from anything seen since in the post–World War II era. Deflationary tendencies that started five years ago have changed many of the traditional intermarket relationships. One of the key relationships that has changed is the link between bonds and stocks. In previous postwar recessions, bond and stock prices fell together. Bond prices turned up before stocks, but not until the economy was well into its down cycle. This meant that long-term rates were still rising even as the economy was weakening. The bear market in stocks that started in 2000, however, saw a major decoupling of bonds and stocks. Bond prices turned up in the spring of 2000 as the stock market peaked. Bond prices continued rising during the next three years as stock prices fell. This unusual behavior is consistent with a deflationary environment. The plunge in long-term rates that started in the spring of 2000 (just as the stock market peaked) gave a double boost to real estate stocks and homebuilders. Both benefit from falling interest rates. REITs also benefit from a falling stock market, especially technology stocks.

REITS TURN UP AS NASDAQ PEAKS

Chapter 7 talks about the rotation into Real Estate Investment Trusts (REITs) that started in the spring of 2000 as the bubble in the Nasdaq market was bursting. (REITs own everything from apartments to offices to shopping malls.) One of the reasons for the 2000 rotation is that REITs have a low correlation to the rest of the stock market. This makes REITs an excellent diversification vehicle, especially when the market is in trouble. Maybe even more importantly, REITs have a tendency to show a *negative* correlation to technology stocks. This means they usually trend in the opposite direction of the Nasdaq market, which is dominated by technology shares. What better place to move some money into when the Nasdaq is peaking? (REITs also pay a high dividend rate, which makes them an excellent defensive sector, especially when interest rates are falling along with stocks.)

ROLE REVERSALS IN 2000

Figure 14.1 plots the Nasdaq market with the Morgan Stanley REIT Index from the start of 2000 to the start of 2003. Their inverse correlation is dramatic when looked at in this fashion. Going into the spring of 2000, the Nasdaq market was soaring while REITs were in decline. During that spring, the peak in the Nasdaq coincided almost exactly with a major upturn in the REIT Index. For the next two years REITs rose while the Nasdaq kept tumbling. The plunging stock market was not the only thing helping REITs. Interest rates also played a big role in the REIT revival. Figure 14.2 positions the REIT

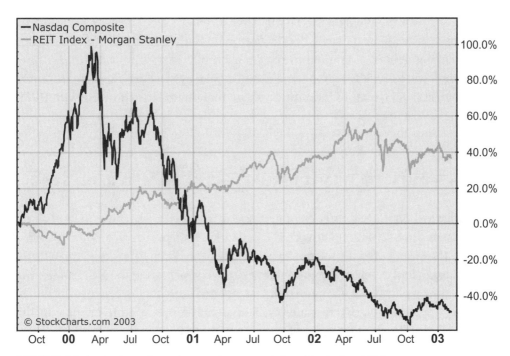

FIGURE 14.1 Both markets show an inverse relationship during 2000.

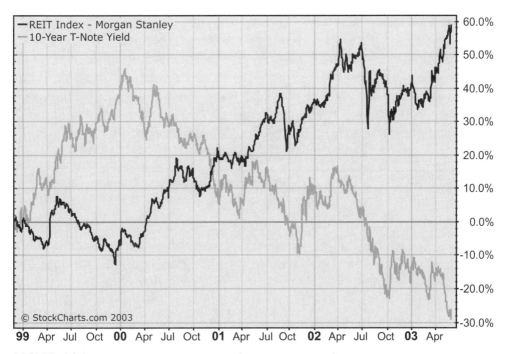

FIGURE 14.2 A clear inverse link is seen between REITs and rates.

Index over the yield on the 10-year Treasury note. Here again, a clear inverse relationship can be seen. REITs bottomed early in 2000 just as rates were peaking. REITs continued to rise as rates fell. Ironically, deflationary pressures were actually helping real estate stocks by pushing interest rates to the lowest levels in more than forty years. Homebuilders rose along with REITs for the same reason.

THINGS START TO CHANGE DURING THE SUMMER OF 2002

Figure 14.3 plots another comparison of the two competing markets—the Nasdaq and REITs. It shows the REIT Index rising through a down trendline in the spring of 2000 just as the Nasdaq was peaking. By the end of 2000, the Nasdaq had fallen to the lowest level in two years while the REIT Index was setting a new all-time high. To the far right of both charts, however, it can be seen that the relative fortunes of the two markets started to change. In July 2002, REITs showed signs of peaking just as the Nasdaq market started to stabilize.

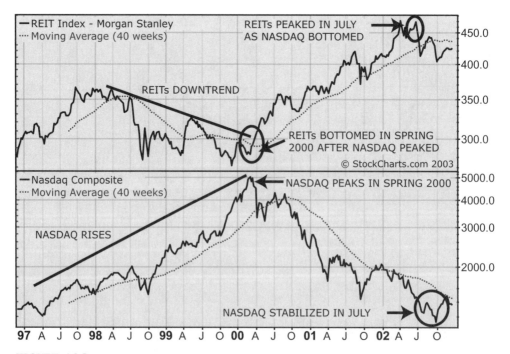

FIGURE 14.3   REITs bottomed as the Nasdaq peaked in 2000.

REITS PEAK IN 2002 AS MARKET BOTTOMS

Figure 14.4 plots three lines: the Dow Jones REIT Index (top line), the yield on the 10-year T-note (middle line), and the Nasdaq Composite Index (bottom line). In order to understand the movement in the REIT market from the summer of 2002 to the summer of 2003, it is necessary to compare all three lines. The peak in the REIT Index occurred right at the start of July 2002. Later that same month, the Nasdaq (and the rest of the market) started a bottoming process that lasted until the following spring when stock prices started to rise. A reverse rotation started in July 2002. Money started moving out of REITs and back into other stocks, especially into technology.

Although the 2002 peak in REITs coincided closely with a bottom in the Nasdaq, the markets moved mostly in tandem from the middle of 2002 to the middle of 2003. They both started moving up in March 2003 and rose together through that June. At least part of the rise in REITs can be attributed to the sharp drop in the Treasury note yield that took place in May of that year. (This sudden drop in long-term rates was precipitated by the Fed's

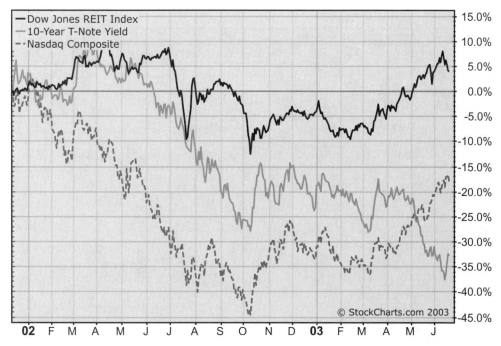

FIGURE 14.4 A comparison of the three markets.

May 6 announcement that it was concerned about the threat of deflation.)
Most of the interest rate decline was seen in long-term rates (especially in the
10-year note), which are the rates that have the most impact on real estate
and housing. It could be argued that the jump in REITs during the spring of
2003 had less to do with a rising stock market and more to do with the plunge
in long-term interest rates.

REITS UNDERPERFORM AFTER SUMMER OF 2002

The REIT rally that started in the spring of 2003 carried prices back to the
highs of the previous spring. This suggested that the REIT rally that started
during the spring of 2003 had reached a critical point in its three-year uptrend.
Any test of a previous high is regarded as a test of an existing uptrend. Most
topping patterns usually start with an inability to exceed a previous peak. Figure 14.5 plots the Dow Jones REIT Index from the start of 2002 to the middle
of 2003; it shows the rally that started during March 2003. It also shows the
REIT Index reaching a crucial chart juncture as it retests the highs formed
the previous year. REITs were also starting to *underperform* the rest of the

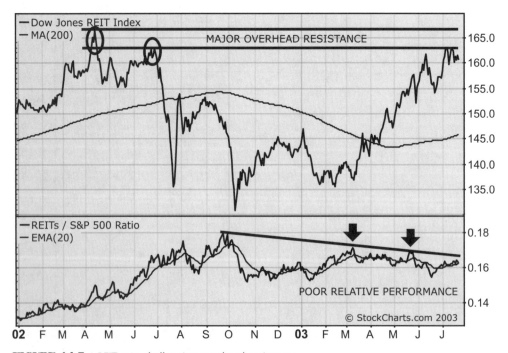

FIGURE 14.5   REITs are challenging overhead resistance.

market by the middle of 2003, another warning sign that investor interest in the group was weakening.[1]

In sector work, *relative* performance is almost as important as *absolute* performance. The line plotted along the bottom of Figure 14.5 is a ratio of the Dow Jones REIT Index divided by the S&P 500 through June 2003. The ratio line started dropping the previous October (just as the stock market was starting to bottom). The ratio line shows a negative slope since that peak. The REIT runup that started in March 2003 was also accompanied by a falling ratio line. This meant that even though the REITs were rising, they were rising more slowly than the S&P 500. It is normally a sign that a market sector has lost its leadership role and is falling out of favor. If that trend continued, it raised two possibilities. One is that the stock market has bottomed, which reduces the need for the defensive qualities of REITs. Another possibility might be that the relative weakness in REITs is an early sign that long-term rates are starting to scrape bottom. Since falling rates have been the driving force in the real estate and housing boom, any hint of higher rates (and a stronger stock market) could prove to be a double negative for REITs and homebuilding stocks.

HOUSING IS INTEREST RATE-SENSITIVE

Real estate and housing are tied very closely to the direction of interest rates. This explains why housing has generally been considered to be *countercyclical*; it moves in the opposite direction of the normal business cycle. Homebuilding activity tends to be strongest when interest rates are falling, which generally happens in a weaker economy. Conversely, a strong economy usually coincides with rising interest rates, which has a dampening effect on the homebuilding industry. Tighter monetary policy in a strong economy has historically had a retraining effect on real estate loans, which tend to weaken even as the economy strengthens. New home sales have in the past also displayed similar countercyclical behavior by turning down during economic expansions (when rates are rising) and bottoming during recessions (when rates are falling). This is primarily due to housing's inverse correlation with long-term interest rates. Housing starts (which measure the number of housing units beginning construction each month) also have a history of falling during economic booms and recovering strongly during economic busts. Again, the determining factor seems to be the direction of long-term rates. However, this has not always been the case.

---

[1] At the start of October 2003 the DJ REIT Index finally exceeded its 2002 peak.

REAL ESTATE DOES NOT ALWAYS FOLLOW INFLATION

Real estate has historically been called an inflation hedge as well as interest rate-sensitive. It has also been said that real estate prices fall when the stock market falls. All of these statements have been made about real estate. And all of them are true—but not always. Home prices and real estate values plunged during the deflationary years of the Great Depression. Home prices fell between 1925 and 1935 and did not start rising until the late 1940s. Land values, especially those in the Midwest, also plunged during the 1930s as farm commodity prices collapsed; they started rising again with the rate of inflation during the 1940s and 1950s. This seems to support the view that housing and real estate are inflation- and deflation-sensitive. Home values also soared during the inflationary 1970s and peaked along with inflation in the early 1980s. The value of farmland plunged after 1981 when agricultural commodity prices peaked. This, too, supports the link with inflation. How, then, do we explain the surge in real estate and home values over the past five years when inflation has been virtually nonexistent and deflation has been the main threat? This is exactly the opposite of what happened during the 1930s. The dramatic increase in real estate values and homebuilding over the past five years cannot be linked to inflation.

REAL ESTATE DOES NOT ALWAYS FOLLOW INTEREST RATES

Real estate's link to interest rates has not always held up. The collapse in real estate and housing during the 1930s coincided with falling long-term rates. The real estate boom of the 1970s took place while long-term rates were rising. In the latter case, the beneficial impact of an inflationary spiral during the 1970s appears to have overcome the harmful effects of rising interest rates. In the 1980s, housing and real estate values weakened as interest rates dropped. During the 1930s, the 1970s, and the 1980s, the link to inflation appears to have been much greater than the link to interest rates.

REAL ESTATE DOES NOT ALWAYS FOLLOW STOCKS

How about the real estate's link to stocks? Stocks fell along with home and land values during the 1930s and turned up with them during the 1940s. Stocks and real estate values rose together until the late 1960s. During the 1970s, however, real estate soared while stocks endured a decade-long secular bear market. Real estate and housing weakened during the early 1980s just as the stock market was starting the biggest bull market in history. Since 2000, real estate and housing has prospered as the stock market endured its worst beating in 70 years. Recent experience contradicts the notion that real estate follows the stock market.

It seems, then, that none of the historical reasons that are normally cited to explain real estate activity—inflation, interest rates, stock prices, and the business cycle—adequately explains the ebbs and flows of real estate and homebuilding. The answer to the puzzle must lie elsewhere. The answer appears to be that real estate moves according to a different cycle than all of the other financial markets and the economy.

THE *LONG CYCLE* IN REAL ESTATE ACTIVITY

In his 1987 book entitled *The Wall Street Waltz* (Contemporary Books, Inc.), Kenneth Fisher (CEO, Fisher Investments, Woodside, CA) describes an 18-year cycle in real estate activity discovered in 1940 by Clarence Long (which is why it is called the Long Cycle). Mr. Fisher blends the 18-year real estate cycle with the 55-year Kondratieff Wave and the four-year business cycle (which is also called the Kitchin Cycle after its inventor Joseph Kitchin). (Both of these cycles are discussed in Chapter 12.)

COMPARISON TO OTHER CYCLES

Long tracked the real estate cycle from 1870 to 1940. Since its length is 18 years (from peak to peak or trough to trough), approximately three Long Cycles take place in one Kondratieff Wave. This also means that one 18-year real estate cycle includes at least four business cycles (which average four years apiece). Fisher points out that business cycles tend to be strongest when the Kondratieff and Long Cycles are in upswings; they tend to be weakest when both longer waves are in downswings. This accounts for some similarities between present-day conditions and those of the 1930s—and some differences.

SIMILARITIES AND DIFFERENCES: PRESENT DAY AND THE 1930s

The 55-year Kondratieff Wave and Long's 18-year real estate cycle both turned down in the late 1920s. As a result of this downward convergence in two major economic cycles, stock values collapsed along with home and land values. The deflationary impact also crushed commodity prices and pushed interest rates sharply lower. This differs from the current situation in that only one of these two major economic cycles turned down. Chapter 12 suggested that the Kondratieff Wave ended its plateau period in 1998 and ushered in the current deflationary cycle. The Long Cycle, however, kept rising. Because homebuilding is so important for economic activity, the fact that real estate kept rising during this economic cycle appears to have cushioned the downturn in the economy since 2000. A critical issue now is how long that real estate cycle continues. The best way to gain insight on this is by studying its history.

HISTORY OF REAL ESTATE CYCLE SINCE 1940

Fisher puts a cycle top in real estate activity in 1945, 18 years after its 1927 peak. Counting forward from the 1945 peak, he puts the next two peaks in 1963 and 1981. He observes that real estate "stumbled badly" starting in 1963 and that farm real estate values collapsed in 1981. (From 1981–1985, farmland in the Midwest lost over 40 percent of its value.) Counting forward from a 1954 trough, he puts the next real estate trough in 1972—just in time for the inflationary surge of the 1970s. Fisher puts the next scheduled real estate cycle trough sometime in the 1990–1992 time frame, which would explain the relative strength in real estate over the past decade. If Fisher's timing of the 18-year cycle is correct, however, it would mean that a peak in real estate activity is overdue. The reason for the current real estate cycle stretching out longer than usual is most likely an unprecedented drop in long-term interest rates to their lowest levels in a half-century. This means that the continuation of the current housing boom may be heavily dependent on interest rates staying low.

ARE HOMEBUILDING STOCKS LINKED TO STOCKS OR RATES?

There are times when homebuilding stocks are in sync with the stock market—and there are times when they are not. This may have more to do with bonds than stocks, however. Homebuilding stocks experienced bear markets in 1990 and 1994 right along with the rest of the stock market. In both instances, however, bond prices fell along with stocks, pushing long-term rates higher. It could be said, then, that homebuilders were reacting to higher rates. It is difficult to say whether the homebuilders were being influenced by the fall in the stock market or the rise in long-term rates. In the two prior bear markets, the correct answer seems to be that homebuilders were being influenced by both markets. An examination of the 1994 bear market in stocks illustrates this point.

Figure 14.6 shows the price of Centex (a homebuilder) at the bottom of the chart, the yield on the 10-year Treasury-note at the top left, and the S&P 500 in the middle left. During that bear market year, Centex fell (as did other homebuilders). In fact, homebuilders did a lot worse than the general market that year. After participating in the stock market downturn, Centex turned up with the S&P 500 near the end of that year. It can be said, then, that Centex (and the other homebuilders) were moving with the stock market. A closer inspection of Figure 14.6, however, suggests that the movement in the homebuilder was more closely correlated with the yield on the 10-year T-note, which turned up at the start of the year and peaked during the fourth quarter.

Rising rates and falling stocks hurt the homebuilders in 1994; falling rates and rising stocks helped them in 1995. Since bonds and stocks were in sync at the time, it did not really matter which one the homebuilders were following. Bond and stock prices were trending in the same direction. So were the homebuilders. The positive link to stocks continued until the start of 1999 when the S&P 500 and Centex started to trend in opposite directions.

FIGURE 14.6 A comparison of the three markets.

HOMEBUILDERS DECOUPLE FROM MARKET DURING 1999

Figure 14.7 shows Centex and the S&P 500 moving in lockstep from 1994 through the end of 1998. From that point on, the homebuilder and the rest of the stock market started trending in opposite directions. In 1999, Centex (and other homebuilders) fell sharply while the S&P 500 rallied. A more dramatic example of the decoupling of homebuilders from the rest of the stock market, however, came in 2000. Figure 14.7 shows the major top in the S&P 500 coinciding that year with a major upturn in Centex. Over the following three years, homebuilders continued rising while the stock market experienced its worst drop in generations.

The positive link between homebuilders and the stock market had been broken. Clearly, the homebuilders (and real estate stocks in general) had started to follow something other than stocks. This "something" was the direction of long-term interest rates. During the prior decade, homebuilders had been moving with both bonds and stocks during bull and bear market cycles. This was only because bonds and stocks were moving in the same direction, though. When bonds and stocks started decoupling during the

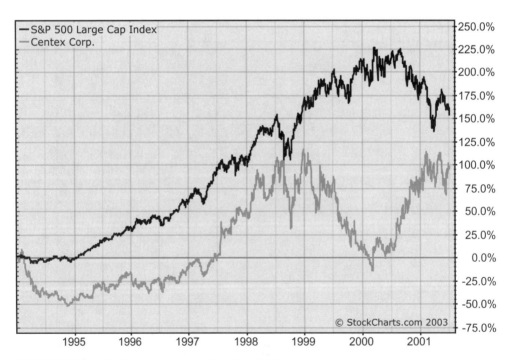

FIGURE 14.7   The two trends decoupled after 1998.

second half of 1998, the homebuilders revealed which one they were really following—and it was not stocks.

HOUSING STOCKS LINK TO INTEREST RATES

Figure 14.8 compares the yield on the 10-year Treasury-note to Centex from the start of 1994 to 2000. The inverse link can be seen very clearly. In fact, they are almost mirror images of each other. The two main turning points on the chart came at the end of 1994 and at the start of 1999. The peak in long-term rates at the end of 1994 coincided with a major upturn in Centex. For the next four years, homebuilders rose while long-term rates fell. The trough in long-term rates at the start of 1999, however, coincided with a peak in the homebuilders. It was right at this point that homebuilders decoupled from stocks. (Bonds and stocks had decoupled during the second half of 1998.) It became clear at the time that homebuilders were more closely tied to bonds than they were to stocks. Bonds and stocks were traveling in opposite directions. The homebuilders had to follow one group. They followed bonds.

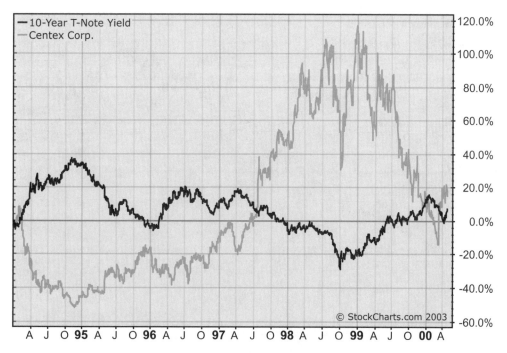

FIGURE 14.8   Centex has moved inversely to rates since 1994.

MARKET ROTATION DURING 2000

Figure 14.9 shows the dramatic market turns in long-term rates and Centex in 2000. The year before, the drop in Centex had coincided with rising rates. (1999 was the year that crude oil and other commodities surged higher, which prompted the Fed to start raising short-term interest rates in the summer.) Long-term rates peaked in the first quarter of 2000—along with the stock market. This was caused by a massive rotation out of stocks and into bonds. The rise in bond prices coincided with a drop in yields. Centex (and the other homebuilders) bottomed as rates were peaking. Once again, homebuilders had shown that they were being influenced more by the direction of long-term interest rates than by the direction of stocks. In so doing, homebuilding stocks fulfilled their historical role as a countercyclical asset class.

The drop in the stock market and interest rates signaled a significant weakening in the economy later that year. The housing industry was moving counter to the stock market, the direction of interest rates, and the business cycle. This is what a countercyclical asset is supposed to do. It is a good thing, too. Throughout the three-year bear market in stocks, accompanied by an historic drop in interest rates, strength in the housing sector was about the

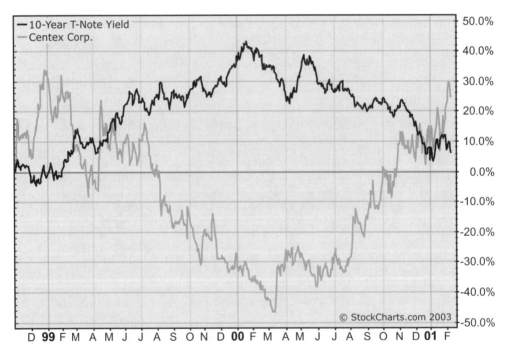

FIGURE 14.9   Centex bottomed as rates peaked in 2000.

only bright spot in an otherwise dismal economic landscape. There seems little doubt that the strong housing sector kept a bad economic situation from getting even worse. As rates plummeted over the next three years, a record level of mortgage refinancing provided consumers with extra money, which they spent primarily on autos, home appliances, and home improvements. The rise in home values largely offset losses in the stock market. From an asset allocation standpoint, the rise in housing during the years after 2000 was an example of the axiom that when one asset is going down, there is usually another one going up.

HOMEBUILDERS AND STOCKS RE-LINK

Although homebuilders continued to do better than the stock market (on a relative basis) in the three years after 2000, they started to track the stock market more closely starting in the middle of 2001. Figure 14.10 compares Centex and the S&P 500 from the middle of 2001 to the autumn of 2002. Centex bottomed with the market after the September 11 tragedy and weakened with the market the following spring. Although homebuilders still did better

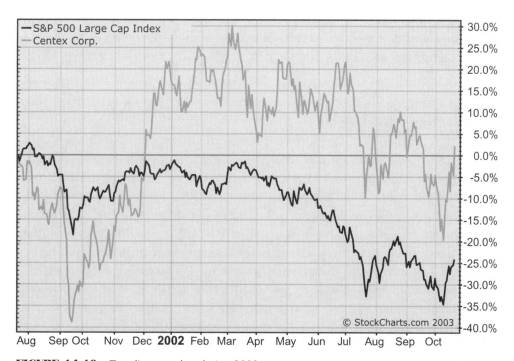

FIGURE 14.10 Trending together during 2002.

than the overall market during that period, their peaks and troughs were more closely correlated. Figure 14.10 also shows that homebuilders hit another big bottom during October 2002, just as the S&P 500 was hitting bottom as well. Although they rose much more strongly than the rest of the market after that lowpoint, housing stocks seemed to benefit from the market's newfound stability. From that October into the following spring, interest rates and stocks moved sideways. In the spring of 2003, two things happened that gave another big boost to housing stocks.

FED'S DEFLATION FIGHT BOOSTS HOUSING STOCKS

In the spring of 2003, the stock market started a rally off a March bottom. This March bottom represented a successful test of the lows hit the previous October. In chart terms, this successful retest increased the odds for a market bottom. Within two months, most of the major stock averages had exceeded the highs formed during the second half of the prior year. This bullish breakout in stocks gave a boost to homebuilders. They got another big boost from rates as well. On May 6, 2003, the Fed announced its intention to fight the threat of deflation. Shortly thereafter, long-term rates plunged. Mortgage rates fell to the lowest level in history. The combination of plunging rates and rising stocks caused an explosive move to record highs in homebuilding stocks.

THE HOUSING TRADEOFF

By the middle of 2003, the housing sector was still the strongest part of the stock market and the economy. It was feeding off a combination of lower long-term rates and a stronger stock market. The trade-off was that a stronger stock market might be hinting at a stronger economy, which could increase the demand for housing. This would be good. The risk was that a stronger economy might result in higher interest rates. This could be bad. The sustainability of the housing boom would probably depend on which of the two markets—bonds or stocks—housing followed. A strong economic recovery could hurt bonds but would help stocks. A weak economic recovery might not be bad for bonds but could hurt stocks. The worst-case scenario for the housing and real estate sector would be a combination of rising rates and a weak stock market.

JAPANESE REAL ESTATE COLLAPSED TWO YEARS AFTER STOCKS

The Japanese stock market peaked in December 1989 and began a 13-year decline that eventually turned into a deflationary spiral. The Japanese real estate market peaked two years after the Japanese stock market. So far, this has not been the case in the United States. However, the Fed's battle against deflation generates some real risks for American real estate and the economy. Its attempt to reflate the U.S. economy has resulted in a weaker dollar and rising commodity prices. Both of these trends threaten to raise long-term U.S. interest rates, which are trading near historic lows. Rising long-term rates could short-circuit a budding U.S. economic recovery. Even more dangerous is the possibility that rising rates could hurt a housing sector that has thrived on plunging rates. Since housing and real estate are countercyclical, it is normal to expect some weakening in this sector as part of an economic recovery. The danger is that rising long-term rates could start to hurt the housing sector before the American economy is in full recovery. A jump in long-term rates starting in mid-June 2003 caused a sizable correction in homebuilding stocks that lasted throughout the third quarter. That may have been a warning that rising rates might not be good for the housing sector.

CHAPTER 15

Thinking Globally

ALL MARKETS ARE RELATED

When I wrote my earlier book on intermarket technical analysis 13 years ago, my purpose was to demonstrate the simple reality that all markets are related. When I first made the claim in 1990, it seemed a little far-fetched. In the new millennium, however, many of the relationships that I described in the earlier book are taken for granted. The link between bonds and stocks is analyzed daily in the financial press and on TV. Intermarket subjects like the impact of a falling dollar on gold are routinely discussed on Bloomberg TV and CNBC. Economists debate the seriousness of the deflation threat and the impact that it could have on the financial markets. I heard one international analyst talking on television the other day about global opportunities in the *dollar bloc* countries like Australia and Canada because of their higher interest rates and strong currencies. Another analyst discussed the benefits that rising commodity prices could bring to emerging markets. This is pretty sophisticated stuff. We have all come a long way since 1990 in our awareness of how any market in the world has an impact on many others. Traders have also learned how to profit from these impacts.

The idea that all global markets are linked in some fashion seems obvious today. If you tune into Bloomberg radio early in the morning, you will get price quotes on key commodities like gold and oil, foreign currencies, foreign bonds, and foreign stock markets. You can hear how American shares are being traded in overseas markets even before they start trading here. In most instances, these early morning quotes determine how the trading day will start in the United States. We have learned to pay attention to overseas trends. Instant communication has made the world seem much smaller and much more interdependent. Some American stock market analysts did not bother watching the overseas markets 10 years ago and did not care what they were doing. Japan could have been on another planet as far as they were concerned. Not anymore. Japan's economy has become a big topic these days because of its deflationary problem, which threatens to become everyone else's problem. The Fed has been busily studying Japan very closely to see what it has tried in the battle against deflation.

Computer terminals and the Internet enable traders to view global trends and watch them trade off each other. Financial data on all global markets (including bonds, stocks, and currencies) are reported instantaneously on quote screens all over the world. A decision by a foreign central bank to lower interest rates (or not to lower them) may have an immediate impact on the trend of the dollar, the stock market, and the gold market here in the states. Much has changed in the financial markets over the past decade on a global scale and in our ability to monitor these changes.

Years ago, traders were not very aware of linkages that existed between the financial markets. Now, with quotes and charts so readily available, traders react much more quickly to changing market trends in Chicago, New York, or Hong Kong. Trading activity in the United States sets the tone for trading overseas and vice versa. How overseas markets react to the American stock market close is an indication of whether or not a move in New York has staying power. If foreign markets follow the U.S. market higher, odds are much better for a higher opening the next day in the United States. If stocks weaken overnight, they will probably do the same thing in New York the next morning.

GLOBAL TRADE INCREASES IMPACT OF EXCHANGE RATES

The "Commodities Corner" page in the July 14, 2003 issue of *Barron's* makes the point that "the share of world commodities traded across borders has risen over time, accentuating the importance of exchange rages." Matthew Shane, a senior economist in macroeconomics at the U.S. Department of Agriculture, is quoted as saying that domestic agricultural prices are becoming increasingly responsive to exchange rates. He calculates that as much as 45 percent of the change in the value of American agricultural exports is attributed to variations in exchange rates. The 1985 figure was 25 percent. This probably explains why agricultural commodity markets had such a good year in 2002 when the dollar started to fall to the lowest level in years.

Another sign of growing global awareness is heavy money flows into emerging markets in recent years.

EMERGING MARKETS

Since interest rates started to plunge three years ago, emerging-market bonds have done extremely well for global investors. Some of the biggest gains have come from Brazil, Mexico, and Russia. Since the 1997–1998 global currency crises in Asia and Russia, emerging-market bonds have gained 134 percent. Since 2001, Russian bonds have returned an impressive 66 percent. American institutional investors were attracted to emerging-market bonds because of their high yields at a time when stock markets were dropping and U.S. bond yields were falling to the lowest levels in over 40 years. By the middle of 2003, however, there were early signs that a global rotation was starting to take place out of bonds and into stocks. Here again, leadership came from emerging-market stocks.

During the first six months of 2003, the Morgan Stanley Capital International Emerging Markets Global Index gained 15.9 percent. This compares with an 11.1 percent return for developed markets over the same period. Two of the factors contributing to the better performance in stock markets of developing countries were a weaker U.S. dollar and stronger commodity markets. For one thing, the weaker dollar increased the profitability of foreign markets to American investors. The weaker dollar also boosted the value of global commodities, which are priced in dollars. Higher commodity prices increase the bottom line of developing countries that are commodity exporters. Mexico and Russia, for example, are exporters of oil and benefit from rising energy prices. Russia exports more oil than any other country with the exception of Saudi Arabia.

In dollar terms, some of the top global performers during the first half of 2003 were Argentina (+65 percent), Brazil (+44 percent), Indonesia (+34 percent), Russia (+28 percent), New Zealand (+20 percent), and Taiwan (+18 percent). These strong overseas gains compared with U.S. returns of 13 percent in the S&P 500 over the same time span. Three of the biggest developing countries showing high growth were China, India, and Russia. (During the first half of 2003, the Chinese GDP had grown by 8 percent with especially big gains in manufacturing. Growth in China is good for the global economy, especially Asia. China has become the biggest importer of goods produced in the rest of Asia, including Japan.) Gains in Asian stock markets (like South

Korea's) during the first half of 2003 were closely tied to a revival of technology stocks as evidenced by a 30 percent gain in the Nasdaq market. Twenty years ago, American investors were just discovering a valuable lesson: foreign markets offer profit opportunities outside of America's borders. Judging from the strong performance of emerging-market bonds and stocks and strong money flows into these markets, that lesson has been well learned.

MORE INTERMARKET EMPHASIS ON SECTOR WORK

My initial intermarket writing focused mainly on the four market groups—bonds, stocks, commodities, and currencies—and how they relate to each other. This is still very important. Over the years, however, more emphasis has been put on intermarket sector work. With the proliferation of Exchange Traded Funds (ETFs), traders are able to slice the market up into smaller parcels in a way that was impossible just a few years ago. Intermarket work plays an important role in sector and industry group rotation. Sector work even plays a role in individual stock selection. It has been estimated that 50 percent of a stock's trend is determined by the sector (or industry group) in which it is found. So if you are looking for a winning stock, find a winning group first. Then pick the strongest stock in that group. Understanding which market sectors do best at different stages of the business cycle is another breakthrough in intermarket work.

Proper asset allocation has become much more important over the past five years. Investors need to have the proper tools to adjust their asset allocation mix to suit market conditions. Those investors who had the foresight to move out of stocks and into bonds in 2000 saved themselves an awful lot of money. Those who moved some money into REITs or gold funds also did quite well while the stock market was falling. The technical tools employed in intermarket analysis are extremely helpful in making the proper asset allocation adjustments.

THE INTERMARKET MODEL IS NOT STATIC

One of the most important lessons to be learned in studying the past five years is that the intermarket relationships outlined in this book are not static. Sometimes they stop working for a period of time before kicking back in again. At times, a lag can exist before a turn in one market starts to exert its influence on another. Sooner or later, however, things have a way of returning to normal. The trick is to recognize when the correlations among markets are working and are exploitable. When they are not working, it is best to give them less weight in one's analysis until correlations start to strengthen again. While most of the lapses in intermarket correlations are temporary, there are some instances where major changes do take place in a traditional intermarket relationship. This was the case with bonds and stocks.

BONDS AND STOCKS DECOUPLE

The biggest change in an intermarket relationship over the past five years has been the major decoupling of bonds and stocks that started in the 1997–1998 period. We now know that it was the result of deflationary pressures not seen since the Great Depression. It took a lot of people a long time to recognize that a major change had taken place in the bond-stock relationship, and even longer to understand why. The decoupling of bonds and stocks over the past five years was not completely new. It happened the last time the world was faced with a deflationary problem. It was not a case of a key relationship no longer working. The relationship between bonds and stocks had reverted to a similar pattern that existed during the 1930s. Those investors who recognized the deflation threat earlier on, and who understood that bonds go up while stocks go down in such an environment, were prepared for market changes after 2000.

WHY WE NEED TO STUDY HISTORY

My first intermarket book examined market trends after 1970. The intermarket relationships described in that earlier text remained pretty constant from the 1970s through the end of the 1990s. Events over the past five years, however, have demonstrated the need to look much further back in time to get a better grasp of intermarket relationships that existed in different economic eras. History does tend to repeat itself. This book examines a very large time span in order to provide a better historical perspective on current trends. Although the news may not always be good, it is reassuring to know that it has happened before.

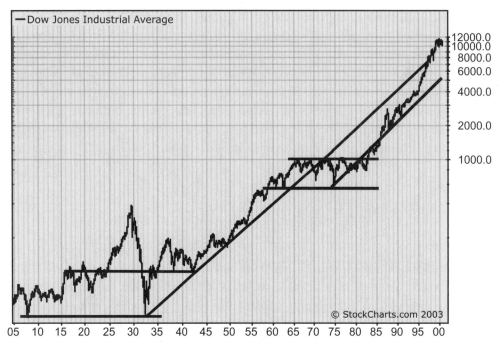

FIGURE 15.1   Shows bear markets during the 1930s and 1970s.

History tells us that stock market booms are usually followed by a long period of stock market underperformance. Figure 15.1 shows that the two previous stock market booms took place during the 1920s and the 1960s. Both were followed by at least a decade of subpar stock market returns. Since the last boom peaked in 2000, history warns us not to expect anything resembling the strong market of the 1990s anytime soon. Figure 15.1 shows the major decline in the stock market during the 1930s, and the sideways action that characterized the 1970s. Both of these weak decades followed big stock market booms. Having ended the third stock market boom of the last century just three years ago, this doesn't augur well for the current decade.

THE DECADE AFTER MARKET BOOMS ARE NOT VERY GOOD

It is always dangerous to compare two different market eras. No two eras are ever exactly alike. Figure 15.2 shows what happened after the major economic expansion of the 1960s ended. The stock market peaked in 1966 and traded in a huge sideways fashion until 1982. This difficult period lasted

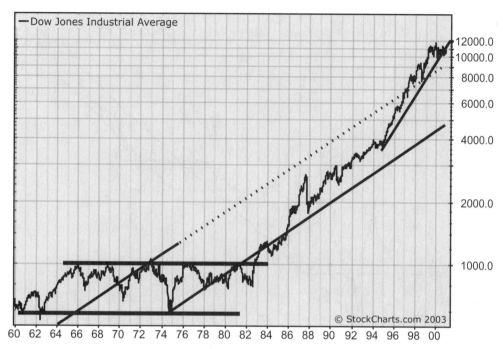

FIGURE 15.2 A closer look at the 1970s.

16 years. The worst loss was suffered in 1973 and 1974 when the S&P 500 lost half its value. Although it bottomed near the end of 1974, it was not until 1982 (eight years later) that the market began another secular bull trend. During the Great Depression, the stock market hit bottom in 1932. It took another 22 years (until 1954) from that bottom for the market to exceed the highs hit during 1929. Measured in *constant dollars* (meaning that the returns are adjusted for inflation), the period from the mid-60s to 1982 was just as damaging as the 1930s.

Figure 15.3 shows the Dow Jones Industrial Average in constant dollars. This does not affect the 1930 collapse since deflation was the main problem during that era. Because the 1970s were marked by hyperinflation, however, the returns on the stock market during that decade look much worse when adjusted for the higher inflation. Measured against inflation, the decline in the Dow from the mid-60s to the early '80s looks almost as bad as it did in the 1930s. In some ways, the 1970s were worse than the 1930s. During the Depression, stocks bottomed only three years after the 1929 peak. During the 1970s, the inflation-adjusted value of the Dow fell for 16 years before turning up in the early 1980s. A closer examination of the 1930s shows the stock market

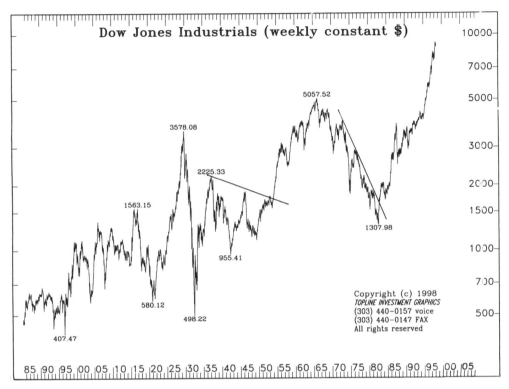

FIGURE 15.3 When adjusted for inflation, the decline in the Dow during the 1970s looks almost as bad as the 1930s.

recovering from 1932 to 1937. After that, however, the Dow lost ground for another 16 years. It took until 1954 for the inflation-adjusted value of the Dow to exceed its 1937 peak. This was 25 years after the stock market boom ended in 1929.

The reason for our examination of these two prior eras is to demonstrate that the decade (or two) after the end of a stock market boom is usually characterized by relatively trendless action. That does not bode well for the coming decade, although it does not mean that money cannot be made in the stock market in the coming years. The important thing is to recognize that the next decade will probably look much different than the last two decades; there will be a need to adjust to the new market environment. It will require a different philosophy, a different set of tools, and a different time horizon.

There is always money to be made in the stock market. The problem is that investors will probably have to work harder to make it over the next decade. The *buy and hold* approach that worked so well over the past 20 years probably is not going to work as well over the next several years.

Investors will need to take a more proactive approach to investing. Bull and bear moves will be shorter in duration. There will be times to buy and times to sell. Simply "holding on" will not work. Successful investing is going to require more skill at market timing.

Sector trading should become even more important in the coming years than it already is. When the market was going up in the 1990s, sector work was not as important. All one needed to do at that time was buy an index fund that tracked the entire market. Sector work was also less important in the three years after 2000 when most sectors fell. In the new market environment that will probably be marked by smaller trends, however, some sectors will undoubtedly do better than others. The difficult part will be learning how to spot the group leaders as soon as possible and rotating into new leaders when the old leaders start to stumble. Needless to say, most of these timing tools that will be needed to do this are technical in nature. This means that some knowledge of technical analysis will be more important than ever.

INTERMARKET IMPLICATIONS FOR TECHNICAL ANALYSIS

Because intermarket work involves looking at so many markets, it has to be done with price charts. Chart analysis is the easiest and most efficient way to study intermarket linkages. It greatly expands the usefulness of technical analysis. It allows analysts like me to talk about things that used to be restricted to security analysts and economists. Some understanding of how bonds, stocks, and commodities rotate in the business cycle allows us to talk about the state of the economy. Sector rotation also sheds light on whether the economy is expanding or contracting.

The financial markets are leading indicators of economic trends. It took the Federal Reserve until the spring of 2003 to acknowledge the threat of deflation. The markets had spotted the threat years earlier. The events surrounding the stock market peak in 2000 also demonstrated the need to incorporate some chart analysis into economic and fundamental forecasting. It took the Wall Street fundamental community a long time to find out what chartists already knew during the first half of 2000. The stock market had peaked and the economy was in trouble. It has often been said that technical analysis is just a shortcut form of fundamental analysis. It is based on the idea that price action is a leading indicator of a market's fundamentals. A lot of Wall Street analysts (and their clients) learned the danger of ignoring the chart signals that the markets gave off in 2000. They learned the danger of ignoring intermarket signals as well.

THE NEED FOR BETTER PERIPHERAL VISION

The greatest contribution made by intermarket analysis is that it improves the market analyst's peripheral trading vision. Trying to trade within the markets without intermarket awareness is like trying to drive a car without looking at the side and rear view mirrors. In other words, it is very dangerous. The application of intermarket analysis extends to all markets everywhere on the globe. By turning the focus of the market analyst outward instead of inward, intermarket work provides a more rational understanding of forces at work in the marketplace. It provides a more unified view of global market behavior. Intermarket analysis uses activity in surrounding markets in much the same way that we use traditional market indicators. Intermarket analysis does not replace traditional market analysis; it adds another dimension to it.

INTERMARKET WORK IS AN EVOLUTIONARY STEP

Technical work has many applications beyond the traditional study of isolated charts and internal market indicators. I like to think that intermarket analysis represents another step in the evolution of technical theory and practice. With the growing recognition that all markets are linked—financial and nonfinancial, domestic and international—traders can take these linkages into consideration more and more in their analyses. Because of its flexibility and its universal application to all markets, technical analysis is uniquely suited to perform intermarket work.

Intermarket analysis provides a more useful framework for understanding how individual markets and sectors relate to one another. Throughout most of the twentieth century, technical analysis had an inward focus. The new century has already started to witness a much broader application of technical principles in the areas of economic and financial forecasting. Even the Federal Reserve has learned to look to the financial markets to get clues about the future course of the economy. It uses charts to do this. The principles presented in this book offer a much broader view of the future of technical analysis. I think it is a bright one. And I believe intermarket analysis will play an increasingly important role in that bright future.

To ignore these interrelationships is to miss enormously valuable price information. What is worse is that it leaves market analysts in the position of not understanding the external forces that are moving the market in which they are trading. The days of following only one market are long gone. Market analysts need to know what is happening in all of the financial markets and must understand the impact of trends in related markets all over the globe. Technical analysis has enormous transferability in moving from one market to another and is extremely useful in comparing these markets' relative performance.

THERE IS STILL A LOT TO LEARN

In concluding the introduction to my earlier book on intermarket analysis, I wrote that the material presented was a "beginning rather than an end." This is even more true today than it was then. As I said at the time, there is still a lot that remains to be done before we can fully understand how markets relate to one another. And just when it seems like we have it all figured out, something changes. This is what happened with bonds and stocks. Nothing changes, however, in a vacuum; there is usually a reason for the change. The changing relationship between bonds and stocks signaled that the recent downturn in the business cycle would be different from other downturns since World War II.

The intermarket principles described in this book are presented as guidelines, not rigid rules. The ability to adapt to changing market circumstances is one of the keys to survival and profitability. This is true in intermarket work just as it is in any other form of market analysis. Although the scope of intermarket analysis is broad, forcing us to stretch our imaginations and expand our vision, I remain excited about the prospects for its future. It is fertile ground for market research and profitable trading opportunities.

Appendix

The start of October 2003 marked the one-year anniversary of the stock market bottom that had formed twelve months earlier. From the first week of October 2002 to the same week a year later, the Dow rose 24 percent while the S&P 500 gained 26 percent. The two best-performing market averages, however, were the Nasdaq Composite Index (+61 percent) and the Russell 2000 small-cap Index (+43 percent). That carried good news for the market. That's because leadership by small caps and technology is a sign of market strength. Sector results were also encouraging. Technology gained 58 percent to take the top spot. The three other market sectors that outperformed the S&P 500 over the prior twelve months were Financials (+32 percent), Basic Materials (+27.3 percent), and Consumer Discretionary (27 percent).

The strong performance by Basic Materials reflected rising industrial commodity prices, which is a sign of economic strength. So is the relative strength in Consumer Discretionary stocks. Their strong performance showed rising consumer confidence, which is an important ingredient in an economic recovery. The gains in the Financials came mainly from brokerage stocks, which were among the top industry group performers (+78 percent). Brokerage stocks are viewed as a leading indicator for the rest of the stock market. Two other leading industry groups were the Internet (+120 percent) and semiconductors (+92 percent). It's a good sign for the technology sector when the semiconductors are in a leadership role. During the third quarter of 2003, precious metals funds gained 24 percent and were that quarter's top performer. Technology funds came in second with a gain of 10 percent. Real estate funds were third with a rise of 9 percent.

2003 GLOBAL TRENDS

Asia was the top performing region during the first three quarters of 2003 (gaining 26 percent in dollar terms). By comparison, North America gained 15 percent while Europe came in last at 14 percent. The stronger performance by Asian markets was also seen during the third quarter of 2003. Japan gained 21 percent to take the top spot among global stock markets. Emerging markets rose 14 percent during the third quarter to also maintain a 2003 leadership role. A lot of the strength in Asia came from semiconductors, which were the top global sector during the first three quarters of 2003 (rising 23 percent). Asia is closely tied to trends in the semiconductor industry. The second best global sector during the third quarter was non-ferrous metals. That's mainly copper and aluminum stocks. A lot of the buying in those commodities was tied to the rising tide in Asia.

CHINA BUYS COMMODITIES FROM LATIN AMERICA

On Monday, September 29, 2003 the *Wall Street Journal* ran a story entitled "Latin America Gets Unexpected Boost from China's Success". The article discussed how China's need to feed its large population and its search for basic materials to fuel its huge manufacturing economy was benefiting Latin America. The Chinese purchase of copper and gold from Chile and Peru boosted the prices of those commodities and helped both economies. Chinese buying of beef from Argentina and soybeans from Brazil had the same beneficial effect on those two countries, and partially explains the strong performance by those two agricultural commodity markets during 2003. The article suggested that buying from China and the rest of Asia could produce a Latin American "export led" recovery over the next few years. That's an example of why stronger commodity prices are usually associated with stronger emerging markets.

INDUSTRIAL METALS LEAD COMMODITY RALLY DURING 2003

A study of how the various commodity markets did during the first three quarters of 2003 carried some positive economic news. That's because the top performing commodity group was Industrial Metals with a gain of 14 percent. This is the group most closely tied to the trend of the global economy. During 2002, the commodity rally was led by agricultural markets, energy, and precious metals. During 2003, the commodity rally was led by economically-sensitive industrial metal markets. Another good sign for the economy was the fact that energy prices lost 2 percent during the first nine months of 2003 and were the weakest of the commodity groups.

2003 INTERMARKET TRENDS FAVOR STOCKS AND COMMODITIES

It's also instructive to compare the prior year's relative performance of the four markets that form the primary basis for intermarket analysis. In the twelve months after October 2002, the stock market was the top gainer (with the S&P 500 up 26 percent). Commodities came in second with a CRB Index gain of 8 percent. The strong performance by those two markets was reflective of an improving economic picture around the globe. Earlier in the book, I talked about the reasons why rising commodity prices were good for stocks coming out of a deflationary environment. Stocks and commodities rose together in the early 1930s and signaled that deflationary pressures were easing. They did the same during 2003. Bonds and the U.S. dollar lost ground during 2003. Bonds lost 4 percent in the twelve months after the stock market bottomed in October 2002. Improving economic conditions during 2003 contributed to a rotation out of bonds and into stocks. That reversed the trend seen during the 2000–2002 bear market when investors bought bonds and sold stocks. The new trend was more consistent with economic growth. The U.S. dollar was the worst of the four markets and lost 12 percent over the prior year. I suggested earlier in the book that the U.S. government was deliberately weakening the dollar to combat deflationary tendencies in the U.S. economy and in an attempt to reinflate the economy. Much of the upward movement in commodities (and gold in particular) over the prior year could be directly traced to the falling U.S. currency. If there was any doubt that the American government wanted a weaker dollar, that doubt was erased during the Group of Seven meeting that took place during September 2003.

MOVE TOWARD FLEXIBLE EXCHANGE RATES BOOSTS YEN

Over the weekend of September 20–21, G7 finance ministers released a statement calling for flexible exchange rates in currency markets. It was clear that the statement was aimed at Asian countries that had been intervening in the foreign exchange markets to keep their currencies from rising. A month earlier the Chinese government had rejected international pressure to allow the yuan to rise to a more reasonable market value. That pressure came from the U.S., but was supported by Japan. The immediate result from the G7 meeting in September 2003 was a jump in the yen versus the dollar to the highest level in three years. It was interesting to see how the world markets reacted. Global stock markets tumbled the first day after the news. The Japanese stock market lost 4 percent on fears that a rising yen would hurt exports. European markets dropped 3 percent on fears that a rising Euro would have the same negative effect on their markets. The U.S. stock market lost a little over 1 percent. The dollar dropped sharply and gold prices jumped to a seven-year high. The rise in the Japanese yen was reflective of an improving Japanese economy, rising Japanese interest rates, and strong money flows into Asian stock markets. The new currency policy, however, could be a mixed blessing.

The United States wanted a weaker dollar to boost exports and create jobs in the American manufacturing sector. A weaker dollar makes U.S. goods more attractive to foreigners. The weaker dollar, however, carried some potential problems. During July, Chinese and Japanese holdings of U.S. Treasuries had risen to a new record. In the third quarter of 2003, the Japanese central bank was the largest foreign holder of U.S. Treasuries. The Japanese had been buying U.S. dollars in an attempt to keep the yen from rising. They re-invested those dollars in U.S. Treasuries. The new fear was that the Japanese would buy fewer dollars in the future, which could result in less buying of Treasuries. That could result in higher U.S. interest rates, which could threaten the budding American economic recovery. Once again, trends in the currency markets had a potential bearing on the direction of interest rates and stock prices here in the United States and elsewhere.

STRONG SEPTEMBER JOBS REPORT BOOSTS STOCKS BUT HURTS GOLD

Another demonstration of intermarket linkages took place on Friday, October 3, 2003. Going into that morning, stock prices had been correcting downward while bond prices were rallying. The dollar was testing its low for the year, while gold prices were flirting with seven-year highs. At 8:30 A.M. (NYT), surprisingly strong employment numbers were reported. The American economy had created new jobs for the first time in eight months. That caused an immediate (but predictable) intermarket reaction in the four markets. The stock market jumped strongly and bond prices fell sharply; the dollar rallied while gold prices fell heavily. There's no way to judge at this time the longer-range consequences of that strong jobs report or the longer-range implications of the new flexible exchange rate policy. In both instances, however, the immediate reactions of the four markets were in line with their normal intermarket pattern. Some went up and some went down. But each of them did what it was expected to do. The trends of the individual markets may change, but their intermarket relationships usually stay pretty constant. Profiting from those relationships is what this book is all about.

OCTOBER 2003 CHARTS

The remaining pages show charts of the major markets through the end of the third quarter 2003. Generally speaking, they paint a more optimistic picture of global market trends. Stocks are stronger and bonds are weaker than the prior year. While the weak dollar carries some potential negative side-effects, it has also given a big boost to commodity markets like gold and, in so doing, diminished deflationary pressures. Deflation appears to be giving way to reflation. The world's deflationary problems started with the Asian currency crisis during 1997. It seems only fitting that 2003 saw Asia leading the world away from deflation. The charts in the Appendix are market snapshots taken at a given point in time. Charts become obsolete, however, as market trends change. What doesn't change is the fact that all of these markets are linked to one another. That's the main message to be learned from intermarket analysis.

Figure A.1

After peaking during the spring and summer of 2002, the REIT sector underwent a downside correction and underperformed the S&P 500 for more than a year. During September 2003, however, the Dow Jones REIT Index exceeded its 2002 peak to reach a new high. The REIT/S&P 500 ratio also turned higher during the third quarter of 2003, which suggested new leadership by REITs. The REIT Index has traded over its 10-week average since March, which is another sign of strength.

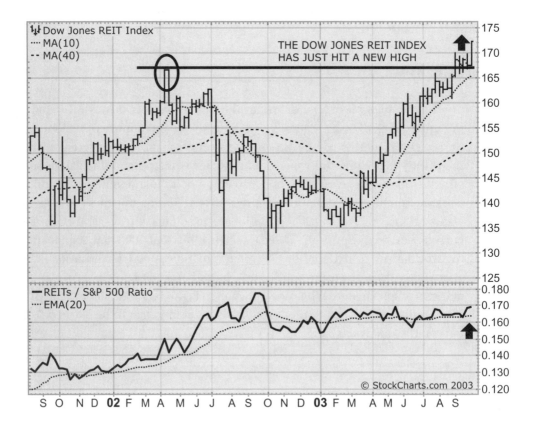

Figure A.2

By the third quarter of 2003, the Nasdaq Composite had gained 70 percent from its October 2002 bottom. The next major resistance level for the Nasdaq is the peak formed at the start of 2002 near 2100. The Nasdaq/S&P 500 ratio has been rising for a year. That kind of relative strength by the Nasdaq is usually good for the stock market. One cautionary note is that fact that the stock market has been rallying for a year. That's the normal time span for cyclical bull markets.

Figure A.3

After registering a five-year high near the start of 2003, the CRB Index spent five months consolidating those gains. During July 2003, however, the CRB starting rising again and reached a six-month high. That suggested that commodity prices were resuming their major uptrend. New weakness in the U.S. dollar during the third quarter of 2003 contributed to the buying of commodity markets (especially precious metals). The rising CRB Index during the summer of 2003 also put upward pressure on long-term interest rates which starting rising as well.

Figure A.4

After plunging during the spring of 2003, the 10-year T-note yield started jumping during June. By July, the long-term yield had exceeded its 40-week moving average and risen to the highest level in a year. Rising commodity prices and a stronger stock market had a lot to do with rising long-term rates. Rising commodity prices are potentially inflationary; rising stock prices are a sign of economic strength. Bond yields jumped all over the world (including Japan) on increasing signs of a global economic recovery. Global funds coming out of bonds moved back into the stock market.

Figure A.5

The 10-year T-note yield is testing the three-year down trendline extending back to the start of 2000. A close over that trendline would confirm that long-term rates have bottomed. Over the prior three years, falling bond yields were a barometer of global economic weakness. Rising bond yields carry a more optimistic message for the economy over the short run. Over the long haul, rising rates could threaten an economic recovery. The jump in bond yields also suggests that deflationary pressures are easing.

THE 10-YEAR T-NOTE YIELD IS TESTING A THREE-YEAR DOWN TRENDLINE

© StockCharts.com 2003

Figure A.6

The Dollar Index peaked at the start of 2002 and broke a seven-year up trend-line at the end of that year. The breakdown in the U.S. currency gave a big boost to commodity markets (gold in particular). At the start of the fourth quarter 2003, the dollar is threatening the low it had formed during second half of 1998. During the first week of October, a rebound off that low caused some profit-taking in the gold market. The major trend of the dollar, however, is still down.

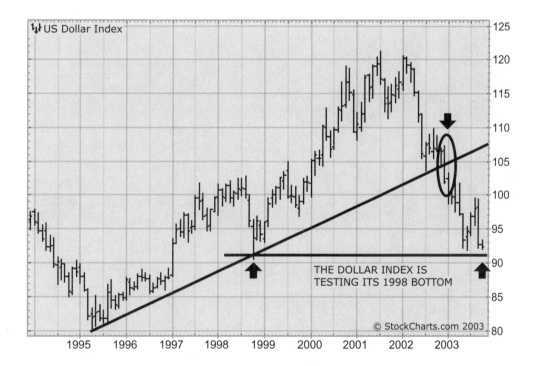

Figure A.7

Gold broke through the $325 level at the end of 2002, which exceeded the previous peak reached during 1999. That launched a new bull market in gold (and gold stocks). After briefly hitting a seven-year high, gold entered a downside correction at the start of October 2003. A surprisingly strong jobs report on October 3, 2003 gave a boost to the stock market and the dollar. That caused profit-taking in gold and gold shares. The early 2003 pullback in bullion stopped at the original breakout point at $325, which is the new floor under the gold market. The major trend of gold is still up.

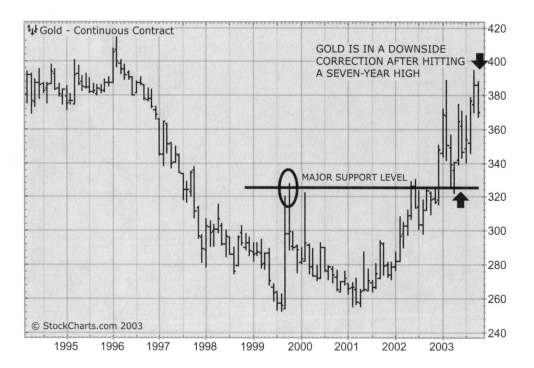

Figure A.8

The Japanese yen surged to a three-year high versus the dollar in mid-September 2003. That was the result of a G7 call for flexible exchange rates. The immediate result was an explosive upmove in the Japanese yen. The rising yen was more reflective of a strengthening Japanese economy and strong money flows into Asian markets. It raised fears, however, that Japan might cut back on purchases of U.S. Treasuries, which could result in higher long-term interest rates in the states. The G7 message left little doubt that the United States wanted a weaker dollar.

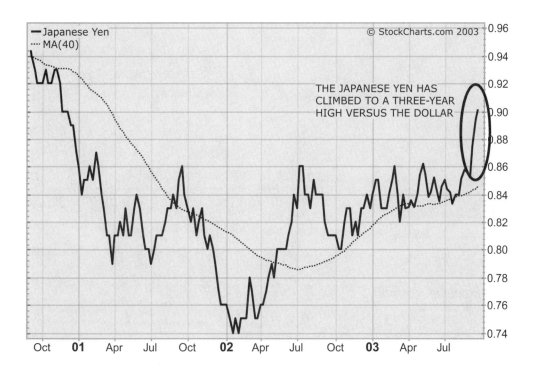

Figure A.9

The Nikkei 225 rose to the highest level in fourteen months during September 2003. Its move over the 40-week moving average during June was a chart sign that the trend was turning higher. The ratio of the Nikkei divided by the S&P 500 started rising in April, which meant that Japanese stocks were outperforming U.S. stocks. Long-term interest rates in Japan started jumping during the summer, which reflected a move out of Japanese bonds and into stocks. It may have also been a strong sign that deflationary trends were easing in Japan and elsewhere on the globe.

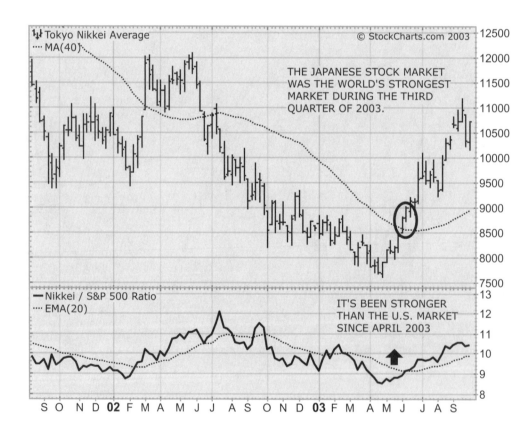

Figure A.10

Industrial Metals peaked during 1997 with the beginning of the Asian currency crisis, and signaled the start of global deflationary problems and economic weakness. Industrial Metals have broken a six-year down trendline. That's a good sign for global economies. It's bad news for bonds, however, since rising Industrial Metals are usually associated with rising long-term interest rates. Rising Industrial Metals also suggest that global deflationary problems that started in 1997 have run their course. That means that deflation has given way to reflation.

Index